THOREAU

A COLLECTION OF CRITICAL ESSAYS

Edited by

Sherman Paul

A SPECTRUM BOOK

Prentice-Hall, Inc., *Englewood Cliffs, N.J.*

Current printing (last digit):
14

Library of Congress Catalog Card Number: 62-13605
PRINTED IN THE UNITED STATES OF AMERICA 93827-C

Table of Contents

INTRODUCTION—*Sherman Paul*   1

THE LAKE ISLE OF INNISFREE—*William Butler Yeats*   8

HENRY DAVID THOREAU (1817-1917)—*the Editors of*
   The Seven Arts   9

FROM *THE GOLDEN DAY*—*Lewis Mumford*   13

THOREAU: NO HERMIT—*Max Lerner*   20

HENRY THOREAU IN OUR TIME—*Stanley Edgar Hyman*   23

THOREAU'S DOCTRINE OF SIMPLICITY—*Leo Stoller*   37

WHAT MUSIC SHALL WE HAVE?—*F. O. Matthiessen*   53

A WEEK ON THE CONCORD AND MERRIMACK RIVERS—
   William Drake   63

WALDEN—*William Drake*   71

FROM *THE AMERICAN ADAM*—*R. W. B. Lewis*   92

A FABLE OF THE RENEWAL OF LIFE—*Sherman Paul*   100

WAYSIDE CHALLENGER: SOME REMARKS ON THE POLITICS
   OF HENRY DAVID THOREAU—*Heinz Eulau*   117

AN EVALUATION OF THOREAU'S POETRY—*Henry W. Wells*   131

THE RED FACE OF MAN—*Edwin S. Fussell*   142

iii

INTRODUCTION—*Laurence Stapleton*   161

LETTER FROM A DISTANT LAND—*Philip Booth*   180

Chronology of Important Dates   185

Notes on the Editor and Contributors   186

Bibliography   187

Introduction

by Sherman Paul

Thoreau's success as a writer is demonstrable: he dramatized the issues of his life so well that for the most part we have been more concerned with taking sides over them than with carefully scrutinizing his work. One book and one essay of his and perhaps one biography in our time have shaped the popular notion of Thoreau; to have read *Walden* and "Civil Disobedience" and Canby's *Thoreau* has often been held sufficient warrant for criticism. Yet there is still no adequate critical text of *A Week on the Concord and Merrimack Rivers* or of the travel books, excursions, and political essays; instead, there is a shortened edition of the *Week,* and deluxe editions. Thoreau has by no means been read in the thorough way in which we have read Hawthorne and Melville or Faulkner and Joyce. A sampling of the criticism in Samuel A. Jones' *Pertaining to Thoreau* (1901), which gathers together early reviews and essays, and in Walter Harding's *Thoreau: A Century of Criticism* (1954), which surveys a century of dispute, confirms the impression that most of the writing on Thoreau has been testimony— appreciation or disparagement.

Having succeeded in waking his neighbors up, Thoreau set them to wrangling, as well he might, for the issues he raised were the uncomfortable ones of life and death. Nature and civilization (civilization and its discontents), self and society, integrity and conformity ("inner" and "other" directedness), play and work, "failure" and success—these are some of the vital issues he raises, issues which show the legacy of Romanticism and around which criticism has polarized. Such criticism as Thoreau has had indicates his challenge as a culture-hero. He is not a simple nature writer but one of those exemplary men who, as Nietzsche suggested, provide the human measure of history. Certainly in our literature he is the pre-eminent self-surpasser. He asks us to consider the rewards and costs of a personally formed life; he asks us to consider not our roles but our vocations, and to find vocations that in the old religious sense are justifiable. He drives life—our life—into a corner. "If we are really dying," he tells us, "let us hear the rattle in our throats and feel cold in the extremities; if we are alive, let us go about our business." Of death-in-life, of the grub-like condition, of the sloth of routine and complacency, and of the trade that curses everything it touches, he is the critic because he has at times been able to surmount them. He believes that man can clarify and concentrate as well as simplify his life, that he can consciously shape the materials of his life and in the shaping transform living into an art and an adventure. His subject is not only the state of men but the promising condition of man.

The critic of Thoreau must respond to these issues first and foremost. He must accept Thoreau's challenge and testify even though the testimony may tell us more about the critic than about Thoreau. Ideally, he should have a fine sensitivity to the words of the text and to what they do as well as a serious commitment to ideas and values —I am thinking of F. O. Matthiessen whose stature as a critic is not fairly gauged by an excerpt from a closely-woven book. But even the critic who has not so fully responded to the work and who may have based his thought on the scholarship of others or on the popular notion of Thoreau will often have something worthwhile to add. At least he adds his voice and thereby helps to create public discussion; he contributes to the on-going assessment which assures us that a writer is still living and has "reputation." Any voice, one might say, is better than silence, for silence closes out discussion, the very quickening of culture.

When a writer is alive, we live in the discussion he arouses. We are interested in the imaginary dialogues of Thoreau and D. H. Lawrence, of Thoreau and Shaw, and in such actual dialogues as those that constitute E. B. White's long engagement with Thoreau. We not only want to know who influenced Thoreau but whom he influenced, especially those significant personalities who make our world with their thoughts and acts. Of such influences, Gandhi's *Satyagraha* is perhaps the most widely known example; yet there are others less spectacular though no less profound. Consider the Walden School that Margaret Naumburg founded; the Appalachian Trail, the work of Benton MacKaye, a philosopher of environment as great as Thoreau, for whom he claimed this distinction; the tradition of the "renewal of the landscape" which Lewis Mumford traced in *The Brown Decades* and has himself notably furthered in his studies of the city and the region; the "neo-functional" critique of

Paul and Percival Goodman's *Communitas: Means of Livelihood and Ways of Life* (New York: 1960), a book that merits a place in the tradition of criticism that includes *Walden* and *The Theory of the Leisure Class;* or the "nerve of failure" with which David Riesman would arm us in our quest for success. These influences are testimonies to a living writer.

I have reprinted little of a testimonial character for several reasons. The best is often the spark that ignites a man's work, but it is too brief, uncapturable. Much, unfortunately, is perfunctory, longwinded and tangential, second-thought, or superficially polemical. Most of it belongs to the kind of criticism that increases in bulk by repetition. Little has distinction of style. And if these are not reasons enough, there is another: the testimonial is inevitable, but fundamental criticism which yields to the object of inquiry is not. After a century of criticism of another sort it is time now to read arduously the works of Thoreau, take their bearings anew, modify the stereotypes that have been handed down, "work and wedge our feet downward through the mud and slush of opinion" to the hard bottom of the text. Then, if the large lines of discussion are not altered, at least the arguments will be refined and reconstituted by the everfresh act of reading—and response.

Thoreau scholarship of course has not been idle. Thoreau's poems, correspondence, and college essays have been collected and edited. The "lost" journal has been printed and the first version of *Walden* has been published and the various stages of its composition carefully analyzed. Monographs have been written on Thoreau's Classicism and Orientalism; theses have been written on individual works like the *Week* and on many aspects of Thoreau's development and thought—for example, his early education, his aesthetics, his interest in travel and early American history; and more complete and deeper, though opposing, interpretations have been offered by two recent studies, *After Walden* and *The Shores of America*. Thoreau is alive—in the seminar, in the few lectures devoted to him in the classroom, in the small bulletin of The Thoreau Society. Bibliographies, even a handbook, acknowledge his importance, although the weekly book reviews of the great metropolitan newspapers (which seldom notice the significant work on Thoreau or other classic American writers) do not. Much of this excellent material deserves recognition; but much of it is either too closely worked for excerpting or not in a form that commands attention in the wider world where criticism does much of its work. The difficulty of finding adequate *essays* on Thoreau's individual works or on special aspects of his thought suggests that there is little public —and lively—critical engagement.

We no longer have the clear (and simple) picture of Thoreau that previous generations have had. One reason may be our cultural uncertainty and thus our difficulty in creating a Thoreau whom we can use to define our aims. Having exploited our world—the landscape, the atmosphere, men—in ways the nineteenth century never dreamed of; having returned in so many ways to what Thoreau called the larval state, we are not so much skeptical as afraid of the Thoreau who talks about the airy freedom of the butterfly. If we think his civil disobedience vain (though it has its current uses), what are we to think of his cultural disobedience? Thoreau would awaken us to what he called the crises of our lives; he does not ask us to go to the woods but to become aware, to cast off complacency, to rouse ourselves from the winter of our content. And if he is unpopular (as Emerson, that arch-foe of moral cowardice, is unpopular), it is because he would recall us, as Randolph Bourne wrote, to the "eternal human tradition of abounding vitality and moral freedom. . . ."

A more salutary reason for our indeterminate picture of Thoreau is the recent scholarly work which has altered the simple chiaroscuro of previous portraits. What has so often been considered dualistically is now considered dialectically. The early Thoreau who dedicated himself to self-culture is now seen to have developed into a spokesman for self-and-culture; indeed we are now beginning to see that the moral life is indivisible, that the dividing lines between the personal, the political, and the cultural are not easily drawn. We now know that Thoreau's life changed and that he did not forever remain as contented as previous interpreters would have us believe. We can no longer dismiss Thoreau as an innocent, a Transcendentalist unfamiliar with evil. As our understanding of Transcendentalism and Romanticism deepens, we realize that much we prize has been denied us by our blindness to the concrete or experiential meaning of old concepts. And as we try to define Thoreau's qualities as a writer, we realize that he is a poet of experience, one who knew well the uses of imagination and of art.

When I planned this book I had hoped for symmetry. Every decade in our century would provide its testimonial to Thoreau as culture-hero; every major work would be represented by a strenuous reading; many aspects of Thoreau's thought, especially his interest in folklore and Orientalism, would have an accounting. This hope, however, proved to be one of those castles in the air that fail for lack of foundation.

Every decade but that of the 1930's offered good substantial essays. Paul Elmer More's "Thoreau's Journal," with which I might have begun, had every virtue of learning and moral concern and reminded one that the New Humanists were not able to dismiss Thoreau as easily as they had Whitman. Indeed, not having many American writers in the tradition they espoused, they were glad to have him. In More's essay, Thoreau's "puritan" character redressed the follies of his romantic thought, just as in the later work of Norman Foerster, Thoreau's education in the Classics and "higher" use of nature redeemed him from romantic "naturism" and sentimentalism—and just as now in Perry Miller's "Thoreau in the Context of International Romanticism" (*Thoreau Society Bulletin*, Fall 1960) all those faults of romantic "consciousness" which Miller relentlessly probed in *Consciousness in Concord* are made good in assertions of Thoreau's greatness as a writer. The New Humanists have monopolized Thoreau; Henry S. Canby's *Thoreau* (1939) is still the standard biography, sharpened and strengthened though it is by Joseph Wood Krutch's *Henry David Thoreau* (1948) and Reginald L. Cook's *Passage to Walden* (1949).

A group of critics who opposed the New Humanists, the critics associated with *The Seven Arts,* also attempted to claim Thoreau. I have included the editorial they published rather than More's essay partly because of the exigencies of space, partly because the New Humanist position is still the academic one, but chiefly because it more sharply defines issues which I think are relevant; and I have reprinted with it Lewis Mumford's essay from *The Golden Day* (1926) because it established Thoreau in the organic tradition which we now recognize as a vital contribution of Romanticism and found in Thoreau a center for the aspirations of a resurgent generation. In a time of genuine cultural stock-taking when literary critics were seeking signs of cultural health, Mumford found in Thoreau (and in Emerson) the welcome assurance of a usable past.

The critics of the 1930's replaced the moral and cultural interpretations of Thoreau with a narrower social one. Much of what was written is now disappointing because it is so obviously doctrinaire. V. F. Calverton's "petty bourgeois individualistic" interpretation of Thoreau in *The Liberation of American Literature* (1930) is not as good as Parrington's study of the "Transcendental Economist" or Lucy Hazard's assessment of Thoreau in terms of the

frontier thesis—earlier studies upon which Calverton drew; and it
lacks the historical authority one finds in later and sounder studies
of Thoreau, for example in Ralph H. Gabriel's *The Course of
American Democratic Thought* and Arthur M. Schlesinger, Jr.'s *The
Age of Jackson*. The best and briefest essay is Max Lerner's
"Thoreau: No Hermit" (1934). It is not doctrinaire, yet distills the
essence of favorable Marxist criticism: that Thoreau rejected the
economics of exploitation, that his political behavior was courageous
and rebellious, and that he knew, as he said, that "to act collectively
is according to the spirit of our institutions." Marxist criticism re-
discovered Thoreau's social conscience, and, as one still sees in
Edwin S. Smith's "A Thoreau for Today" (*Mainstream,* 1960), it
submerged the individual conscience in the social conscience. Society
became the norm, and the individual conscience that tried society
was not necessarily a social conscience. Though Lerner had opened
a wide vista for critics when he wrote that Thoreau's "thought effected an almost Nietzschean transvaluation of values," few saw its
possibilities. They waited on history, on the next discontinuity in
our culture, the period of the 1940's and 1950's when critics began
to respond again to the demands of what Lionel Trilling called
"the opposing self."

The critical landmark of this period is F. O. Matthiessen's *American Renaissance: Art and Expression in the Age of Emerson and
Whitman* (1941). Informed by the critical experience of the century
—at once moral, cultural, and social—it demonstrated the most
needed lesson: that the moral, cultural, and social values we seek
in art must be found by sensitive awareness of the work as art and
by an equally sensitive awareness of the continuities and deter-
minants of history. Matthiessen's fertile work stimulated the study
of Thoreau in many ways. It made the writing critically central; it
defined the organic aesthetic and by relating its exemplars in the
past to those of the present made the study of "influence" significant.
Following Matthiessen, critics re-examined the cultural matrix of
Transcendentalism and Romanticism, and returned to the text and
to Thoreau as writer. What they began to do can be seen in Stanley
Edgar Hyman's "Henry Thoreau in Our Time" and in R. W. B.
Lewis' interpretation of the cultural significance of *Walden* in *The
American Adam*.

I say "what they began" because this work is not yet completed.
Even for *Walden* I have been able to find only tentative explorations—first readings. As for the remainder of Thoreau's writings,
the lack of similar readings reveals the general neglect. My rep-

resentation is admittedly spotty, but what I have included either provides a reading by which one can test his own or opens new areas of investigation. I am especially grateful for the opportunity to publish for the first time the work of William Drake and Edwin Fussell. Mr. Drake's master's thesis, "A Formal Study of H. D. Thoreau" (University of Iowa, 1948), is pioneer work; researchers have found it and have been indebted to it, and now a good part of it is available to the public. Professor Fussell's essay on the Indian, prepared especially for this collection, is a condensation of a chapter in a literary study he is now completing. With Laurence Stapleton's introduction to *H. D. Thoreau: A Writer's Journal*, which treats Thoreau's explorations in Concord (as well as his relationships to modern writers), it extends the study of Thoreau beyond the usual limits of the Walden period to the last decade of his life when his major concern was with the aboriginal American environment—with the discovery and exploration of America and his "Kalendar" of the phenomena of Concord.

Some of the remaining selections, although justified by general considerations already discussed, deserve further comment. Henry Wells' essay is the fullest treatment of Thoreau's poetry; Heinz Eulau's essay on Thoreau's politics is one of the few serious considerations by a political scientist; and Leo Stoller's "Thoreau's Doctrine of Simplicity," which suggests the argument of his *After Walden,* is the best critique of Thoreau's ideal of self-culture. The poems by Yeats and Philip Booth speak for all the unrecorded testimony and for those states of feeling that always accompany ideas. They span the time limits of this collection and provide a symmetry of a different—and a better—kind than my editorial art can provide.

The Lake Isle of Innisfree

by William Butler Yeats

I will arise and go now, and go to Innisfree,
And a small cabin build there, of clay and wattles made:
Nine bean-rows will I have there, a hive for the honeybee,
And live alone in the bee-loud glade.

And I shall have some peace there, for peace comes dropping slow,
Dropping from the veils of the morning to where the cricket sings;
There midnight's all a glimmer, and noon a purple glow,
And evening full of the linnet's wings.

I will arise and go now, for always night and day
I hear lake water lapping with low sounds by the shore;
While I stand on the roadway, or on the pavements grey,
I hear it in the deep heart's core.

Henry David Thoreau (1817-1917)

by the Editors of The Seven Arts

It is a hundred years this month since Thoreau was born (July 12, 1817). Perfectly self-coherent as he was and, unlike most writers, the embodiment of all his ideas, he marks better perhaps than any other figure in our social history the distance we have travelled in our progress from the unity of the one to the unity of the many. "The universe," he said, "is always on the side of the most sensitive." The world, in the long run, is always on the side of those who have been able to contrive some definite pattern out of life. Thoreau's pattern was that of the pioneer mind itself, which in him realized its height and depth. Unwilling as he was to yield his allegiance to any ideas which the instincts of his fellow-countrymen had not entitled them to, he gave no hostages to the ever-shifting fabric of a society that had no fund of ideals verified in the general experience of the race. That is why he has outlasted so many of his more gifted contemporaries, lightly caught out of themselves, lightly undone. He knew how primitive at bottom was the life that surrounded him, and like Whitman the only men he really respected were men close to the elements, the forest, the sea, the soil. It was among such alone that he was able to discover the perfect integrity which he exacted from living things and found in such abundance in trees and animals.

It was this that led him to look with the aloofness of an immortal upon the world out of which he had grown like a resinous and vibrant little hemlock, solitary and disdainful among the ephemeridae of an April meadow. For Thoreau, whose imagination never compassed the gelatinous mass of human kind, society meant nothing but the infringement of the individual. "Blessed are the young," he said, "for they never read the President's message." He was an anarchist not through the wisdom of the serpent but the

"Henry David Thoreau (1817-1917)." From *The Seven Arts*, II (July 1917), 383-385.

innocence of the dove, a skeptical innocence that allowed nothing to pass without proof. Our original "man from Missouri," he never forgot, however, that skepticism degrades itself when it stands guard not over the ends but over the means of life. So far as the means were concerned, it was impossible for Thoreau to take them seriously at all; he was literally "out from under" society by virtue of a continence like that of a lone goldfish in a glass of ice-water. And he was as unsinkable as a cork, thanks to the universal tinker's genius with which his nimblehanded forebears had endowed him. His disdainfulness, no doubt, came a little cheap, and his immortal airs would not have been less convincing had they been put to the test of mortal desire. But then he would not have been the perfectly typical man he was, he would not have been able to flatter us now with a sense of our own immeasurable advance in frank self-knowledge and free experience.

As it is, he flatters us quite enough. In much that our generation holds dear, Thoreau was poor indeed. His emotional rigidity, for example, must have been unique even in Concord. A young girl once complained that having taken her to the top of a mountain, he fixed his earnest gaze on a distant point in the landscape and remarked, "How far is it in a bee-line to that spot?" It is conceivable, of course, that he had other thoughts then and on similar occasions, but they never found expression even in his verse. Practical enough to be able to regulate even the beating of his pulse, he kept the chambers of his mind in perfect order by packing everything that got in his way up into the attic of Transcendentalism. A capacious attic that was indeed, without which Concord could hardly have existed at all. It contained, among other things, a veritable Pandora's box full of all the amorous plagues that confuse and terrify mankind. But never a germ escaped. It had been locked for generations and the key had been hidden away, heaven knows where, in the old world, and the dust had gathered on it, and it had been forgotten. Yet how much they owed to that box, the philosophers of Concord! Never before or since have high thinkers and plain livers had smoother sailing.

With regard to the objective world, moreover, Thoreau leaves off where we begin. But might it not be added that we begin on the hither side of a great many important things the secret of which he possessed and we have lost? His imagination, unlike Emerson's, absolutely concrete, required a commensurate field of fact of a sort that society only affords where a certain number of people have disengaged themselves from necessity and accepted parts in the tragicomedy of the free life. Half a dozen of his contemporaries had taken this step: Thoreau made the most of them. John Brown, Whitman, and one or two others, as we know, appealed to him even more than bumblebees; but one swallow does not make a summer and a handful of individuals cannot make the corporate life significant if it has no significance without them. Besides, to the beasts of the field Thoreau could allow a certain latitude; precisely because, having no souls, they never whine about them, as Whitman said, they offered him an unlimited scope for a purely pagan delight. The sensuous and dramatic in man could not have passed the censorship of his multifarious principles; toward the rest of creation he could adopt without compunction the role of the free spectator, "clear of the nets of right and wrong."

I have said that he possessed a secret which we have lost. It was the secret of the sensuous life in a rich objective world. The life of nature meant more to Thoreau than the life of man has meant to any of our novelists, in its appeal, I mean, to the eye, the ear, the touch, the taste. There are pages in "Walden" which, by contrast, show up our American fiction, despite its occasional glamour, its frequent finesse, for the poor unpalatable straw it mostly is. To Thoreau there was a perceptible music in the universe, an Æolian music, and it was not through the contemplative inner ear that he received it, as Emerson did,—he heard it as plainly as a sensitive modern ear hears the music of humankind in the rhythm of city streets. It was this that gave him his marvellous power, like that of Saint Francis, over the lower orders, in which he divined an unconscious aspiration. The fox he characterized as "a rudimentary, burrowing man" and it disturbed him that we treat horses merely as automata to get work from, without any sense of responsibility to the spark of life that glimmers in them. It would be easier to find these complaints altogether absurd were they not bound up with a certain faculty possessed by Thoreau which testified to a profound grasp of the invisible forces. Rowing on Walden Pond, for example, he would put his hand into the water and gently lift out a fish which, after a moment's caress, would lie motionless across his palm for the space of half an hour. Feats like this gave him in the eyes of the village children a glamour like that which surrounded Virgil in the Middle Ages. The spiritual powers that made them possible, translated to the written page, constitute a lost province in our literary mind.

It is not this, however, it is not even his atavistic and half animal simplification of life, so alluring in certain ways just now, for which we remember him; it is the firmness of his personal texture, the force with which he enclosed and cultivated the little garden-plot of his own character. Stevenson called him a "skulker," Lowell said that his whole life was a search for the doctor. But there is something solid in Thoreau, beside which these two engaging literary entertainers of an optimistic and highly self-delusive past ring exceedingly hollow. He was as queer as Dick's hatband and he rubs most modern philosophy the wrong way. As for his prose, it contains passages of the kind which people used to call imperishable and which our contemporaries take a special delight in forgetting just for that reason. But in spite of everything he has never quite lost his tenacious grip on our imagination. Is it because of the conscientious objector in him, which our indeterminate and facile democracy has always found it so hard to forgive? At bottom we love self-discipline, we love obstacles, we love austerity, and Thoreau is a perpetual reminder, the most vivid reminder our history affords us, that it is the toughness, the intransigence of the spiritual unit which alone gives edge to democracy. As our epoch of expansion draws to its close and we are obliged more and more to test the mettle of our social consciousness, we shall be brought back to this truth, apprehended in so many ways by our fathers in the forest. The day will come when easy solutions no longer have any charm for us and we shall have attained the strength to fashion ourselves in the face of the multitudinous modern world. Then Thoreau will delight us anew,—not least because the gate of *his* Utopia was a needle's eye.

From *The Golden Day*

by Lewis Mumford

The pioneer who broke the trail westward left scarcely a trace
of his adventure in the mind: what remains are the tags of pioneer
customs, and mere souvenirs of the past, like the Pittsburg stogy,
which is our living connection to-day with the Conestoga wagon,
whose drivers used to roll cigars as the first covered wagons plodded
over the Alleghenies.

What the pioneer felt, if he felt anything, in the midst of these
new solitudes; what he dreamt, if he dreamt anything; all these
things we must surmise from a few snatches of song, from the com-
monplace reports issued as the trail was nearing its end, by the
generation of Mark Twain and Hamlin Garland, or by the reflections of their sons and daughters, romantically eager, like John G.
Neihardt's, critically reflective, like Susan Glaspell's, or wistfully
sordid, like Edgar Lee Masters' Anthology. Those who really faced
the wilderness, and sought to make something out of it, remained
in the East; in their reflection, one sees the reality that might have
been. Henry David Thoreau was perhaps the only man who paused
to give a report of the full experience. In a period when men were
on the move, he remained still; when men were on the make, he remained poor; when civil disobedience broke out in the lawlessness
of the cattle thief and the mining town rowdy, by sheer neglect,
Thoreau practiced civil disobedience as a principle, in protest
against the Mexican War, the Fugitive Slave Law, and slavery itself.
Thoreau in his life and letters shows what the pioneer movement
might have come to if this great migration had sought culture
rather than material conquest, and an intensity of life, rather than
mere extension over the continent.

Born in Concord about half a generation after Emerson, Thoreau

From *The Golden Day: A Study in American Experience and Culture* by Lewis
Mumford (New York: Liveright Publishing Corp.), pp. 107-120. Copyright 1926
by Lewis Mumford. Reprinted by permission of the author.

found himself without the preliminary searchings and reachings of the young clergyman. He started from the point that his fellow-townsman, Emerson, had reached; and where he first cleared out of his mind every idea that made no direct connections with his personal experience, Thoreau cleared out of his life itself every custom or physical apparatus, to boot, which could not stand up and justify its existence. "A native of the United States," De Tocqueville had observed, "clings to the world's goods as if he were certain never to die; and he is so hasty at grasping at all within his reach, that one would suppose he was constantly afraid of not living long enough to enjoy them. He clutches everything, he holds nothing fast, but soon loosens his grasp to pursue fresh gratifications." Thoreau completely reversed this process: it was because he wanted to live fully that he turned away from everything that did not serve towards this end. He prized the minutes for what they brought, and would not exercise his citizenship at the town meeting, if a spring day by Walden Pond had greater promise; nor would he fill his hours with gainful practices, as a maker of pencils or a surveyor, beyond what was needed for the bare business of keeping his bodily self warm and active.

Thoreau seized the opportunity to consider what in its essentials a truly human life was; he sought, in Walden, to find out what degree of food, clothing, shelter, labor was necessary to sustain it. It was not animal hardihood or a merely tough physical regimen he was after; nor did he fancy, for all that he wrote in contempt of current civilization, that the condition of the woodcutter, the hunter, or the American Indian was in itself to be preferred. What he discovered was that people are so eager to get the ostentatious "necessaries" of a civil life that they lose the opportunity to profit by civilization itself: while their physical wants are complicated, their lives, culturally, are not enriched in proportion, but are rather pauperized and bleached.

Thoreau was completely oblivious to the dominant myths that had been bequeathed by the Seventeenth Century. Indifferent to the illusion of magnitude, he felt that Walden Pond, rightly viewed, was as vast as the ocean, and the woods and fields and swamps of Concord were as inexhaustible as the Dark Continent. In his study of Nature, he had recourse on occasion to the scientific botanists and zoölogists; but he himself had possession of a method that they were slow to arrive at; and it is easier for us to-day to understand the metaphysical distinction of Thoreau's kind of na-ture study than it would have been for Gray or Agassiz. Like

Wordsworth before him, like Bergson after him, he realized that in current science "we murder to dissect," and he passed beyond the artful dismemberments of contemporary science to the flower and the bird and the habitat themselves. "Not a single scientific term or distinction," he wrote once in his notebook, "is the least to the purpose. You would fain perceive something and you must approach the object totally unprejudiced. You must be aware that nothing is what you take it to be. . . . Your greatest success will be simply to perceive that such things are, and you will have no communication to make to the Royal Society." In other words, Thoreau sought in nature all the manifold qualities of being; he was not merely in search of those likenesses or distinctions which help to create classified indexes and build up a system. The aesthetic qualities of a fern were as important for his mode of apprehension as the number of spores on a frond; it was not that he disdained science, but that, like the old herbalists and naturalists he admired, he would not let the practical offices of science, its classification, its measurements, its numerations, take precedence over other forms of understanding. Science, practiced in this fashion, is truly part of a humane life, and a Darwin dancing for joy over a slide in his microscope, or a Pupin, finding the path to physics through his contemplation of the stars he watched as a herd-boy through the night, are not poorer scientists but richer ones for these joys and delights: they merely bow to the bias of utilitarianism when they leave these things out of their reports. In his attitude toward scientific truth Thoreau was perhaps a prophetic figure; and a new age may do honor to his metaphysics as well as to his humanity.

The resolute acceptance of his immediate milieu as equal to the utmost that the earth could offer stood by Thoreau in his other activities, too. He captained huckleberry parties as he might have led a battle, and was just as much the leader in one as he would have been in the other. His courage he reserved for better occasions than the battlefield, for he was ready to go to jail for his principles, and to mock Emerson for remaining outside. As for his country, he loved the land too well to confuse it with the shifting territorial boundaries of the National State. In this, he had that vital regional consciousness which every New Englander shared: Hawthorne himself had said that New England was as large a piece of territory as could claim his allegiance. Thoreau was not deceived by the rascality of politicians, who were ready to wage war for a coveted patch of Mexico's land; nor did he side with those who, for the sake of the Union, were ready to give up the principles that alone had made the Union valuable. What he loved was the landscape, his friends, and his companions in the spirit: when the Political State presumed to exercise a brass counter-claim on these loyalties it might go to the devil.

Thoreau's attitude toward the State, one must note, was just the opposite to that of the progressive pioneer. The latter did not care what sort of landscape he "located" in, so long as he could salute the flag of his country and cast his vote: Thoreau, on the contrary, was far too religious a man to commit the idolatry of saluting a symbol of secular power; and he realized that the affairs controlled by the vote represented only a small fraction of an interesting life, while so far from being indifferent to the land itself, he absorbed it, as men have absorbed legends, and guarded it, as men preserve ceremonies. The things which his contemporaries took for the supreme realities of life, matter, money, and political rights, had only an instrumental use for Thoreau: they might contribute a little to the arrangement of a good life, but the good life itself was not contained, was not even implied in them. One might spend one's life pursuing them without having lived. "There is not one of my readers," he exclaimed, "who has yet lived a whole human life."

In Thoreau's time, industrialism had begun to puff itself up over its multiplication of goods and the increase of wants that it fostered, in order to provide the machine with an outlet for its ever-too-plentiful supply. Thoreau simply asked: "Shall we always study to obtain more of these things, and not sometimes be content with less?" "If we do not get our sleepers and forge rails and devote long days and nights to work," he observed ironically, "but go tinkering with our lives to improve *them*, who will build the railroads?" Thoreau was not a penurious fanatic, who sought to practice bare living merely as a moral exercise: he wanted to obey Emerson's dictum to save on the low levels and spend on the high ones. It is this that distinguishes him from the tedious people whose whole existence is absorbed in the practice of living on beans, or breathing deeply, or wearing clothes of a vegetable origin: simplification did not lead in Thoreau to the cult of simplicity: it led to a higher civilization.

What drove Thoreau to the solitude of the woods was no cynical contempt for the things beyond his reach. "Before we can adorn our houses with beautiful objects, the walls must be stripped, and our lives must be stripped, and beautiful housekeeping and beautiful living be laid for a foundation: now, a taste for the beautiful is most cultivated out of doors, where there is no house, and no housekeeper." The primeval woods were a favorable beginning for the search; but Thoreau did not think they could be the end of it. The land itself, however, did stir his imagination; he wrote:

> *All things invite this earth's inhabitants*
> *To rear their lives to an unheard of height,*
> *And meet the expectation of the land.*

"The expectation of the land!" One comes upon that phrase, or its equivalent, in almost every valid piece of early American thought. One thinks of moorland pastures by the sea, dark with bayberries and sweet fern, breaking out among the lichened rocks; and the tidal rivers bringing their weedy tang to the low meadows, wide and open in the sun; the purple pine groves, where the needles, bedded deep, hum to the wind, or the knotted New England hills, where the mountain laurel in June seems like upland snow, left over, or where the marble breaks through into clusters of perpetual laurel and everlasting; one sees mountain lakes, giant aquamarines, sapphires, topazes, and upland pastures where the blue, purple, lavender and green of the huckleberry bushes give way in autumn to the fringe of sumach by the roadside, volcanoes of reds and crimsons; the yellow of September cornfields, with intenser pumpkins lying between the shocks, or the naked breasts and flanks of the autumn landscape, quivering in uneasy sleep before the white blanket puts it to rest. To smell this, taste this, and feel and climb and walk over this landscape, once untouched, like an unopened letter or a lover unkissed—who would not rise to meet the expectation of the land? Partly, it was the challenge of babyhood: how will it grow up and what will become of it? Partly, it was the charm of innocence; or again, it was the sense of the mighty variety that the whole continent gives, as if between the two oceans every possible human habitat might be built, and every conceivable variety of experience fathomed.

What the aboriginal Indian had absorbed from the young earth, Thoreau absorbed; what the new settlers had given her, the combing of the plow, the cincture of the stone fence or the row of planted elms, these things he absorbed too; for Thoreau, having tasted the settled life of Concord, knew that the wilderness was not a permanent home for man: one might go there for fortification, for a quickening of the senses, for a tightening of all the muscles; but that, like any retreat, is a special exercise and wants a special occasion: one returned to Nature in order to become, in a deeper sense, more cultivated and civilized, not in order to return to crudities that men had already discarded. Looking ahead, Thoreau saw what was needed to preserve the valuable heritage of the American wilderness. He wrote:

> The kings of England formerly had their forests to hold the king's game, for sport or food, sometimes destroying villages to create and extend them; and I think that they were impelled by a true instinct. Why should not we, who have renounced the king's authority, have our national preserves, where no villages need be destroyed, in which the bear and panther, and some even of the hunter race, may still exist, and not be "civilized off the face of the earth,"—our own forests, not to hold the king's game merely, but to hold and preserve the king himself also, the lord of creation,—and not in idle sport of food, but for inspiration and our own true recreation? or shall we, like the villains, grub them all up, poaching on our own national domain?

These pregnant suggestions of Thoreau, which were to be embodied only after two generations in our National and State Parks, ·and in projects like Mr. Benton MacKaye's great conception of the Appalachian Trail, make the comments of those who see in him only an arch-individualist, half-Diogenes, half-Rousseau, seem a little beside the point. The individualism of an Emerson or a Thoreau was the necessary complement of the thoroughly socialized existence of the New England town; it was what prevented these towns from becoming collections of yes men, with never an opinion or an emotion that differed from their neighbors. He wrote for his fellow-townsmen; and his notion of the good life was one that should carry to a higher pitch the existing polity and culture of Concord itself.

> As the nobleman of cultivated taste surrounds himself with whatever conduces to his culture—genius—learning—wit—books—paintings—statuary—music—philosophical instruments, and the like; so let the village do—not stop short at a pedagogue, a parson, a sexton, a parish library, and three selectmen, because our pilgrim forefathers got through a cold winter once on a bleak rock with these. To act collectively is according to the spirit of our institutions; and I am confident that our circumstances are more flourishing, our means are greater than the nobleman's.

Do not those sentences alter a little our stereotype of homespun New England, of Individualistic America?

Just as Thoreau sought Nature, in order to arrive at a higher state of culture, so he practiced individualism, in order to create a better order of society. Taking America as it was, Thoreau conceived a form, a habitat, which would retain what was unique in the American contact with the virgin forest, the cultivated soil, and the renewed institutions of the New England town. He understood the precise thing that the pioneer lacked. The pioneer had exhausted himself in a senseless external activity, which answered no inner demands except those for oblivion. In his experiment at Walden Pond, Thoreau "learned this, at least . . . that if one advances confidently in the direction of his dreams, and endeavors to live the life which he has imagined, he will meet with success unexpected in the common hours. . . . In proportion as he simplifies his life, the laws of the universe will appear less complex, and solitude will not be solitude, nor poverty poverty, nor weakness weakness. If you have built castles in the air, your work need not be lost; that is where they should be. Now put the foundations under them."

In short, Thoreau lived in his desires; in rational and beautiful things that he imagined worth doing, and did. The pioneer lived only in extraneous necessities; and he vanished with their satisfaction: filling all the conditions of his environment, he never fulfilled himself. With the same common ground between them in their feeling towards Nature, Thoreau and the pioneer stood at opposite corners of the field. What Thoreau left behind is still precious; men may still go out and make over America in the image of Thoreau. What the pioneer left behind, alas! was only the burden of a vacant life.

Thoreau: No Hermit

by Max Lerner

When just out of Harvard, Thoreau came under the powerful sway of Emerson's mind and did his formative thinking as a member of the Concord group of transcendentalists. He eventually liberated himself, however, from Emerson's influence, and at no time was he taken in by the transcendentalist excesses of the Concord group or by the millennial dreams that grew thick as huckleberries on the Concord bushes. The sources of strength in his thinking came rather from other strains—an absorption with the Greek classics, a prolonged study of the Oriental teachings, the Graeco-British tradition of individualism, the nature-worship of the French and German philosophers and the English romantic poets, and finally a conscious modeling upon the way of life of the American Indians.

But Thoreau was not one to be too deeply influenced. He was impervious to anything that did not fit into that continual quest for a practical solution of the problems of his own individual life which he called his philosophy. But implicit in his highly personal essays and nature soliloquies and journal entries is a devastating attack upon every dominant aspect of American life in its first flush of industrial advance—the factory system, the corporations, business enterprise, acquisitiveness, the vandalism of natural resources, the vested commercial and intellectual interests, the cry for expansion, the clannishness and theocratic smugness of New England society, the herd-mindedness of the people, the unthinking civic allegiance they paid to an opportunist and imperialist government.

He despised everything derivative and secondary. His criticism of American society sprang from the rebellion of the pioneer spirit. For he was seeking on an intellectual and moral frontier the zest and immediacy of the original pioneer effort and protesting passionately against the cultural crudity and the materialism of the pioneer in an industrial age. He rejected the factory system because it meant the exploitation of others; he rejected the cult of success and the Puritan creed of persistent work because it meant the exploitation of oneself. His economics anticipated Ruskin's by defining the cost of a thing as the amount of life that has to be exchanged for it; his aesthetics anticipated William Morris's by declaring that no beauty can exist in commodities that does not flow from a creativeness in the lives of those who fashion them. He recounts in *Walden* (1854) a two-year experiment in living in a hut in the woods, stripping the husk of civilization to the core, and setting up his own economy of wants and satisfactions. He found that the economic system was making unreasonable demands on him, and so he proceeded to sabotage it, entering upon a conscientious withdrawal of efficiency which was none the less earnest because it was restricted to his own life. Similarly he sabotaged the government by refusing to pay taxes, and he spent a night in the village jail as an exultant political prisoner. His essay "Civil Disobedience" (1849) is a sharp statement of the duty of resistance to governmental authority when it is unjustly exercised; read by Gandhi in 1907, it became the foundation of the Indian civil disobedience movement. Thoreau's three speeches on John Brown (1859-1860; republished in Vol. X of the *Collected Works*) extol his insurrectionary attempt at Harpers Ferry and denounce the shortsighted coercion of the government that martyred him.

As a social critic Thoreau was uncompromising: his thought was tighter than Emerson's, less optimistic, less given to the resolution of opposites. It was a taut, astringent rejection of everything, that could not pass the most exacting tests of the individual life. In that sense there was something of the nihilist about Thoreau, and his thought effected an almost Nietzschean transvaluation of values.

But his hermit-like individualism may easily be overemphasized, just as his absorption with nature has been overemphasized. Both must be seen as part of a rebellion against the oversocialized New England town, in which the individual was being submerged, and against the factory system which saw nature only as so much raw material and sought to subdue it to the uses of profit. He was not so limited as to believe that the individual could by his own action stem the heedless onrush of American life, or succeed wholly in rechanneling it; yet, being a transcendentalist, he believed that a sharp moral protest such as that of John Brown, once clearly made, is ultimately irresistible. While he regarded individual development as the only aim of society, and the individual's moral sense as the only test and ultimately the only safeguard of institutions, he did not envisage the individual as the necessary cadre of society. "To act collectively is according to the spirit of our institutions," he wrote in *Walden,* and he follows this with a plea to extend the social services of the community and to make every New England village the basis of a venture in adult education. Nor did he wholly turn his back on the machine as an instrument of production: his emphasis was rather on its cultural consequences in his own day.

It was one of his characteristic paradoxes that the man who could solemnly call his fellow-townsmen together to read them a protest against the imprisonment of John Brown or the return of a fugitive slave could also profess an unconcern with most of the burning political issues of the day, and insist that his business was not to change the world but to solve the problem of living in it. He could say: "God does not sympathize with the popular causes," and at the same time have so deep a sense of the relation between a great culture and the common concerns of life that he has come down as perhaps the leading American nativist; commenting on the fact that no literature had yet grown up around "the Man of the Age, come to be called workingman," he remarks that "none yet speaks to his condition, for the speaker is not yet in his condition." It was his tragedy to be forced by the crudities of an expanding capitalism into a revulsion against society and its institutions that has until recently obscured the real force of his social thought. But there is about that thought a spare and canny strength and a quality of being unfooled that will survive even such a tragedy.

Henry Thoreau in Our Time

by Stanley Edgar Hyman

1

In July, 1945, we celebrated the centennial of Henry David Thoreau's retirement to Walden Pond. Almost twice as many old ladies as usual made the pilgrimage to Concord, to see the shrine containing his furniture, and to Walden, where they had the privilege of adding a rock to the cairn where his hut once stood and of opening a box lunch in the picnic ground that stands as his monument. The American Museum of Natural History staged a Walden Pond exhibit. The *Saturday Evening Post* ran an illustrated article. And to add the final mortuary touch, a professor of English published a slim volume called *Walden Revisited*. All in all, it was a typical American literary centennial. Henry Thoreau would probably not have enjoyed it.

A more significant Thoreau centenary would have been July, 1946, the hundredth anniversary of his going to jail. Every reader of *Walden* knows the story. Thoreau had not paid a poll tax for several years, as a sign that he had renounced his allegiance to a government that protected slavery and made war on Mexico, and one day when he walked into Concord to get a mended shoe from the cobbler he was seized and put into jail. That night the tax was paid for him, and the next morning he was freed, obtained his mended shoe, and went back to the woods to pick some berries for dinner. While he was in jail, placidly meditating on the nature of state coercion, Emerson is supposed to have come by and asked: "Henry, what are you doing in *there?*" To which Thoreau is supposed to have replied, "Waldo, what are *you* doing *out there?*"

"Henry Thoreau In Our Time" by Stanley Edgar Hyman. From *The Atlantic Monthly*, CLXXVIII (November 1946), 137-146. Copyright 1946 by *The Atlantic Monthly*. Reprinted by permission.

It takes not much investigation into the story to discover that the actual details of Thoreau's first great political gesture were largely ridiculous. For one thing, the act itself was both safe and imitative, Bronson Alcott having given Thoreau the idea three years before by refusing to pay his taxes and going to jail, where he was treated quite well. For another, Thoreau in jail seems to have been not at all the philosophic muser he makes himself out to be, but, as the jailer later reported, "mad as the devil." For a third, Emerson certainly engaged in no such pat dialogue with him, for the jailer allowed no visitors, and Emerson's actual reaction to the event was to tell Alcott he thought it was "mean and skulking, and in bad taste." Finally, the person who "interfered" and paid his tax was Thoreau's old Aunt Maria, disguised with a shawl over her head so that Henry would not be angry with her for spoiling his gesture.

Why, then, celebrate the centenary of this absurd event? For only one reason. As a political warrior, Thoreau was a comic little figure with a receding chin, and not enough high style to carry off a gesture. As a political writer, he was the most ringing and magnificent polemicist America has ever produced. Three years later he made an essay called "Civil Disobedience" out of his prison experience, fusing the soft coal of his night in jail into solid diamond. "Civil Disobedience" has all the power and dignity that Thoreau's political act so signally lacked. "Under a government which imprisons any unjustly, the true place for a just man is also a prison," he writes in a line Debs later echoed, ". . . the only home in a slave state in which a free man can abide with honor." "I saw that the State was halfwitted, that it was timid as a lone woman with her silver spoons, and that it did not know its friends from it foes, and I lost all my remaining respect for it, and pitied it." He summarizes his position reasonably, even humorously, but with finality:—

> I have never declined paying the highway tax, because I am as desirous of being a good neighbor as I am of being a bad subject; and as for supporting schools, I am doing my part to educate my fellow-countrymen now. It is for no particular item in the tax-bill that I refuse to pay it. I simply wish to refuse allegiance to the State, to withdraw and stand aloof from it effectually. I do not care to trace the course of my dollar, if I could, till it buys a man or a musket to shoot with,—the dollar is innocent,—but I am concerned to trace the effects of my allegiance. In fact, I quietly declare war with the

State, after my fashion, though I will still make what use and get what advantage of her I can, as is usual in such cases.

In the relative futility of Thoreau's political act and the real importance of his political essay based on it, we have an allegory for our time on the artist as politician: the artist as strong and serviceable in the earnest practice of his art as he is weak and faintly comic in direct political action. In a day when the pressure on the artist to forsake his art for his duties as a citizen is almost irresistible, when every painter is making posters on nutrition, when every composer is founding a society devoted to doing something about the atom bomb, when every writer is spending more time on committees than on the typewriter, we can use Henry Thoreau's example.

In the past century we have had various cockeyed and contradictory readings of Thoreau's "essence." But from them we can reach two conclusions. One is that he is probably a subtler and more ambiguous character than anyone seems to have noticed. The other is that he must somehow still retain a powerful magic or there would not be such a need to capture or destroy him, to canonize the shade or weight it down in the earth under a cairn of rocks. It is obvious that we shall have to create a Thoreau for ourselves.

The first thing we should insist on is that Thoreau was a writer, not a man who lived in the woods or didn't pay taxes or went to jail. At his best he wrote the only really first-rate prose ever written by an American, with the possible exception of Abraham Lincoln. The "Plea for Captain John Brown," his most sustained lyric work, rings like *Areopagitica,* and like *Areopagitica* it is the product of passion combined with complete technical mastery. Here are two sentences:—

> The momentary charge at Balaklava, in obedience to a blundering command, proving what a perfect machine the soldier is, has, properly enough, been celebrated by a poet laureate; but the steady, and for the most part successful, charge of this man, for some years, against the legions of Slavery, in obedience to an infinitely higher command, is as much more memorable than that as an intelligent and conscientious man is superior to a machine. Do you think that that will go unsung?

Thoreau was not only a writer, but a writer in the great stream of the American tradition, the mythic and non-realist writers, Hawthorne and Melville, Mark Twain and Henry James, and, in our own day, as Malcolm Cowley has been most insistent in pointing out, Hemingway and Faulkner. In pointing out Hemingway's kinship, not to our relatively barren realists and naturalists, but to our "haunted and nocturnal writers, the men who dealt in images that were symbols of an inner world," Cowley demonstrates that the idyllic fishing landscape of such a story as "Big Two-Hearted River" is not a real landscape setting for a real fishing trip, but an enchanted landscape full of rituals and taboos, a metaphor or projection of an inner state.

It would not be hard to demonstrate the same thing for the landscape in *Walden*. One defender of such a view would be Henry Thoreau, who writes in his *Journals,* along with innumerable tributes to the power of mythology, that the richest function of nature is to symbolize human life, to become fable and myth for man's inward experience. F. O. Matthiessen, probably the best critic we have devoting himself to American literature, has claimed that Thoreau's power lies precisely in his re-creation of basic myth, in his role as the protagonist in a great cyclic ritual drama.

2

Central to any interpretation of Thoreau is Walden, both the experience of living by the pond and the book that reported it. As he explains it in the book, it was an experiment in human ecology (and if Thoreau was a scientist in any field, it was ecology, though he preceded the term), an attempt to work out a satisfactory relationship between man and his environment. He writes:—

> I went to the woods because I wished to live deliberately, to front only the essential facts of life, and see if I could not learn what it had to teach, and not, when I came to die, discover that I had not lived. I did not wish to live what was not life, living is so dear; nor did I wish to practice resignation, unless it was quite necessary. I wanted to live deep and suck out all the marrow of life, to live so sturdily and Spartan-like as to put to rout all that was not life, to cut a broad swath and shave close, to drive life into a corner, and reduce it to its lowest terms, and, if it proved to be mean, why then to get the whole and genuine meanness of it, and publish its meanness to the world; or if it were sublime, to know it by experience, and be able to give a true account of it in my next excursion.

And of his leaving:—

> I left the woods for as good a reason as I went there. Perhaps it
> seemed to me that I had several more lives to live, and could not spare
> any more time for that one.

At Walden, Thoreau reports the experience of awakening one
morning with the sense that some question had been put to him,
which he had been endeavoring in vain to answer in his sleep. In
his terms, that question would be the problem with which he begins
"Life Without Principle": "Let us consider the way in which we
spend our lives." His obsessive image, running through everything
he ever wrote, is the myth of Apollo, glorious god of the sun, forced
to labor on earth tending the flocks of King Admetus. In one sense,
of course, the picture of Henry Thoreau forced to tend anyone's
flocks is ironic, and Stevenson is right when he notes sarcastically:
"Admetus never got less work out of any servant since the world
began." In another sense the myth has a basic rightness, and is,
like the Pied Piper of Hamelin, an archetypal allegory of the artist
in a society that gives him no worthy function and no commensurate reward.

The sun is Thoreau's key symbol, and all of *Walden* is a development in the ambiguities of sun imagery. The book begins with the
theme: "But alert and healthy natures remember that the sun rose
clear," and ends: "There is more day to dawn. The sun is but a
morning star." Thoreau's movement from an egocentric to a socio-
centric view is the movement from "I have, as it were, my own
sun, and moon, and stars, and a little world all to myself" to "The
same sun which ripens my beans illumines at once a system of earths
like ours." The sun is an old Platonist like Emerson that must set
before Thoreau's true sun can rise; it is menaced by every variety
of mist, haze, smoke, and darkness; it is Thoreau's brother; it is
both his own cold affection and the threat of sensuality that would
corrupt goodness as it taints meat; it is himself in a pun on s-o-n,
s-u-n.

When Abolitionism becomes a nagging demand Thoreau can
no longer resist, a Negro woman is a dusky orb rising on Concord,
and when John Brown finally strikes his blow for Thoreau the
sun shines on him, and he works "in the clearest light that shines
on the land." The final announcement of Thoreau's triumphant
rebirth at Walden is the sun breaking through mists. It is not to
our purpose here to explore the deep and complex ambiguities of
Thoreau's sun symbol, or in fact to do more than note a few of
many contexts, but no one can study the sun references in *Walden*

without realizing that Thoreau is a deeper and more complicated
writer than we have been told, and that the book is essentially
dynamic rather than static, a movement *from* something *to* something, rather than simple reporting of an experience.

Walden is, in fact, a vast rebirth ritual, the purest and most
complete in our literature. We know rebirth rituals to operate
characteristically by means of fire, ice or decay, mountains and pits,
but we are staggered by the amount and variety of these in the
book. We see Thoreau build his shanty of boards he has first purified in the sun, record approvingly an Indian purification ritual
of burning all the tribe's old belongings and provisions, and later
go off into a description of the way he is cleansed and renewed
by his own fireplace. We see him note the magic purity of the ice
on Walden Pond, the fact that frozen water never turns stale, and
the rebirth involved when the ice breaks up, all sins are forgiven,
and "Walden was dead and is alive again." We see him exploring
every phase and type of decay: rotting ice, decaying trees, moldy
pitch pine and rotten wood, excrement, maggots, a vulture feeding
on a dead horse, carrion, tainted meat, and putrid water.

The whole of *Walden* runs to symbols of graves and coffins, with
consequent rising from them, to wombs and emergence from them,
and ends on the fable of a live insect resurrected from an egg long
buried in wood. Each day at Walden Thoreau was reborn by
his bath in the pond, a religious exercise he says he took for purification and renewal, and the whole two years and two months
he compresses into the cycle of a year, to frame the book on the
basic rebirth pattern of the death and renewal of vegetation, ending
it with the magical emergence of spring.

On the thread of decay and rebirth Thoreau strings all his pre-
occupations. Meat is a symbol of evil, sensuality; its tainting sym-
bolizes goodness and affection corrupted; the shameful defilement
of chastity smells like carrion (in which he agreed with Shakespeare); the eating of meat causes slavery and unjust war. (Thoreau, who was a vegetarian, sometimes felt so wild he was tempted
to seize and devour a woodchuck raw, or yearned like a savage
for the raw marrow of kudus—those were the periods when he
wanted to seize the world by the neck and hold it under water like
a dog until it drowned.)

But even slavery and injustice are a decaying and a death, and
Thoreau concludes "Slavery in Massachusetts" with: "We do not
complain that they *live,* but that they do not *get buried.* Let the
living bury them; even they are good for manure." Always, in

Thoreau's imagery, what this rotting meat will fertilize is fruit, ripe fruit. It is his chief good. He wanted "the flower and fruit of man," the "ripeness." The perfect and glorious state he foresees will bear men as fruit, suffering them to drop off as they ripen; John Brown's heroism is a good seed that will bear good fruit, a future crop of heroes. Just as Brown, in one of the most terrifying puns ever written, was "ripe" for the gallows, Thoreau reports after writing "Civil Disobedience," as he dwells on action and wildness, that he feels ripe, fertile: "It is seedtime with me. I have lain fallow long enough." On the metaphor of the organic process of birth, growth, decay, and rebirth out of decay, Thoreau organizes his whole life and experience.

I have maintained that *Walden* is a dynamic process, a job of symbolic action, a moving *from* something *to* something. From what to what? On an abstract level, from individual isolation to collective identification—from, in Macaulay's terms, a Platonic philosophy of pure truth to a Baconian philosophy of use. It is interesting to note that the term Bacon used for the utilitarian ends of knowledge, for the relief of man's estate, is "fruit." The Thoreau who went to Walden was a pure Platonist, a man who could review a Utopian book and announce that it was too practical, that its chief fault was aiming "to secure the greatest degree of gross comfort and pleasure merely." The man who left Walden was the man who thought it was less important for John Brown to right a Greek accent slanting the wrong way than to right a falling slave.

Early in the book Thoreau gives us his famous Platonic myth of having long ago lost a hound, a bay horse, and a turtle dove. Before he is through, his symbolic quest is for a human being, and near the end of the book he reports of a hunter: "He had lost a dog but found a man." All through *Walden* he weighs Platonic and Baconian values: men keep chickens for the glorious sound of a crowing cock "to say nothing of the eggs and drumsticks"; a well reminds a man of the insignificance of his dry pursuits on a surface largely water, and also keeps the butter cool. By the end of the book he has brought Transcendentalism down to earth, has taken Emerson's castles in the air, to use his own figure, and built foundations under them.

3

Thoreau's political value, for us, is largely in terms of this transition from philosophic aloofness. We see in him the honest artist struggling for terms on which he can adjust to society *in his capacity as artist.* As might be expected from such a process, Thoreau's social statements are full of contradictions, and quotations can be amputated from the context of his work to bolster any position from absolute anarchism to ultimate toryism, if indeed they are very far apart. At his worst, he is simply a nut reformer, one of the horde in his period, attempting to "improve" an Irish neighbor by lecturing him on abstinence from tea, coffee, and meat as the solution to all his problems, and the passage in *Walden* describing his experience is the most condescending and offensive in a sometimes infuriating book. At his best, he is the clearest voice for social ethics that ever spoke out in America.

One of the inevitable consequences of Emersonian idealism was the ease with which it could be used to sugar-coat social injustice, as a later generation was to discover when it saw robber barons piling up fortunes while intoning Emersonian slogans of Self-Reliance and Compensation. If the Lowell factory owner was more enslaved than one of his child laborers, there was little point in seeking to improve the lot of the child laborer, and frequently Emerson seemed to be preaching a principle that would forbid both the rich and the poor to sleep under bridges. Thoreau begins *Walden* in these terms, remarking that it is frivolous to attend to "the gross but somewhat foreign form of servitude called Negro Slavery when there are so many keen and subtle masters that enslave"; that the rich are a "seemingly wealthy, but most terribly impoverished class of all," since they are fettered by their gold and silver; that the day laborer is more independent than his employer, since his day ends with sundown, while his employer has no respite from one year to another; even that if you give a ragged man money he will perhaps buy more rags with it, since he is frequently gross, with a taste for rags.

Against this ingenious and certainly unintentional social palliation, *Walden* works through to sharp social criticism: of the New England textile factory system, whose object is, "not that mankind may be well and honestly clad, but, unquestionably, that the corporations may be enriched"; of the degradation of the laboring class of his time, "living in sties," shrunken in mind and body; of the worse condition of the Southern slaves; of the lack of dignity and privacy in the lives of factory girls, "never alone, hardly in their dreams"; of the human consequences of commerce and technology; of the greed and corruption of the money-mad New England of his day, seeing the whole world in the bright reflecting surface of a dollar.

As his bitterness and awareness increased, Thoreau's direct action became transmuted. He had always, like his friends and family, helped the Underground Railway run escaped slaves to Canada. He devotes a sentence to one such experience in *Walden,* and amplifies it in his *Journal,* turning a quiet and terrible irony on the man's attempt to buy his freedom from his master, who was his father, and exercised paternal love by holding out for more than the slave could pay. These actions, however, in a man who disliked Abolitionism, seem to have been simple reflexes of common decency, against his principles, which would free the slave first by striking off his spiritual chains.

From this view, Thoreau works tortuously through to his final identification of John Brown, the quintessence of direct social action, with all beauty, music, poetry, philosophy, and Christianity. Finally Brown becomes Christ, an indignant militant who cleansed the temple, preached radical doctrines, and was crucified by the slaveowners. In what amounts almost to worship of Brown, Thoreau both deifies the action he had tried to avoid and transcends it in passion. Brown died for him, thus he need free no more slaves.

At the same time, Thoreau fought his way through the Emersonian doctrine that a man might wash his hands of wrong, providing he did not himself commit it. He writes in "Civil Disobedience":—

> It is not a man's duty, as a matter of course, to devote himself to the eradication of any, even the most enormous wrong; he may still properly have other concerns to engage him; but it is his duty, at least, to wash his hands of it, and, if he gives it no thought longer, not to give it practically his support. If I devote myself to other pursuits and contemplation, I must first see, at least, that I do not pursue them sitting upon another man's shoulders. I must get him off first, that he may pursue his contemplations too.

Here he has recognized the fallacy of the Greek philosopher, free because he is supported by the labor of slaves, and the logic of this realization was to drive him, through the superiority and smugness of "God does not sympathize with the popular movements," and "I came into this world, not chiefly to make this a good place to live in, but to live in it, be it good or bad," to the militant fury of "My thoughts are murder to the State, and involuntarily go plotting against her."

Thoreau's progress also involved transcending his economics. The first chapter of *Walden,* entitled "Economy," is an elaborate attempt to justify his life and views in the money terms of New England commerce. He speaks of going to the woods as "going into business" on "slender capital," of his "enterprise"; gives the reader his "accounts," even to the halfpenny, of what he spends and what he takes in; talks of "buying dear," of "paying compound interest." He accepts the ledger principle, though he sneaks into the Credit category such unusual profits on his investment as "leisure and independence and health." His money metaphor begins to break down when he writes of the Massachusetts citizens who read of the unjust war against Mexico as sleepily as they read the prices-current, and he cries out: "What is the price-current of an honest man and patriot today?" By the time of the John Brown affair he has evolved two absolutely independent economies, a money economy and a moral economy. He writes:—

> "But he won't gain anything by it." Well, no, I don't suppose he could get four-and-sixpence a day for being hung, take the year round; but then he stands a chance to save a considerable part of his soul,— and *such* a soul!—when you do not. No doubt you can get more in your market for a quart of milk than for a quart of blood, but that is not the market that heroes carry their blood to.

What, then, can we make of this complicated social pattern? Following Emerson's doctrine and example, Thoreau was frequently freely inconsistent. One of his chief contradictions was on the matter of reforming the world through his example. He could disclaim hoping to influence anyone with "I do not mean to prescribe rules to strong and valiant natures" and then take it back immediately with "I foresee that all men will at length establish their lives on that basis." Certainly to us his hatred of technological progress, of the division of labor, even of farming with draft animals and fertilizer, is backward-looking and reactionary. Certainly he distrusted cooperative action and all organization. But the example of Jefferson reminds us that a man may be economically backward-looking and still be our noblest spokesman, just as Hamilton reminds us that a man may bring us reaction and injustice tied up in the bright tissue of economic progress.

To the doctrine of naked expediency so tempting to our time, the worship of power and success for which the James Burnhams among us speak so plausibly, Thoreau opposes only one weapon— principle. Not policy or expediency must be the test, but justice and principle. "Read not the Times, read the Eternities." *Walden* has been a bible for the British labor movement since the days of

William Morris. We might wonder what the British Labor Party, now that it is in power, or the rest of us, in and out of power, who claim to speak for principle, would make of Thoreau's doctrine: "If I have unjustly wrested a plank from a drowning man, I must restore it to him though I drown myself."

4

All of this takes us far afield from what must be Thoreau's chief importance to us, his writing. The resources of his craft warrant our study. One of his most eloquent devices, typified by the crack about the Times and the Eternities, is a root use of words, resulting from his lifelong interest in language and etymology, fresh, shocking, and very close to the pun. We can see the etymological passion developing in the *Journal* notes that a "wild" man is actually a "willed" man, that our "fields" are "felled" woods. His early writings keep reminding us that a "saunterer" is going to a "Sainte Terre," a Holy Land; that three roads can make a village "trivial"; that when our center is outside us we are "eccentric"; that a "landlord" is literally a "lord of the land"; that he has been "breaking" silence for years and has hardly made a "rent" in it.

By the time he wrote *Walden* this habit had developed into one of his most characteristic ironic devices: the insistence that telling his townsmen about his life is not "impertinent" but "pertinent," that professors of philosophy are not philosophers, but people who "profess" it, that the "bent" of his genius is a very "crooked" one. In the "Plea for Captain John Brown" the device rises to a whiplash power. He says that Brown's "humanities" were the freeing of slaves, not the study of grammar; that a Board of Commissions is lumber of which he had only lately heard; of the Governor of Massachusetts: "He was no Governor of mine. He did not govern me." Sometimes these puns double and triple to permit him to pack a number of complex meanings into a single word, like the "dear" in "Living is so dear." The discord of goose-honk and owl-cry he hears by the pond becomes a "concord" that is at once musical harmony, his native town, and concord as "peace."

Closely related to these serious puns in Thoreau is a serious epigrammatic humor—wry, quotable lines which contain a good deal of meaning and tend to make their point by shifting linguistic levels. "Some circumstantial evidence is very strong, as when you find a trout in the milk." To a man who threatened to plumb his

depths: "I trust you will not strike your head against the bottom."
"The partridge loves peas, but not those that go with her into the
pot." On his habit of exaggeration: "You must speak loud to those
who are hard of hearing."

He reported that the question he feared was not "How much
wood did you burn?" but "What did you do while you were warm?"
Dying, to someone who wanted to talk about the next world: "One
world at a time"; and to another, who asked whether he had made
his peace with God: "We have never quarrelled." When Emerson
remarked that they taught all branches of learning at Harvard: "All
of the branches and none of the roots." Refusing to pay a dollar for
his Harvard diploma: "Let every sheep keep but his own skin."
Asked to write for the *Ladies' Companion:* "I could not write anything companionable." Many of these are variants of the same joke,
and in a few cases, the humor is sour and forced, like the definition
of a pearl as "the hardened tear of a diseased clam, murdered in its
old age," or a soldier as "a fool made conspicuous by a painted
coat." But those are penalties any man who works for humor must
occasionally pay, and Thoreau believed this "indispensable pledge
of sanity" to be so important that without some leaven of it "the
abstruse thinker may justly be suspected of mysticism, fanaticism or
insanity." "Especially the transcendental philosophy needs the
leaven of humor," he wrote, in what must go down as understate-
ment.

Thoreau was perhaps more precise about his own style and more
preoccupied generally with literary craft than any American writer
except Henry James. He rewrote endlessly, not only, like James, for
greater precision, but unlike James, for greater simplicity. "Simplify, Simplify, Simplify," he gave as the three cardinal principles
of both life and art. Emerson had said of Montaigne: "Cut these
words and they would bleed," and Thoreau's is perhaps the only
American style in his century of which this is true. Criticizing De
Quincey, he stated his own prose aesthetic, "the *art* of writing," demanding sentences that are concentrated and nutty, that suggest far
more than they say, that are kinked and knotted into something
hard and significant, to be swallowed like a diamond without
digesting. "Sentences which are expensive, towards which so many
volumes, so much life, went; which lie like boulders on the page,
up and down or across; which contain the seed of other sentences,
not mere repetition, but creation; which a man might sell his
grounds and castles to build."

In another place he notes that writing must be done with gusto, must be vascular. A sense of Thoreau's preoccupation with craft comes with noting that when he lists "My faults" in the *Journal*, all seven of them turn out to be of his prose style. Writing for Thoreau was so obsessive, so vital a physical process, that at various times he describes it in the imagery of eating, procreation, excretion, mystic trance, and even his old favorite, the tree bearing ripe fruit. An anthology of Thoreau's passages on the art of writing would be as worth compiling as Henry James's prefaces and certainly as useful to both the writer and the reader.

Thoreau's somewhat granite pride and aloofness are at their most appealing, and very like James Joyce's, when he is defending his manuscripts against editorial bowdlerizing, when he stands as the embattled writer against the phalanx of cowardice and stupidity. He fought Emerson and Margaret Fuller on a line in one of his poems they printed in the *Dial*, and won. When the editor of *Putnam's Monthly* cut passages from an article, Thoreau wrote to a friend: "The editor requires the liberty to omit the heresies without consulting me, a privilege California is not rich enough to bid for," and withdrew the series. His letter to Lowell, the editor of the *Atlantic*, when Lowell cut a "pantheistic" sentence out of cowardice, is a masterpiece of bitter fury, withering Lowell like a premature bud in a blast.

Henry Thoreau's and John Brown's personalities were as different as any two personalities can be; one the gentle, rather shy scholar who took children huckleberrying, the other the harsh military Puritan who could murder the children of slavers in cold blood on the Potawatomie, with the fearful statement: "Nits grow to be lice." Almost the only things they had in common, that made Thoreau perceive that Brown was his man, his ideas in action, almost his Redeemer, were principle and literary style. Just as writers in our own day were drawn to Sacco and Vanzetti perhaps as much for the majesty of Vanzetti's untutored prose as for the obvious justice of their case, Thoreau somehow found the most convincing thing about Brown to be his speech to the court. At the end of his "Plea" he quotes Brown's "sweet and noble strain":—

> I pity the poor in bondage that have none to help them; that is why I am here; not to gratify any personal animosity, revenge, or vindictive spirit. It is my sympathy with the oppressed and the wronged, that are as good as you, and as precious in the sight of God.

adding only: "You don't know your testament when you see it."

"This unlettered man's speaking and writing are standard English," he writes in another paper on Brown. "It suggests that the one great rule of composition—and if I were a professor of rhetoric I should insist on this—is, to *speak the truth*." It was certainly Thoreau's great rule of composition. "He was a speaker and actor of the truth," Emerson said in his obituary of Thoreau. We have never had too many of those. He was also, perhaps as a consequence, a very great writer. We have never had too many of those, either.

Thoreau's Doctrine of Simplicity

by Leo Stoller

The simple life, by whose gauge Henry Thoreau measured men and economies, aims at the most complete realization of the perfectibility innate in every person. The man who strives for it is not trying to find the way to wealth but the way "to invent and get a patent for himself." [1] In his youth, Thoreau sought the conditions for such a life in an idealized distortion of the economic order then being displaced by the industrial revolution. After his experiment at Walden Pond, he moved toward a reconciliation between simplicity and an economy of machines and profit. This goal he never reached. But he left behind elements of a critique of our society and intimations of an undiminishable ideal to be fought for.

1

The immediate antecedent of Thoreau's doctrine of simplicity appears to have been the self-culture preached by the Unitarians and especially by William Ellery Channing. Channing transmitted to a later and a different age the faith in human perfectibility which he had learned of the Enlightenment. "Let us not disparage that nature which is common to all men," he declared, "for no thought can measure its grandeur. It is the image of God, the image even of his infinity . . . no limits can be set to its unfolding." [2] He subsumed the whole virtue of individual life under the ideal of an integral perfection, in striving toward which "all the principles of

"Thoreau's Doctrine of Simplicity" by Leo Stoller. From *The New England Quarterly*, XXIX (December 1956), 443-461. Copyright 1956 by *The New England Quarterly*. Reprinted by permission.

[1] *The Writings of Henry David Thoreau*, 20 vols. (Boston and New York, 1906), xx, 282. Later references to this edition will be indicated in parentheses in the text. Volumes VII through XX are the Journal.

[2] *The Works of William E. Channing, D.D.* (Boston, 1875), 13.

our nature grow at once by joint, harmonious action, just as all parts of the plant are unfolded together." [3]

The devotion of young Henry Thoreau to this ideal of self-culture is amply attested by his writings. Elements of the doctrine are to be found scattered through the fragmentary journals of the late thirties and early forties, and a complete statement is in Thoreau's early essay "The Service." [4] Here, in imagery derived chiefly from light, spheres, and sound, Thoreau has embodied the whole of his early transcendentalism, which strove to perfect mankind by centering earth on the single man and urging him on to a correspondence with the goodness of the enveloping over-soul. The spiritual sphere which enclosed all horizons was to be expressed microcosmically in perfected men through whom its divine light would be shed on others to effect the redemption of the world.

The whole duty of man—workman, thinker, artist—was to perfect his own unique self: "every stroke of the chisel," proclaimed young Thoreau, "must enter our own flesh and bone." [5] Moreover, it was the entire man who was to be perfected, not some single aspect of the character whose development would be at the expense of the rest. The "coward," the man who does not aspire to correspondence with the over-soul, is "wretchedly spheroidal at best, too much educated or drawn out on one side, and depressed on the other," but the "brave man" is "a perfect sphere," concentric, as it were, with the great sphere of the over-soul.[6] To the music of this great sphere—that is, to the higher law—each man must attune his life.

These views which Thoreau expressed in his writing he unhesitatingly set about to realize in his life. His art and his Yankee pragmatism—bound together by temperament and the organic theory—demanded alike that he reduce all abstract truths to practice.

He found very quickly that the fruit which the divine spirit had given him to mature would have no buyers. The editors in Boston and New York accepted few of his essays and did not pay for all they printed. Almost immediately, therefore, he was forced to test the mode of self-culture which Channing and his adherents had suggested for men whose employment did not contribute to their development. Its key was the disciplined exploitation of spare time. "The

[3] *The Works of William E. Channing, D.D.,* 15.
[4] F. B. Sanborn, editor (Boston, 1902).
[5] F. B. Sanborn, editor, 24.
[6] F. B. Sanborn, editor, 6.

winter," Channing had advised, "brings leisure to the husband-man, and winter evenings to many laborers in the city," and "a single hour in the day, steadily given to the study of an interesting subject, brings unexpected accumulations of knowledge." [7] Similarly Frederic Henry Hedge, proclaiming in *The Dial* that "the work of life" is "the perfect unfolding of our individual nature," went on to explain that since the business of society "is not the highest culture, but the greatest comfort," the best which the aspirant might get from it was to be let alone after work. He "must expect nothing from Society, but may deem himself happy, if for the day-labor, which necessity imposes, Society will give him his hire, and beyond that leave him free to follow his proper calling, which he must either pursue," Hedge ironically concluded, "with exclusive devotion, or wholly abandon." [8]

In testing this advice, Thoreau became increasingly convinced of an incompatibility between his own self-culture and a profit-centered civilization. After his graduation from Harvard, he taught school and learned that the thinking of a schoolteacher and the thinking of an artist were not complementary. When he returned from Staten Island early in 1844 he worked for a while at pencil-making and later summed up this experience with the remark that he had tried trade but "found that it would take ten years to get under way" in it and that he would probably be on his way "to the devil" (II, 77). In the years which preceded his removal to Walden Pond, Thoreau saw himself being drawn into the pit which had already engulfed his neighbors, whose lives were wasted in seeking wealth or in earning a living.

Concord was economically rusticated, a backwater town relatively free of the evils of industrialism then becoming evident in other areas of Massachusetts. But Thoreau, penetrating deeply into this small world, found the souls of his townsmen encrusted and en-slaved, their potential freedom perverted into desperation. He learned that the laboring man, striving to maintain the market-value of his hands and brain, had "no time to be anything but a machine" (II, 6). He found society devoted to ends which made it inevitable that some do "all the exchange work with the oxen, or, in other words, become the slaves of the strongest" (II, 63). After the smoke of the railroad is blown away, he declared, "it will be perceived that a few are riding, but the rest are run over" (II, 59). For "we do not ride on the railroad, it rides upon us" (II, 102), and

[7] *The Works of William E. Channing, D.D.,* 33.
[8] "The Art of Life,—the Scholar's Calling," *Dial,* 1 (October, 1840), 176-179.

each of the sleepers that tie the tracks is a man. "The rails are laid on them, and they are covered with sand, and the cars run smoothly over them" (II, 103).

Seeking to avoid the fate of his fellows for himself and to discover a way by which all men might labor toward perfection, Thoreau attempted to establish a social order which would not reduce men to animals and machines but would be consistent with the devoted pursuit of self-culture. He was not alone among the transcendentalists to undertake this task. George Ripley, for example, hoped equally with Thoreau for a new world in which mankind might practice self-culture successfully. The "great object of all social reform," he wrote, is "the development of humanity, the substitution of a race of free, noble, holy men and women, instead of the dwarfish and mutilated specimens which now cover the earth." [9] And both Ripley and Thoreau established their experimental orders on the same ultimate principles.

Neither provided a place for the relationship of employer and wage-earner or for the conflicts associated with the existence of social classes. In economics their highest aim was that each man should receive the whole product of his labor.[10] Their common ethical ideal was to eliminate the conflict between work of the hands and work of the mind, so that a man's whole activity might contribute to his integral perfection. They applied these principles, as all know, in different manners, one basing himself on individual labor, the other on cooperative labor. But too much has perhaps been made of this difference. Neither application was practical in its own day, nor can an exact imitation of either be successful in any later day. The prescriptions of the utopian experimenters become in the end merely curious; it is only their ideals that can remain meaningful.

The principle that each man should receive the whole product of his labor became at Walden a life based on subsistence agriculture and on handicrafts to the exclusion of all trading and all wage-earning. It seemed to Thoreau that the "complex" way of earning a living (as he was later to call it) introduced between a man and the goods and services he actually needed a whole series of unnecessary intermediate activities. The farmer is poor, he wrote in *Walden*, because he "is endeavoring to solve the problem of a

[9] John T. Codman, *Brook Farm: Historic and Personal Memoirs* (Boston, 1894), 147f.
[10] For the history of this idea see Anton Menger, *The Right to the Whole Produce of Labour: the Origin and Development of the Theory of Labour's Claim to the Whole Product of Industry* (London, 1899).

livelihood by a formula more complicated than the problem itself. To get his shoestrings he speculates in herds of cattle" (II, 36). What Thoreau was suggesting was that as far as possible the farmer make his own shoestrings, weave his own cloth, grow his own food, and build his own house. "Who knows," he asked, "but if men constructed their dwellings with their own hands, and provided food for themselves and families simply and honestly enough, the poetic faculty would be universally developed, as birds universally sing when they are so engaged?" (II, 50). At the pond Thoreau had built his own house and believed that he had demonstrated that he could "avoid all trade and barter" (II, 71) in obtaining his food. And like him, he thought, "every New Englander might easily raise all his own breadstuffs in this land of rye and Indian corn, and not depend on distant and fluctuating markets for them" (II, 70). The "complex" economy of commerce and industry was to be restored to the "simplicity" of a more primitive era.

The ethical ideal behind Thoreau's experiment proved less susceptible of concrete embodiment. Having found the available modes of earning a living subversive of the great end of self-culture, Thoreau dreamed of a life all integral, whose every activity would help ripen the unique product lying potential in the soul. "The whole duty of life," he had once written, "is contained in the question how to respire and aspire both at once" (VII, 300). In his vision the labor which supported the body, by being also an end in itself—"industry . . . its own wages" (VII, 157)—would simultaneously enlarge the soul.

His favorite way of giving this difficult concept expression was through the image of time and eternity. The man who does not aspire to perfection and labors only to maintain his body works within the limits of a time which is external to him. Since his soul marches in place, his life shows no true sequence, and his actions "do not use time independently, as the bud does," which helps "lead the circle of the seasons" (VII, 215). The aspirant man whose labor contributes steadily to his perfection creates his own time, which has nothing in common with ordinary time, but is a sequence established by incremental activity against the background of eternity. "As time is measured by the lapse of ideas, we may grow of our own force," he wrote, "as the mussel adds new circles to its shell" (VII, 206). The achievement of the "artist in the city of Kouroo" (II, 359) who devoted his entire life to making a walking-stick was that by striving after perfection in his manual task he overcame the contradiction between time and eternity and did not age but continued to develop and become more nearly perfect in a perennial youth.

Whatever its metaphysical overlay, here is an ancient ideal of mankind, often frustrated and as often expressed again: the liberation of man from the everlasting pecking after corn which denies his mind full freedom, and the elevation of the labor imposed as a necessity by nature to an artistic activity which will discipline the spirit.

2

The economy which Thoreau established at Walden to provide an adequate base for the pursuit of self-culture, like all the other experimental economies of its day, failed to achieve its objective. What he had spoken of was a simple life in which a man would neither work for another nor hire another, but live to himself, eating only what he grew, growing only what he ate, and avoiding as much as possible all trade and barter. What he did in actuality was to set himself up in an unproductive and by-passed corner of Massachusetts as a marginal commercial farmer whose cash crop did not bring in enough money to satisfy his needs and who therefore hired himself out as a day-laborer in order to make ends meet. He learned, he says, that he could easily raise a "bushel or two of rye and Indian corn . . . and grind them in a hand-mill, and so do without rice and pork" and that if he needed a "concentrated sweet" he could make molasses out of pumpkins or beets or perhaps set out a few maple trees (II, 71). But what he actually did was to plant a cash crop to which even he could apparently not limit his diet—beans—and with its proceeds buy the rice and the pork, the rye and Indian meal, the sugar and molasses.

But although he was forced to retreat from his experiment in the simple economy and to live in the only social structure which history had made available to him, Thoreau did not abandon the ideal which had originally led him to the pond. Unlike George Ripley, who after Brook Farm divorced himself from social problems, Thoreau refused to make his peace with a society inimical to self-culture, and he continued to denounce the evil practices of his countrymen with passion.

The public expression of his prophet's anger was "Life Without Principle," an essay whose title is Thoreau's epitome of his America and his world. He had learned Concord by heart and was not slow to discover that the rest of mankind were simply his townsmen multiplied—"warped and narrowed by an exclusive devotion to trade and commerce and manufactures and agriculture and the like, which are but means, and not the end" (IV, 477). Their truest symbol he found in the Gold Rush, that great gamble which was simply an extension of the other lottery called trade and of "all the common modes of getting a living" (IV, 463). After reading an "account of the Australian gold-diggings one evening," he had in his mind's eye, "all night, the numerous valleys, with their streams, all cut up with foul pits, from ten to one hundred feet deep, and half a dozen feet across, as close as they can be dug, and partly filled with water,—the locality to which men furiously rush to probe for their fortunes,—uncertain where they shall break ground,—not knowing but the gold is under their camp itself,—sometimes digging one hundred and sixty feet before they strike the vein, or then missing it by a foot,—turned into demons, and regardless of each other's rights, in their thirst for riches,—whole valleys, for thirty miles, suddenly honeycombed by the pits of the miners, so that even hundreds are drowned in them,—standing in water, and covered with mud and clay, they work night and day, dying of exposure and disease" (IV, 465). "The philosophy and poetry and religion of such a mankind," he declared, "are not worth the dust of a puffball. The hog that gets his living by rooting, stirring up the soil so, would be ashamed of such company" (IV, 463).

In his effort to live in the civilization whose aims and methods he thus denounced and yet to avoid being part of it, Thoreau returned to the divided life advocated by Channing and Hedge. His stay at the pond, which had failed when measured by its high utopian ideal, had succeeded in an immediately practical way by teaching Thoreau how to make a living in the mornings and to seek bread for his soul in the afternoons and evenings. He still believed, after his return to Concord, that the "rarest success" would be to support both "body" and "essence" by "one and the same means" (VI, 181), but he accepted the plain fact that this success was beyond him and limited himself to reducing as far as possible the time expended on the body in order to enlarge that available for the spirit.

Basing itself on this division, one aspect of the doctrine of simplicity demanded voluntary poverty and the practice, as often as possible, of the primitive arts of life. The poverty was a necessary consequence once acquisition was rejected and a maximum amount of energy devoted to the higher goal of self-culture. Thoreau practiced it with moderation and wrote of it in his journal with polemic excess, reaching at times the questionable principle that "just in proportion to the outward poverty is the inward wealth" (IX, 114f).

Praise and practice of the activities of primitive economic life fill the later years in Concord with a reverberating echo of the experiment by Walden Pond. Not long after he himself had returned to the town and abandoned all efforts at becoming an independent small producer, Thoreau began to write enthusiastic tributes to the few men of the old school still struggling for a living in out-of-the-way corners of the township. The chief subject of his praise was George Minott, an aged subsistence farmer who apparently made a personal idiosyncrasy of the localism characteristic of his group. In 1854 he told Thoreau that he had last visited Boston in 1815—and, added a Concord gossip, "had not been ten miles from home since" (XII, 175). A self-conscious opponent of commercial agriculture, Minott claimed never to have brought produce to market in his lifetime (XV, 131) and ridiculed his successful neighbor Baker who gave his own excellent corn to his stock and bought cheaper southern corn to make bread for his family and farmhands (IX, 67). The world in which this old man had grown up was dying along with him, and the new was something he could not understand. There were still a few places in the woods that remained as they had been when he was a boy, "but for the most part," he said, "the world is turned upside down" (IX, 67). To Henry Thoreau, Minott was "perhaps the most poetical farmer," who most realized to him "the poetry of the farmer's life" (IX, 41).

Thoreau spoke with particular approval of the fact that Minott had a woodlot in which he felled his own trees and thus provided his own fuel. It seemed to him to be "more economical, as well as more poetical, to have a woodlot and cut and get out your own wood from year to year than to buy it at your own door" (XV, 178). Thoreau never owned a woodlot, but when he wrote this sentence at the end of 1856 he had for several years been collecting much of his own firewood from forest and river and had made the gathering of fuel a regular activity of his autumn.

Together with collecting fuel belong other experiments of the post-Walden years in which for a given moment and over a small area of his life Thoreau once again followed the pattern of George Minott. He made his own maple sugar (XIV, 207ff). He tried to eat acorns, both raw and cooked (IX, 56-59). In *Walden* he tells of the ground-nut which he discovered in the fall of 1852 and whose tubers he had eaten "roasted and boiled at supper time" (X, 384). In the day of market agriculture, "of fatted cattle and waving grain-fields," this "humble root" had been forgotten, but to Thoreau it seemed "like a faint promise of Nature to rear her own children and feed them simply here at some future period" (II, 264).

Consistent with the approval of Minott's subsistence agriculture are the journal passages in praise of the handicraft manufacture which was its historical counterpart. Thoreau was an occasional visitor at Barrett's sawmill, and there one day he noticed the miller's apprentice making birch and maple trays by hand. He was "pleased with the sight of the trays because the tools used were so simple" and because they were "made by hand, not by machinery." The relation between the apprentice and his work he called "poetic" (XVII, 227).

Thoreau himself thus provided an adequate example of the kind of simplicity that was based on the divided life. He made his living as a surveyor, part of the machinery, that is, for the definition and exchange of property rights and an essential member of a community devoted to acquisition. But denying this aim and practicing voluntary poverty, he strove (with unequal success) to limit his surveying to the mornings and to devote the greater part of his time to the activities whose end product was his essays.

3

This first aspect of the doctrine of simplicity, which condemned the aims and the systems of production of industrial society, dealt with the problem of the individual who wished to devote his life to higher ends than those sought by his contemporaries. A second aspect, whose development began late and was never completed, groped for methods by which the new system of production could be combined with the noble aim of self-culture.

The first hint of this new direction is to be found early in 1851, the day after Thoreau lectured before a Mechanics' Institute and was taken on a tour of a gingham mill by some of his audience. His report shows a certain breathlessness. "Saw at Clinton last night," he writes, "a room at the gingham-mills, which covers one and seven-eighths acres and contains 578 looms, not to speak of spindles, both throttle and mule. The rooms all together cover three acres. They were using between three and four hundred horse-power, and kept an engine of two hundred horse-power, with a wheel twenty-three feet in diameter and a band ready to supply deficiencies, which have not often occurred. Some portion of the machinery . . . revolved eighteen hundred times in a minute." He goes on to a brief description of the manufacture, beginning with the need for long-staple cotton "clean and free from seed" and concluding with the cloth "measured, folded, and packed." At the end of the journal entry he writes, "I am struck by the fact that no work has been shirked when a piece of cloth is produced. Every thread has been counted in the finest web; it has not been matted together. The operator has succeeded only by patience, perseverance, and fidelity" (VIII, 134-36). About four years after this he toured a steel-mill and again entered a circumstantial account in the journal reflecting his admiration of the skill and power embodied in the productive methods of modern industry (XIII, 100-02). The spirit of these entries is certainly not the same as that which in 1839 led Thoreau and his brother John to row as quickly as possible past the factories on the shores of the Merrimack, as if anxious to escape contamination.

The ambivalence which creeps into Thoreau's attitude to industrial and commercial civilization in the eighteen-fifties is expressed by indirection in his comments on the telegraph. Thoreau denounced the telegraph, along with the railroad and the steamboat, as an instrument by which the old subsistence farming was being debased into commercial agriculture that produced crops for the market and for profit and thus became indistinguishable from trade (XII, 108). What else, indeed, but denunciation would be consistent with his attitude toward the messages of profit and loss that the telegraph was designed to carry? At the end of August, 1851, the first telegraph line through Concord was completed and Thoreau wrote characteristically in his journal that the atmosphere was full of other telegraphs and that men need not be restricted to the lines erected by people like Morse (VIII, 442). The next day he walked under the new line and "heard it vibrating like a harp high overhead. It was as the sound," he wrote, "of a far-off glorious life, a supernal life, which came down to us, and vibrated the lattice-work of this life of ours" (VIII, 450). Again and again in the years that followed he heard the divine music of the spheres through this instrument designed to serve the devil's ends. He wrote quite truly that it was not Mr. Morse who had invented *this* music (IX, 220), but he plainly recognized the possibility that given the proper ear one could detect sounds not intended by the inventor or the telegrapher. The vibrations of the telegraph wire were "like the hum of the shaft, or other machinery, of a steamboat, which at length might become music in a divine hand" (IX, 248).

Thoreau did not apply this dialectic of coinciding higher and lower ends to industry. Here, as in other aspects of his thinking, the forward element is his relation to nature. In the mid-fifties, after he had again and again surveyed woodlots in preparation for their auction to lumber dealers, Thoreau became interested in the problem of the conservation of forests. He had believed from his youth in the unique role played by nature in the education of the mind, and this belief, though somewhat modified, did not change essentially as he grew older. But the method by which he sought to keep men in contact with nature underwent a radical transformation.

To the younger Thoreau it had seemed that nature and modern society were in complete contradiction and that to accept one meant to reject the other. Then, however, he was speaking of a settled America which was surrounded by unmodified nature and which still included oases of wildness within its borders. He had himself retreated to a patch of woods within earshot of the railroad whistle, and after his trip to Maine in 1846 he reminded his contemporaries that they were within easy reach of a "bran-new country" where a man might "live, as it were, in the primitive age of the world" (III, 87).

The recession of the frontier, which made itself evident in New England long before it pressed the nation as a whole, brought to an end the historical context in which young Thoreau had spoken and created a new problem. If it was essential for the education of men to be in continuous association with nature, then it was essential to find some way to preserve nature itself.

When there was still wilderness beyond a frontier, Thoreau had urged men to remove to nature by arguing from the principle that there they would find the best life. In attacking the problem of the preservation of nature he did not argue from principle but from expediency. "The Succession of Forest Trees" led men to the most profitable method of managing woodlots. The most profitable method, however, based as it was on a natural succession of one type of growth by another, was also the one most likely to preserve the forest itself from extinction.

In "Higher Laws," relying on the power of nature to affect the unconscious, Thoreau had advised fathers to bring up their sons as hunters and fishermen in the hope that having been led to seek out nature for low ends they might in time become aware of the higher purposes of their relation to her. Similarly his work on sylviculture shows that he was ready to employ the dialectic of lower and higher in relation to a branch of the economy intimately related to nature. He was more concerned with ends than with means, and if the times showed that they would not abandon agriculture aimed at markets and money, Thoreau was willing to make use of this economy which he had long condemned in order to achieve ends not dreamed of by its practitioners.

Thoreau's thinking about the second aspect of the doctrine of simplicity shows only the first stages of this evolution whose goal was the union of expediency with principle. He made some progress toward separating the ideal itself from the "simple" economy with which it had been linked in the testing at Walden, but he failed— or perhaps did not live long enough—to anchor it in the "complex" economy which he had begun to accept.

After leaving Walden, Thoreau never again attempted to derive his livelihood from the simple economy whose activities he continued to praise in his journal. He wished occasionally that he were back in the woods, and he envied the men who explored the Maine forests for cuttable timber—but he stayed put in Concord. "I hate the present modes of living and getting a living," he exclaimed. "Farming and shopkeeping and working at a trade or profession are all odious to me. I should relish getting my living in a simple, primitive fashion" (XIV, 7). "But," he concluded, "what is the use in trying to live simply, raising what you eat, making what you wear, building what you inhabit, burning what you cut or dig, when those to whom you are allied insanely want and will have a thousand other things which neither you nor they can raise and nobody else, perchance, will pay for? The fellow-man to whom you are yoked is a steer that is ever bolting right the other way" (XIV, 8).

The form of the simple life in which self-culture rested on an economic foundation of handicrafts and subsistence agriculture had ceased to be programmatic, and Thoreau neither practiced it himself nor advocated it for society at large. And side by side with the knowledge that a return to the old order was no longer possible came also the realization that the preindustrial economy in itself was of a true simplicity.

In 1853, Thoreau found in a book on the Hawaiian Islands the remark that one main obstacle to improvement was "the extremely limited views of the natives in respect to style of living." They were contented with so little that they had no desire for the civilization which would bring commodities in abundance. "But this," said Thoreau, "is putting the cart before the horse, the real obstacle being their limited views in respect to the object of living." Their simplicity of living did not come from philosophy but from ignorance. In their case, outward simplicity was accompanied by "idleness" and "its attendant vices" and was no better than the complex life of civilized society, and perhaps not even as good. For it is not the appearance of simplicity which is the essential. "There are two kinds of simplicity,—one that is akin to foolishness, the other to wisdom. The philosopher's style of living is only outwardly simple, but inwardly complex. The savage's style is both outwardly and inwardly simple. . . . It is not the tub that makes Diogenes, the Jove-born, but Diogenes the tub" (XI, 410-12).

When Thoreau found a hut in the Acton woods, he did not jump to the conclusion that its inhabitant was leading a truly simple life but asked instead, "Is he insane or of sound, serene mind? Is he weak, or is he strong?" Only if he knew "that the occupant was a cheerful, strong, serene man" would he rejoice to see his shanty (IX, 467).

This separation of the concept of simplicity from its original economic foundation in the pre-industrial order, as well as the beginning of a new acceptance of industrial production and commercial agriculture mentioned earlier, prepares the way for a synthesis of the aims of simplicity and the methods of complexity. This synthesis, however, toward which he was groping, Thoreau never reached, and he continued to the end to draw examples of simplicity from handicrafts and subsistence agriculture, these being the only concrete approximations of the ideal available. It is important, therefore, to separate the concept itself from the forms in which the artist Thoreau illustrated it.

The keystone of the doctrine of simplicity is the principle of self-culture. At the end of his career as at the beginning, Thoreau believed that "the object of life is something else than acquiring property" (XVII, 196), that the man approaching success is not he who "has got much money, many houses and barns and wood-lots," but he who has been "trying to better his condition in a higher sense than this, has been trying to invent something, to be somebody,—*i.e.*, to invent and get a patent for himself" (XX, 281f). The journals of his last years and such late lectures as "Wild Apples" and "Autumnal Tints" are rich with variation of this central theme. Obsessed as he had long been with the analogy between the life of man and the seasons of nature, he turned in his own maturity to the image of ripeness and in paragraphs free of the stridency of his youth guided his hearers to the conclusion that they too must grow toward a ripeness and must mature their own harvest.

Inseparable from self-culture in its later stage as in the earlier was the ideal of an integral existence, in which there would be no division between labor for the body and labor for the spirit. The economic activities which assist in perfecting the unique contribution of a man's character Thoreau termed life in the present, distinguishing them from all those others which merely sustain the body and are postponements of life's proper business. The distinction between them he illustrated by the analogy of the artist and the artisan. He noticed one evening a horse which during the day powered a sawing-machine through a treadmill and was let out at night to graze: at each step the animal lifted his hind legs "convulsively high from the ground, as if the whole earth were a treadmill continually slipping away from under him while he climbed its convex surface." To Thoreau the horse was "symbolical of the moral condition . . . of all artisans in contradistinction from artists, all who are engaged in any routine; for to them also the whole earth is a treadmill, and the routine results instantly in a similar painful deformity. The horse may bear the mark of his servitude on the muscles of his legs, the man on his brow" (XI, 276f). The ideal which he had in mind, and which he could not find in production based on division of labor, was an economy whose workers would no longer be mere artisans.

Thoreau kept returning to the activities of a more primitive economy because only there could he find that wholeness of relationship between a man and his work whose highest realization is in the life of the artist. One March day he found an Indian basket woven of osiers. The man who was "weaving that creel," he wrote, "was meditating a small poem in his way. It was equal to a successful stanza whose subject was spring" (XVI, 313f). Considered abstractly, a subsistence economy in which the individual does not produce commodities for exchange but only articles for his own consumption provides the condition under which a man may always be an artist. For the true craftsman, like the artist, conceives his task in its entirety, selects the raw materials, and transforms them into the article which had been foreseen from the beginning. Artistic activity of this kind, not aimed at the market, becomes an end in itself, and through it the man disciplines and develops his own mind at the same time that he is maturing its product. With the division of labor, the productive process is separated into stages and each man acts upon the raw materials in only one stage or in several at most, and the task of conceiving the cycle of production and viewing it in its totality becomes itself a stage and the province of a specialist. The individual producer cannot maintain his relation to the productive process as a whole or make his labor an end in itself. He does not produce articles for consumption but commodities for sale and must exchange the products for his specialized labor in order to obtain the necessities of life. His daily work is thus no longer life in the present, but postponed life, and if he wishes to develop the potentialities of his soul he must do so after hours.

In addition to the restoration of a creative relationship between man and labor, Thoreau sought the elimination of a certain depersonalizing of human relations which he associated with the replacement of barter by business transactions and of the relation between man and man by that between man and market. "How rarely," he exclaimed in his journal, are we "encouraged by the sight of simple actions in the street! We deal with banks and other institutions, where the life and humanity are concealed,—what there is. I like at least to see the great beams half exposed in the ceiling or the corner" (XIX, 169).

These ideals Thoreau was never able to combine with the methods of production insisted upon by his contemporaries. The failure of the Walden experiment had cut the doctrine of simplicity off from any economic foundation. Thoreau could no longer advise mankind to resign from the industrial and agricultural revolutions and head for the woods. Neither, however, could he reconcile his philosophical anarchism with any form of socialism. He was left with a critique of industrial and commercial civilization but with no associated program of action. His concept of simplicity became, like the Old Marlborough Road, "a direction out there" (V, 215), away from the definable evils of the social order but with no clear goal in sight.

The audiences at his lectures, their practical American minds looking for a program, complained that they could not understand him. All they could find was the obviously unbelievable implication that mankind should return to the life of the savage. Thoreau's friend Ricketson, constituting himself their spokesman, asked the lecturer why, "having common sense," he did not "write in plain English always" and "teach men in detail how to live a simpler life" (VI, 259). Thoreau replied that he was not interested in giving men instructions but in inspiring them with ideals. "As a preacher," he wrote, "I should be prompted to tell men, not so much how to get their wheat bread cheaper, as of the bread of life compared with which *that* is bran. . . . Don't spend your time in drilling soldiers, who may turn out hirelings after all, but give to undrilled peasantry a *country* to fight for" (VI, 260).

What Music Shall We Have?

by F. O. Matthiessen

"Talk about learning our *letters* and being *literate!* Why, the roots of *letters* are *things.* Natural objects and phenomena are the original symbols or types which express our thoughts and feelings, and yet American scholars, having little or no root in the soil, commonly strive with all their might to confine themselves to the imported symbols alone. All the true growth and experience, the living speech, they would fain reject as 'Americanisms.' "

—Thoreau's *Journal* (1859)

In this rejected essay ["The Service"] (1840), he was trying his wings in the cloudy air of transcendental symbolism. Margaret Fuller found it "rich in thoughts," but protested that these thoughts were "so out of their natural order" that it could not be read without pain. She agreed with Emerson that "essays not to be compared with this have found their way into *The Dial.*" But those had been more unassuming in their tone; Thoreau's attempted so much that it needed to be "commanding." It was not printed during his lifetime, or until long after his death.[1] And certainly most of it provides evidence for Lowell's gibe that when Thoreau ejaculated, in the *Week,* "Give me a sentence which no intelligence can understand," he received a plentiful award.

Yet this essay is of cardinal value since it lets us follow the very process by which Thoreau found what he wanted to do with language. It has been suggested that the title, underscored by those of its first and last sections, "Qualities of the Recruit" and "Not How Many, but Where the Enemy Are," was the product of Thoreau's

[1] It was issued separately by Sanborn in 1902.

private reaction to current discourses on pacifism. The repeated imagery of a crusade seems borrowed from Tasso's *Jerusalem Delivered,* which had been one of his favorites in college, and whose hero Godfrey is cited here. However, the campaign that Thoreau urges is quite other. The first section sounds the theme, "For an impenetrable shield, stand inside yourself." The final pages are a trumpet blast to rouse the soul hovering on the verge of life, to call man not to action against others, but to the realization of his submerged potentialities. All such passages are what Emerson found in Thoreau at this time, simply Emerson's own thoughts originally dressed. But the middle section, "What Music Shall We Have?" hints, if somewhat obscurely, at Thoreau's special qualities, and at the way by which he was to arrive at them. One of its sentences, "A man's life should be a stately march to an unheard music," may seem a vague enough acceptance of the romantic belief in such melodies. But it meant something compelling to Thoreau, since it became a recurrent image throughout his work. He varied it a decade later in his journal: "It is not so much the music as the marching to the music that I feel." He picked it up again in the conclusion to *Walden:* "Let him step to the music which he hears, however measured or far away." He obviously did not mean merely the disembodied harmony of thought, and it is worth trying to see upon what he grounded his image since it came to epitomize for him the relation between his life and his writing.

In "The Service" Thoreau seems groping to convey his recognition, which was to grow increasingly acute, that a deep response to rhythm was his primary experience. He tried to develop it in this fashion: "To the sensitive soul the Universe has her own fixed measure, which is its measure also, and as this, expressed in the regularity of its pulse, is inseparable from a healthy body, so is its healthiness dependent on the regularity of its rhythm." The first statement is the usual transcendental doctrine of the merging of the individual with the Over-Soul; the remainder of the sentence, blurred as it is by its loose pronouns, still adumbrates what is going to be Thoreau's particular forte, his grasp of the close correspondence, the organic harmony between body and spirit. Emerson perceived this trenchantly when he said: "The length of his walk uniformly made the length of his writing. If shut up in the house he did not write at all." The context of the demand that Lowell mocked is nearly always forgotten: "Give me a sentence which no intelligence can understand. There must be a kind of life and palpitation to it, and under its words a kind of blood must circulate forever." Thoreau's first conviction about the artist was that his words should speak not to the mind alone but to the whole being. He made himself more explicit (1852) in this distinction between the thinker and the artist: "Poetry *implies* the whole truth. Philosophy *expresses* a particle of it." He said in the *Week* that "a true account of the actual is the rarest poetry, for common sense always takes a hasty and superficial view"—a remark not far from the strictness upon which modern poets have again insisted. While still at college Thoreau had noted the Greek poets' "appetite for visible images" in contrast to the tendency of the northern imagination to "the dark and mysterious" and its consequent "neglect of the material." [2] His admiration continued to develop for the type of writer who "was satisfied with giving an exact description of things as they appeared to him, and their effect upon him." He found this ability pre-eminently in Homer, in the way he could convey the physical sensation of action: "If his messengers repair but to the tent of Achilles, we do not wonder how they got there but accompany them step by step along the shore of the resounding sea." [3]

Thoreau's emergence from the cloud-land of "The Service" onto similar solid earth was due in large part to his having clung fast to his perception that both language and rhythm have a physical basis. His theory of language, in so far as he recorded one, seems at first

[2] The manuscript of Thoreau's review of H. N. Coleridge's *Introductions to the Study of the Greek Classic Poets*, dated October 1, 1836, is in the Huntington Library. This library also possesses, among much other Thoreau material, the entire manuscript of *Walden*.

[3] Thoreau's convictions about the nature of art look forward to Hemingway's. Compare the sentences quoted in the paragraph above with Hemingway's suggested tests for determining the difference between reporting and creating: "When you describe something that has happened that day the timeliness makes people see it in their own imagination. A month later that element of time is gone and your account would be flat and they would not see it in their minds nor remember it. But if you can make it up instead of describe it you can make it round and whole and solid and give it life. You create it, for good or bad. It is made, not described. It is just as true as the extent of your ability to make it and the knowledge you put into it." (*Esquire*, October 1935.) Also: "All good books are alike in that they are truer than if they had really happened and after you are finished reading one you will feel that all that happened to you and afterwards it all belongs to you: the good and the bad, the ecstasy, the remorse and sorrow, the people and the places and how the weather was. If you can get so you can give that to people, then you are a writer." (*Esquire*, December 1934.) Despite his wide divergence in philosophy, T. E. Hulme would also have agreed with the core of these passages. They are in line with what he implied by saying that "Plain speech is essentially inaccurate. It is only by new metaphors . . . that it can be made precise."

glance to approximate Emerson's. He held that the origin of words is in nature ("Is it not as language that all natural objects affect the poet?") and that they are symbols of the spiritual. He spoke of the difficulty in finding the word that will exactly name and so release the thing. But he had a more dogged respect for the thing than any of his companions, and limitless tenacity in waiting to find the word. He remarked, for instance, how Channing called their walks along the banks of the river *"riparial* excursions. It is a pleasing epithet, but I mistrust such, even as good as this, in which the mere name is so agreeable, as if it would ring hollow ere long; and rather the thing should make the true name poetic at last. Alcott wished me to name my book *Sylvania!"*

Thoreau knew that the farmer's lingo surpassed the scholar's labored sentences. He had a relish for old sayings and for rural slang, and set down many fragments of conversation with his friends the woodchoppers and the farmers.[4] He hated writers who did not speak out of a full experience but used "torpid words, wooden or lifeless words, such words as humanitary, which have a paralysis in their tails." To those who think of him only as the extreme individualist it may come as a surprise to find that from the beginning of his career he asserted the social foundations of language:

"What men say is so sifted and obliged to approve itself as answering to a common want, that nothing absolutely frivolous obtains currency . . . The analogies of words are never whimsical and meaningless, but stand for real likenesses. Only the ethics of mankind, and not of any particular man, give point and vigor to our speech."

[4] Examples crop up everywhere in his journals. "When it snowed yesterday very large flakes, an inch in diameter, Aunt said, 'They are picking geese.' This, it seems, is an old saying." Thoreau's conversations with his friends Minott and Therien could be arranged into type-characters of the Farmer and of the Lumberman. Minott in particular provided Thoreau's journal with many fresh turns of phrase. For instance, "I asked M. about the Cold Friday. He said, 'It was plaguy cold; it stung like a wasp.'" Or again, Minott "says that some call the stake-squelcher 'belcher-squelcher,' and some, 'wollerkertoot.' I used to call them 'pump-er-gor.' Some say 'slug-toot.'"

Everyday idioms found readier access into Thoreau's writing than into Emerson's. Still he seems to have responded involuntarily to the age's tendency to refine, for he made a few excisions even from *Walden.* For example, in the description of the teamster, near the opening of "Economy," he left out "He rolls out of his cradle into a Tom and Jerry and goes at once to look after his team." In "What I Lived For" he eliminated an even more characteristic Yankee colloquialism by dropping an instance of how "our life is frittered away by detail." The omitted sentence read: "Its dish consists almost entirely of 'fixings,' and very little of the chicken's meat."

Thus far nothing has really differentiated his position from what Emerson developed with much greater wealth of detail. But while discussing the primitive sense of words he made a remark that suggests what carried his practice such a considerable distance from his master's: "We reason from our hands to our head." Thoreau was not inclined to rate language as superior to other mediums of expression on the ground that it was produced solely by the mind and thence could share more directly in the ideal. On the contrary, he insisted upon its double parentage:

"A word which may be translated into every dialect, and suggests a truth to every mind, is the most perfect work of human art; and as it may be breathed and taken on our lips, and, as it were, become the product of our physical organs, as its sense is of our intellectual, it is the nearest to life itself."

According to Channing, in much that Thoreau wrote "there was a *philological* side,—this needs to be thoughtfully considered." He was always eager to probe roots and etymologies, and in some passages we can find him doing something more dynamic than that ordinarily amounts to. Even in a few notes on Latin terminations he dwelt on their closeness to physical life and revealed the kind of movement he wanted to catch in his own writing:

"This termination *cious* adds force to a word, like the lips of browsing creatures, which greedily collect what the jaw holds; as in the word "tenacious" the first half represents the kind of jaw which holds, the last the lips which collect. It can only be pronounced by a certain opening and protruding of the lips; so "avaricious." These words express the sense of their simple roots with the addition, as it were, of a certain lip greediness . . . When these expressive words are used, the hearer gets something to chew upon . . . What is *luscious* is especially enjoyed by the lips. The mastiff-mouthed are tenacious. To be edacious and voracious is to be not nibbling and swallowing merely, but eating and swallowing while the lips are greedily collecting more food."

What separates Thoreau most from Emerson is his interest in the varied play of all his senses, not merely of the eye, a rare enough attribute in New England and important to dwell on since it is the crucial factor in accounting for the greater density of Thoreau's style. You think first, to be sure, of his Indian accuracy of sight that could measure distances like the surveyor's instrument and tell

time almost to the minute by the opening of the flowers. This alert-
ness remained constant. Indeed, the last notation in his journal, before it was broken off by the consumption from which he died, con-
siders the precise shape of some furrows made by the rain and
concludes: "All this is perfectly distinct to an observant eye, and yet
could easily pass unnoticed by most." But usually he felt that sight
alone was too remote for the kind of knowledge he wanted, that "we
do not learn with the eyes; they introduce us, and we learn after by
converse with things." He held that scent was "a more primitive
inquisition," "more oracular and trustworthy." It showed what was
concealed from the other senses: by it he detected earthiness. Taste
meant less to him, though eating became a kind of sacrament and
out in the berry field he could be thrilled to think that he owed
a perception to this "commonly gross sense," that he had been inspired through the palate. Just what he implied by that needs a
longer declaration:

> "Let not your life be wholly without an object, though it be only to
> ascertain the flavor of a cranberry, for it will not be only the quality
> of an insignificant berry that you will have tasted, but the flavor of
> your life to that extent, and it will be such a sauce as no wealth can
> buy."

Even in this fragile instance we can see his determination never
to record an abstraction, but to give himself and his reader the full
impression of the event.

He became ecstatic as he talked about touch: "My body is all
sentient. As I go here or there, I am tickled by this or that I come
in contact with, as if I touched the wires of a battery." He knew,
like Anteus, that his strength derived from ever renewed contact
with the earth. But he wanted more than contact with nature, he
wanted the deepest immersion, and his delight mounted at being
drenched in the summer waters of the pond, or when he could
wonder whether "any Roman emperor ever indulged in such luxury
as . . . walking up and down a river in torrid weather with only
a hat on to shade the head." But as his preoccupation in "The
Service" has told us, he gave his most rapt attention to sounds.
These alone among his sense impressions were to have a chapter
devoted to them in *Walden*. He can hardly find enough verbs of
action to describe what they do to him. They melt and flow, and
he feels himself bathed in their surge. The sharp scream of the jay
rasps at him like steel; the first faint peep of the hyla leaks into

his ear. The liquid notes of a bobolink are as refreshing "as the first distant tinkling and gurgling of a rill to a thirsty man." On hearing an Italian boy with his hand organ, he expresses an intensity of pleasure equal to what Whitman felt in the opera: "these delicious harmonies tear me to pieces while they charm me." The most exquisite flavor is not to be compared to the sweetness of the note of the wood thrush. As he listens, it seems to take him out of himself: he leaves his body in a trance and has the freedom of all nature. After such an experience he can say, measuring his words, "The contact of sound with a human ear whose hearing is pure and unimpaired is coincident with an ecstasy."

It is no wonder, therefore, that he often failed to convey what it meant to him. One of his earliest essays, parts of which he used in the closing pages of the *Week,* was on "Sound and Silence," wherein he made an impossible effort to catch the evanescent rippling of the one into the other, and added the Carlylean reflection that so the most excellent speech finally falls away into the perfect stillness that it has disturbed and intensified. He kept returning to the theme that "there is all the romance of my youthfulest moment in music. Heaven lies about us, as in our infancy." But the articulation of such a theme could quickly vaporize into an exaltation of the vague, which Thoreau's age so often identified with the essence of music. He can carry us with him much more surely when he talks of his simple joy in playing the flute, of how its echo lends detachment and so enchantment to his life. He has much to say about the good cheap music of nature, the hum of insects, the booming of ice, the fall of a distant tree, or the voice of a neighbor singing. He recounts the endless excitement that the humming of the telegraph wire brought him. It is his Aeolian harp, and reminds him of Anacreon and will make him read the Greek poets again. It is the poetry of the railroad, the heroic thoughts that the Irishmen had at their toil now given expression. The frequency of his concern with it is extraordinary. He writes about it at length no less than thirty times; and when in contrast he says that "one will lose no music by not attending the oratorios and operas," and that only in proportion as a man has a poor ear for music must he go to art for it, we are faced, as so often in Thoreau, with the odd balance between the poverty of the materials of his experience and the fertility of his resource.

He himself had no doubts on this score, either for his life or for his art: "Men commonly exaggerate the theme . . . The theme is nothing, the life is everything. All that interests the reader is the

depth and intensity of the life excited." [5] He was therefore intent
to study the exact evidence of his senses, since he believed that
only through their concrete reports could he project his inner life.
Sometimes he felt a danger involved in forming too exact habits
of observation, for they could run to excess and yield him, instead
of fresh knowledge, merely a flat repetition of what he already
knew. His remedy for this was what he called a free "sauntering
of the eye." The poetic knowledge he wanted would come only
through something like Wordsworth's "relaxed attention," only if
he was not a scientific naturalist, "not prying, nor inquisitive, nor
bent upon seeing things." He described his desired attitude towards nature by calling it one of indirection, by repeating frequently that the most fruitful perception was "with the unworn
sides of your eye." We remember Keats' delight in "the sidelong
glance," and his feeling that his ripest intuitions came through
indolence. Thus nonchalantly, almost unconsciously, Thoreau could
catch the most familiar scene in new perspective, with possibilities
hitherto untold to his direct scrutiny, and with a wholeness of impression that could give it composition in writing.

It is true that in the later volumes of the journals, increasingly
in the years after *Walden,* he felt that his senses were less buoyant
than when he was young, that his moments of inspiration were
much rarer, and that, in spite of himself, he was being narrowed
to a round of external facts. This forces the question, which he
would not admit, of whether he had not exhausted a too limited
range of experience. Thoreau's own answer would be what Emerson's was when reflecting on the description of the telegraph wire
in *Walden:* "The sensibility is all . . . To prize sensibility, see the
subjects of the poet; they were insignificant until he raised them."
And to the end, even in his most sterile moods, he could respond
to such never stale melodies as those of the wood thrush, though
he could not recapture quite this earlier pitch: "Where was that

---

[5] Again Thoreau approximates the kind of concentration Hulme has demanded: "There are then two things to distinguish, first the particular faculty
of mind to see things as they really are, and apart from the conventional ways
in which you have been trained to see them. This is itself rare enough in all
consciousness. Second, the concentrated state of mind, the grip over oneself which
is necessary in the actual expression of what one sees. To prevent one falling
into the conventional curves of ingrained technique, to hold on through infinite
detail and trouble to the exact curve you want. Wherever you get this sincerity,
you get the fundamental quality of good art without dragging in infinite or
serious."

strain mixed into which this world was dropped but as a lump of sugar to sweeten the draught? I would be drunk, drunk, drunk, dead drunk to this world with it forever."

In that moment Thoreau approached Keats, but, in the act of making the comparison, you recall that Thoreau's idea of luxury was to stand up to his chin in a retired swamp and be saturated with its summer juices. This man, who, unlike Whitman, hated to lie with the sun on his back, was constant in his dislike of sensuality. His desire was for "no higher heaven than the pure senses can furnish, a *purely* sensuous life." The double suggestion here of the need for clarified perception and of the vision into which it could lead him brings out the mystical element that always remained part of his experience. Yet even when he was swept beyond his moments of physical sensation he did not forget his debt to them. The triumphal strains to which he was set marching in "The Service" were not a nebulous fancy. They were the imaginative transformation of a rhythm he had actually heard and which he was trying to symbolize in words:

"In our lonely chambers at night we are thrilled by some far-off serenade within the mind, and seem to hear the clarion sound and clang of corselet and buckler from many a silent hamlet of the soul, though actually it may be but the rattling of some farmer's waggon rolling to market against the morrow."

The checkrein of his senses was what held even such a passage from gliding away into a romantic reverie of escape. Their vigilance constituted his chief asset as an artist. It brought his pages out of the fog into the sunlight in which he wanted them to be read. He came near to defining his own ideal of style when he objected to DeQuincey's as too diffuse and flowing in detail, not sufficiently "concentrated and nutty." What he wanted were "sentences which suggest far more than they say, which have an atmosphere about them, which do not merely report an old, but make a new, impression; sentences which suggest as many things and are as durable as a Roman aqueduct." These lines tend to soar beyond bounds, until their swaying looseness is fortunately given ballast by the concluding example. If Thoreau at his best achieved weight and permanence, it was because he was always being called back from thoughts to the miracle of surfaces, because he lived up to his resolve:

"Whatever things I perceive with my entire man, those let me record, and it will be poetry. The sounds which I hear with the consent and coincidence of all my senses, these are significant and musical; at least, they only are heard."

His remarks about music all lead to this point. He is never really talking about the art of music, of which he knew next to nothing, but about this close co-ordination, which alone made him feel that his pulse was beating in unison with the pulse of nature and that he could therefore reproduce it in words. By this analogy of the pulses he also emphasized the fact that resilient rhythm comes only from restfulness. And so he preached a gospel of leisure to Yankees, telling them that "the truly efficient laborer will not crowd his day with work, but will saunter to his task, surrounded by a wide halo of ease." Agreeing with Emerson that the poet's work needs "a frolic health," he understood much more intimately how style is based on physical aplomb. He had learned by the time he was twenty-two that "the wise man . . . abides there where he is, as some walkers actually rest the whole body at each step, while others never relax the muscles of the leg till the accumulated fatigue obliges them to stop short." Melville was to master the same thing from his experience: "To ensure the greatest efficiency in the dart, the harpooners of this world must start to their feet from out of idleness, and not from out of toil."

A Week on the Concord
and Merrimack Rivers

by William Drake

This is the shift, then, that we can trace in the use Thoreau made of the metaphor. It was at first a structure that simply drew a parallel between a "truth" about human experience and an analogous fact in nature. It reflected to some extent the dualism of "spirit" and "nature." But gradually it becomes clear that "spirit" for Thoreau is not a separate world; "soul" should be read simply as "self." The key metaphor is that of exploring the unknown land of one's self. It is important that self-exploration for Thoreau is metaphorically identified with exploration of the natural world: it is not a dualism which he expresses, but an integration.

This strategic metaphor offers us the key to the structural plans of his books. Several of them are, literally and simply, travel books; as *Cape Cod,* for example. In every case, including the *Week* and *Walden,* he adopts for fundamental framework a narrative account of an episode in his life that was a period of exploration and discovery. We have seen how he avoided at first the merely literal record, and strove to integrate in some way the realities he observed and the "truths" he subsequently learned, and an effort has been made to explain the underlying problem in his thought that this evidences.

In his *Journal* he accumulated day by day the material that he expected to draw from in arranging a book that would represent the fruits of his thinking. We know that he considered himself an essayist and that he attempted to follow Emerson's example in writ-

"A Week on the Concord and Merrimack Rivers" and *"Walden."* From "A Formal Study of H. D. Thoreau" by William Drake (Unpublished Master's Thesis, University of Iowa, 1948). Reprinted by permisison. In the preceding chapter, Mr. Drake discusses Thoreau's appropriation of the doctrine of correspondence and his strategic metaphor of exploration.

ing and delivering lectures. His books are still thought of by some primarily as collections of essays, and in an extreme view, paragraphs. The critical commonplaces that have been applied to Emerson's literary method have also been applied, less critically, to Thoreau.

During the years Thoreau was gradually conceiving the plan for the *Week,* he could have been satisfied with writing a series of essay-lectures. But why, in spite of his work in this direction, did he attempt over-all schemes of organization for his books? He did, indeed, incorporate several such essays into his first book, and in recent editions of his selected writings the *Week* does not appear as a whole, and "The Christian Fable" and "Friendship" are printed separately. But the *Week* seems to have been designed as more than a collection of essays and opinions. The fact that he chose to give the book a unified structural framework is important. It is evidence of the strategic metaphor: this journey on the Concord and Merrimack is an exploratory journey into thought.

The excursion itself begins to appear in commentary in the *Journal* nine months after the trip was made, in a way that suggests that Thoreau was already probing its possibilities as material for a book. The *Journal* entry which describes their setting sail from Concord throws clearest light on the reason why this excursion should provide the narrative scheme for his first book:

> So with a vigorous shove we launch our boat from the bank, while the flags and bulrushes curtsy God-speed, and drop silently down the stream. As if we had launched our bark in the sluggish current of our thoughts and were bound nowhither. (*J,* I, 136)[1]

River and lake images are the most fundamental in Thoreau, and have implications not yet fully read. The river "of our thoughts" is the dominant figure for the *Week,* and stress may be laid on the words "bound nowhither." His first book is indeed a striking out into new territory, and remains somewhat inconclusive and disorganized in its findings. Can any image represent better the voyages of exploration that the young man feels obliged to make in hopes of finding himself, setting out from what has been his home without knowing exactly what it is he will learn? One realizes how necessary it is to approach Thoreau as an artist, when un-

[1] Footnotes in this and the following essay refer to the standard edition, *The Writings of Henry David Thoreau,* Boston, 1906, xx volumes which includes the *Journals,* indicated by *J.*

covering these images that strike most deeply into his life. *Walden* is companion to the *Week,* and its image is as fundamental for a later stage of his experience; after the river journey is the pond, an ocean in miniature, which seems bottomless, but whose depths are measured.

The importance of the river symbol increases as we learn how the *Week* took shape. The ideas that were lifted into the *Week* were the product of the ten-year interval between the actual excursion in the late summer of 1839, and the publication of the book in 1849. Poems, also, which had been previously printed in *The Dial* reappear in the text of this book. But in addition, not only are the materials of essay and poetry used to fill in the *Week,* but actual incidents from later in his experience are described as occurring during the voyage. One notable example is that of his dream, "which had reference to an act in my life in which I had been most disinterested and true to my highest instinct but completely failed in realizing my hopes; and now, after so many months, in the stillness of sleep, complete justice was rendered me." (*J,* I, 177) This is recorded in his *Journal* on January twenty-sixth, 1841, but attributed in the *Week* to the Wednesday night of camping on the journey. (*W,* I, 315)

A brief sample might be taken here of another such passage, to compare its treatment in the *Journal,* as it was originally recorded, to its handling in the *Week.* The date of the *Journal* entry is March 30, 1840.

Journal	*Week*
Pray, what things interest me at present? A long, soaking rain, the drops trickling down the stubble, while I lay drenched on a last year's bed of wild oats, ruminating. These things are of moment. To watch this crystal globe just sent from heaven to associate with me. While these clouds and this somber drizzling weather shut all in, we two draw nearer and know one another. The gathering in of the clouds with the last rush and dying breath of the wind, and then the regular dripping of twigs and leaves the country o'er, the impression of in-	At present, the drops come trickling down the stubble while we lie drenched on a bed of withered wild oats, by the side of a bushy hill, and the gathering in of the clouds, with the last rush and dying breath of the wind, and then the regular dripping of twigs and leaves the country over, enhance the sense of inward comfort and sociableness. (*W,* I, 320)

ward comfort and sociableness, the
drenched stubble and trees that
drop beads on you as you pass,
their dim outline seen through the
rain on all sides drooping in sympathy with yourself. (*J*, I, 132)

In the *Journal* entry there is a curious ambiguity about time, so
that one does not know whether this experience did take place the
previous September on the excursion with his brother, and is rec-
ollected, or whether it is more recent, as it seems. The account is
highly impressionistic, as the incomplete sentence indicates. As he
re-writes it for the *Week*, he not only gathers into one exact sentence the main impressionistic details, but omits the fanciful at-
tribution of sympathy to the raindrops and trees. The identification
of his own mood with the weather is changed to a description of
the weather which merely "enhances" the mood. Also, the archaic
form "o'er" is modernized to "over."

In this careful reworking, the account of the actual and original
journey begins to take on the character, almost, of fiction. The
river of his thought is surveyed over a ten-years' flow; the symbol
becomes quite clear.

In spite of the skillful transformation of many passages, such
as quoted above, from the *Journal* to the context of the *Week*, and
in spite of the obvious technical advances they indicate, some problems remain only partially and awkwardly solved. Thoreau was
never satisfied, as should already be clear, with pure symbol; the
river of the *Week* was intended to operate on both levels, of natural
fact and of metaphor. His difficulty lay in making the poetry and
speculation about friendship, favorite authors, Christianity, and
the art of writing, develop naturally out of the context of the experience on its naturalistic level. This he obviously failed to do.

He did, however, attempt it. It is doubtful that he could have
been satisfied with merely loading the book, regardless of continuity. The simplest method he uses is that of association; a discussion of ideas develops, suggested by some observation along the
way. In this way also he brings in tales out of the early colonial
history of the region, and anecdotes from his own previous experience. The effort to tie in material of a definite essay character is
frequently more transparent. Long digressions are attributed to the
thoughts of "one of," even when these are rather formal essays.
For example, after a discussion of his favorite reading matter, the
Hindu scriptures, he continues:

> While engaged in these reflections, thinking ourselves the only naviga-
> tors of these waters, suddenly a canal-boat, with its sail set, glided
> round a point before us, like some huge river beast, and changed the
> scene in an instant . . . (*W*, I, 150)

But even this must be admitted to have some dramatic force, and
a strong sense of the necessity of keeping to the narrative framework.

Again, a rambling essay on the past and the present-day appeal
of great books of antiquity is followed immediately with this:

> Thus did one voyageur waking dream, while his companion slum-
> bered on the bank. Suddenly a boatman's horn was heard echoing
> from shore to shore, to give notice of his approach to the farmer's
> wife with whom he was to take his dinner, though in that place only
> muskrats and kingfishers seemed to hear. The current of our reflec-
> tions and slumbers being thus interrupted, we weighed anchor once
> more. (*W*, I, 165)

The attempt Thoreau makes throughout, of which the above are
representative examples, is that of relating all the speculative asides
and anecdotal digressions to the concrete and dramatic present
tense. This often involves a free and imaginative handling of his
material, as though it were fiction.

The first chapter of the *Week* introduces the Concord River by
its Indian name, the "Grass-ground River," as more descriptive of
this natural phenomenon than "Concord," a name borrowed from
the settlement on its banks and representing a hope for success in
human affairs. It is one of Thoreau's best pieces of simple factual
description, and he is at ease in it because he can articulate the
relation between men and nature. The river, with its permanent
flow, represents what in nature is constant and most rewarding to
investigate. "It will be Grass-ground River as long as grass grows
and water runs here; it will be Concord River only while men lead
peaceable lives on its banks." (*W*, I, 3) The history of white settlements on its banks, of Indian settlements before that, bears the
same relation to this river as Egypt to the Nile.

> As yesterday and the historical ages are past, as the work of today is
> present, so many flitting perspectives and demi-experiences of the life
> that is in nature are in time veritably future, or rather outside to
> time, perennial, young, divine, in the wind and rain that never
> die. (*W*, I, 7)

It is this relationship, which the primitive man fulfills unconsciously and civilized thinking man wants to understand consciously,
that Thoreau aims to bring into focus. Throughout the book, the
farmers who live beside the river, the boatmen, and other travel-
lers, are seen in the perspective of the facts of the river itself. This
opening depiction of natural details sets the level of reference for
the rest of the book. It rises to an over-all survey—"a huge volume
of matter, ceaselessly rolling through the plains and valleys of the
substantial earth" (*W*, I, 10)—and concludes with his decision to
set sail upon it, relaying the sense of excitement and willingness
to submit to a common and natural fate, whose outcome is not
predictable:

> I had often stood on the banks of the Concord, watching the lapse
> of the current, an emblem of all progress, following the same law
> with the system, with time, and all that is made; the weeds at the
> bottom gently bending down the stream, shaken by the watery wind,
> still planted where their seeds had sunk, but erelong to die and go
> down likewise; the shining pebbles, not yet anxious to better their
> condition, the chips and weeds, and occasional logs and stems of trees
> that floated past, fulfilling their fate, were objects of singular interest
> to me, and at last I resolved to launch myself on its bosom and float
> whither it would bear me. (*W*, I, 11)

It might be well to point out here the idea of progress and improvement that is implied in this figure; and also, the fact that this
symbol of "fate" is not arbitrarily chosen. The complex phenomenon of the river follows "the same law with the system, with time,
and all that is made . . ." It is a symbolism that functions first of all
on the level of natural fact.

On surveying the book as a whole, this present tense of observed
fact which is set at the beginning does not seem to hold up all the
way through. The interludes of speculation and story-telling may
be solidly framed by concrete fact, but they do not always grow out
of it naturally. One feels too strongly the simple alternation between one level and the other. Thoreau's reading, too, interferes
with his own thought and observation. The *Week* is the work of a
very literary-minded young man, who is enthusiastic about books
and authors. There is hardly a page without at least one quotation
from poetry, ranging from Pindar to Tennyson, with a great many
scattered lines from the metaphysical poets of the Seventeenth Century.

His own poems interrupt the page time after time, and he does not yet realize that he is more successful at metaphorical prose than verse. The rhyming tendency seems to have been irrepressible at the time he moved to his hut at Walden Pond, where he wrote a great deal of the *Week*; a fact that is borne out by the *Journal* of that period. But if rhyme satisfied his sense of elation, it resulted in verses inferior to his prose, where he could handle metaphor much more skillfully. His poems suffer stylistically from the archaisms he borrowed from his reading; so does the prose often, but in it are sometimes buried lines whose formal poetic quality he must have undervalued. This passage, for example, is prose only by virtue of its typography. When printed as follows it is a better poem than many he wrote:

> What have I to do with plows?
> I cut another furrow than you see.
> Where the off-ox treads, there it is not,
> It is farther off;
> Where the nigh-ox walks, it will not be,
> It is nigher still.
> If corn fails, my crop fails not,
> And what are drought and rain to me? (*W*, I, 54)

These inconsistencies in style and in structure reveal Thoreau's failure to integrate thought and experience. The dichotomy of "truth" and "fact" has been traced through his handling of metaphor to its integration in the strategic metaphor of the self-explorer. The structural plan of the *Week* is basically an elaboration of that metaphor. But Thoreau still does not manage to hold together all the materials of his book. The metaphor of exploration which seemed definite at the beginning is indefinite at the end:

> It is easier to discover another such a new world as Columbus did, than to go within one fold of this which we appear to know so well. (*W*, I, 409)

What is not clear in the *Week* is how the exploration of this world "we appear to know so well" does lead one to the more important world within. Is this still a hint of the "higher" realm of the idealist? Curiously, he concludes the book with the attempt to heal the idealistic split in the suggestion that one may literally experience the ideal through the senses:

May we not *see* God? Are we to be put off and amused in this life, as it were with a mere allegory? Is not Nature, rightly read, that of which she is commonly taken to be the symbol merely? (*W*, I, 408)

This is a point in his thought midway between the first speculation of the *Journal* and *Walden*, wherein he clearly believes that nature is the final fact, and not a symbol. Thoreau would not admit that another world lies beyond the senses. It is but another step from this hope of literally experiencing what seems as yet hidden and unexplained, but from which appear to come our ideas, to the definition of the limits of knowledge, admission of ignorance and the unknown, and exploration of the natural self. It is a step that Thoreau takes. *Walden* is the full flowering of the strategic metaphor.

Walden

by William Drake

Walden, like the *Week,* has for structure an elaborated metaphor. It is that of the traveller who, instead of leaving home, explores the very ground he lives on. Only now the end of exploration is in sight, and the book points to it from the beginning. Its successful organization, especially pronounced in comparison with the *Week,* indicates the decisiveness of Thoreau's thought. It is not only the narrative that holds *Walden* together, but also the singleness of the problem explored, the definiteness of aim, and the mature development of his metaphorical prose.

The *Week* concluded, as we saw, with the expectation of literally experiencing the ideal through the senses. Unless Thoreau were to go on and discard this lingering dualism, he would likely have been bound to retreat to the dualistic position. *Walden* shows that he did go on. There is less emphasis on knowing, the passive mind-centered attitude that characterizes the idealist. *Walden* describes a practical experiment, to discover how far the "higher potentialities of a human being can be developed, when one lives deliberately." These are not simply the insights of one's thought, but a solution of the problems that cause anxiety, conflict, or sluggishness.

The geometric symbol for *Walden* is the upward curve. The background one would chart it against is the single knowable world of nature and experience. The lower part of the line is lost in an unknown beginning, just as the upper part continues potentially into the unknown. Underlying Thoreau's thought is the assumption of evolution, in both geological history and human affairs. His knowledge of geology was, incidentally, fairly extensive and accurate by present day standards, and seems not to have been commented on or credited with an important influence on his thinking. He appears to believe that this development means improvement; hence the *upward* curve. It is better, for example, that men are no longer cannibalistic, strictly speaking, and are even beginning to find any animal food distasteful:

> Whatever my own practice may be, I have no doubt that it is a part of the destiny of the human race, in its gradual improvement, to leave off eating animals, as surely as the savage tribes have left off eating each other when they came in contact with the more civilized. (*W*, II, 239)

Human evolution therefore means "spiritual" evolution. Thoreau knew full well how slowly men improve their condition, and how formidable are the entrenched traditions and customs that hold men back. Hence his experiment, to see how far one man can go in the desired direction. *Walden* begins with a discussion of the means utilized, and concludes with an invitation to all to wake up, explore themselves, find out exactly who they are.

The constant theme in *Walden* is that of "spiritual" awakening. It appears in metaphor in almost every chapter, the commonest symbols being those of spring, morning, and restorative medicines. It is reflected in the overall structure of the book. Although Thoreau lived at Walden Pond for more than two years, his book is an ideal account of a single year, following the seasons from summer to spring. The seasonal change from winter to spring is exploited metaphorically at the end to describe the awakening of the human being to self-realization, well-being, and development. It is time, he means, for the whole human race to awaken, and assume a consciousness it has rarely shown yet, and seize its opportunity to live.

Although Thoreau's vocabularly still retains the words "soul," "divine," and "spiritual," they must be understood in quotation marks. In the chapter "Higher Laws" he refers to the "higher, or, as it is named, spiritual life . . ." (*W*, II, 232) In a later letter, a few years after the publication of *Walden,* he says, "our souls (I use this word for want of a better) . . ." (*W*, VI, 347) If he was at a loss to find new words for what the twentieth century is still too embarrassed to describe accurately, in naturalistic terms, he may possibly be excused. His direction, however, should be clear in spite of this. Since the writing of the *Week,* the word "God" has disappeared from his vocabulary almost entirely, and he refers only vaguely and anonymously to whatever force is responsible for the universe. This, it is true, suggests that he still feels some single force is responsible, but it is impossible to determine exactly what he imagines the character of that force to be. He uses the artisan-image of nature as

God's handiwork occasionally, but this contradicts his otherwise natural universe, and he clearly does not develop a pantheistic position. Probably it is only a way of expressing the reverence he believed men should feel toward their world. In the main, one may say he was uninterested in the deity, and is more interested in the mythical and metaphorical use of religious terminology, seeing the gods of Greece, India, and Christendom as equally important projections, imaginative attempts to describe and explain.

Two paradoxes need to be analyzed. First, why Thoreau sought out the most primitive conditions of living, in order to measure the furthest possible spiritual advance; and why the study of nature teaches a man to know himself. To the former, he provides an adequate answer in "Economy." Man's relation to nature has a permanent character: he is dependent on her for the basic means of keeping himself alive. This is the root of the problem of how to live well, because only when one has managed his economic life successfully is he able to develop his higher potentialities. He needs leisure and energy to enjoy his life, especially if work cannot always be entirely a labor of love. The enjoyment of life is the predominant theme of *Walden*; it is what men must wake up to, and attain by conscious direction of the lives. It is comparable to the "joy of life" theme in Ibsen and Hardy, where it is also ascribed the status of a natural right, if not obligation. By simplifying all his relations, Thoreau is able to define their fundamental character, their functions and possibilities. "Economy" is an essay not on economics, but on the economic utilization of one's time and energy.

One can trace to this end the dualism of Thoreau's early thought. What originally were the "higher" and "lower" halves of life are now, in *Walden,* the two ends of a single rising scale, which stays within nature and is continuous with it. This, to repeat, is only fully understood when related to his assumption of evolution. Men in his opinion are scarcely developed from the savage state: "The civilized man is a more civilized and experienced savage"; (*W,* II, 44) we go "a step or two beyond instinct." (*W,* II, 280) We are "still a little afraid of the dark, though the witches are all hung, and Christianity and candles have been introduced." (*W,* II, 145) We prefer our fond habitual superstitions to the truth, which we could easily get by means of patient investigation: "It is remarkable how long men will believe in the bottomlessness of a pond without taking the trouble to sound it." (*W,* II, 315) The higher life is the highest point of our evolutionary development, and there is farther yet to go: "But man's capacities have never been measured; nor are we to judge of what he can do by any precedents, so little has been tried." (*W*, II, 11) *Walden* calls for us to enter a new stage of conscious development, to act deliberately in problems we have hitherto tried to settle blunderingly. But before we can know where we are, we must first have the courage to lose ourselves deliberately, freeze in for a winter alone, investigate the state of our ignorance. Primitive nature, which "puts no questions and answers none which we mortals ask," (*W*, II, 312) can thus define the extent of our development and clarify the direction we may most profitably go.

Man can find himself by exploring nature because of this clarification of his relations; man knows himself only through relations to things outside himself. Our thought may be humbler when we realize that "The universe is wider than our views of it"; (*W*, II, 352) but the bringing into true and accurate focus of the world of nature about us, that is, what we *can* know, at least tells us what we are, and this is indeed a waking up, a revelation.

Metaphor is for Thoreau at last the means of expressing relations: "My thought is a part of the meaning of the world, and hence I use a part of the world as a symbol to express my thought." (*J*, IV, 410) In *Walden* the metaphor almost invariably has its matter-of-fact root in the literal context of the narrative; there is no sense of two separated levels, as in the *Week*, one of narrative and one of thought. The metaphor expresses a relation rather than a parallel. Again, "He is richest who has the most use for nature as raw material of tropes and symbols with which to describe his life." (*J*, V, 135) This may be contrasted with Emerson's assertion of correspondence. The word "use" here is important, as it eliminates the possibility of nature's actually reflecting man's thought. Thoreau's nature, like that of the twentieth century scientist's, has as its regularities not those of human thought, but laws which human thought can discover, and which we yet only partially know.

Language

The first technical advance over the *Week* that one notices in the style of *Walden* is its freedom from literary self-consciousness. The poetic archaisms "o'er," "yon," "methinks," "ye," "e'er," "oft," make a negligible appearance now. *Walden* has, still, more quotations from poetry and Hindu scripture than may be evident at first, but their volume has been reduced considerably and they are less conspicuous in context. But these are evidences of a shift in attitude, which thus has its shaping effect on style. *Walden* is addressed directly to the reader, as though Thoreau means simply to hold a conversation. It is a report which he intends to deliver in person. He must not be taken too much at his word, if he seems to ignore the technical problems of the literary artist and pursue only philosophy. Actually, he worked hard to develop his own personal style. This was vitiated in the *Week* by his poetizing, and the passages of "fine" prose. They indicate an embarrassment in facing the facts of his subject matter, an inclination to decorate and "improve" with literary and fanciful allusions. The style of *Walden* is purified of such literary gingerbread by Thoreau's intention to speak in the first person as directly as he can.

This attitude of conversational informality implies a diction closer to common spoken language, and figures drawn from the commonplaces of experience rather than from literary models. The vocabulary of informal speech is heavily weighted with words that refer to common objects of use in household and trade. It is out of these that Thoreau constructs his metaphors. The *Week* revealed his love of memoirs, semi-illiterate histories written by soldiers and colonists who took part in the events they described, tales handed down by word of mouth, old sayings, myths, and legends. This is the folk literature and philosophy of the formally uneducated. In the *Week* he observed that

> There is a sort of homely truth and naturalness in some books which is very rare to find, and yet looks cheap enough. There may be nothing lofty in the sentiment, or fine in the expression, but it is careless country talk . . . The scholar is not apt to make his most familiar experience come gracefully to the aid of his expression. (*W*, I, 11)

Walden is his chief success in adapting formal literary style to the "homely" expression of familiar and common experience, and it is a document which is related in spirit more closely to folk literature than to formal literary tradition.

One characteristic of the spoken language of common people is its reliance on proverbs, old saws, and catch phrases, with which stories are described and given their point. Thoreau in *Walden* not only investigates many such old saws to see how much truth there is in them, but gives them an ironic twist for his own purposes. A catalogue could very well be made of Thoreau's "new saws," which have all the character of proverbs. Such as:

A man sits as many risks as he runs. (*W*, II, 170)

. . . speech is for the convenience of those who are hard of hearing; (*W*, II, 156)

Old deeds for old people, new deeds for new. (*W*, II, 9)

If you have any enterprise before you, try it in your old clothes. (*W*, II, 26)

Thoreau was especially fond of drawing out the opinions of the uneducated, judging the wisdom of the customs they adhered to, and the extent to which they relied on practices devised by their own learning. He speaks of winter fishermen,

> wild men, who instinctively follow other fashions and trust other authorities than their own townsmen . . . They never consulted with books, and know and can tell much less than they have done. The things which they practice are said not yet to be known. (*W*, II, 313)

The education of the mass of men is by custom and practical experience, rather than by theory and school; Thoreau in *Walden* speaks as one reporting the results of his own practical education. He strikes at times the attitude of the wise old codger, though always ironically: "I have lived some thirty years on this planet. . ." (*W*, II, 10) When reporting information he has read or has been told, he generally qualifies it with "as they say," or "it is said," to indicate how useful knowledge or expressive myths circulate among mankind, he helping to pass them along; such lore being not unlike that of the fisherman who knows how to find worms in winter. Even the Bible is no better qualified as an authority: ". . . they are employed, as it says in an old book, laying up treasures which moth and rust will corrupt . . ." (*W*, II, 6)

On its narrative level *Walden* is a record of practical experiments in building, cooking, planting, keeping warm, and measuring things out of sheer curiosity. The price of nails, the recipe for bread, the best bait for fishing, the exact dates of the pond's freezing and melting, represent the kind of detail he feels obliged to account for with exactness. *Walden* is, on this level, a compendium, or handbook on how to arrange economically the practical details of one's life. The curiosity that leads one beyond simply useful facts also has its folk character in Thoreau, in his reliance on first-hand information and his love of myth and hearsay.

If Thoreau early came to the conclusion (1841) that the best thought was "without sombreness," he clearly believes now that it should have the positive quality of humor. In the metaphors of *Walden* there is a deliberate amused extravagance:

> My bricks being second-hand ones required to be cleaned with a trowel . . . The mortar of them was fifty years old, and was said to be still growing harder; but this is one of those sayings which men love to repeat whether they are true or not. Such sayings themselves grow harder and adhere more firmly with age, and it would take many blows with a trowel to clean an old wiseacre of them. (*W*, II, 266)

Or:

> We meet at meals three times a day, and give each other a new taste of that old musty cheese that we are. (*W*, II, 151)

When humor is not involved in metaphor, it exploits the shock of paradox and contradiction: "I have a great deal of company in my house; especially in the morning, when nobody calls." (*W*, II, 151) Serious-minded people perhaps read *Walden* without realizing how humor qualified throughout Thoreau's personal extravagances and overstatement, since one aspect of his humor is the pose of dead seriousness.

The force of his metaphors is frequently due to the empathic shock of an extravagant and ironic image:

> If the legislature regards it [the pond], it is chiefly to regulate the number of hooks to be used there; but they know nothing about the hook of hooks with which to angle for the pond itself, impaling the legislature for a bait. (*W*, II, 236)

Or:

> The bullet of your thought must have overcome its lateral and ricochet motion and fallen into its last and steady course before it reaches the ear of the hearer, else it may plough out again through the side of his head. (*W*, II, 156)

The metaphor in *Walden* rarely draws on literature, formal learning, or iconographic symbols for its point; a practice that may be contrasted, for example, with contemporary "metaphysical" poetry. Its image is ordinarily not visual, but, as the samples above indicate, empathic, involving physical action-weight, force, movement. In the chapter "Sounds," the train being fitted out to plow through deep snow is described as follows:

> If the snow lies deep, they strap on his snowshoes, and, with the giant plough, plough a furrow from the mountains to the seaboard, in which the cars, like a following drill-barrow, sprinkle all the restless men and floating merchandise in the country for seed. (*W*, II, 130)

The metaphor thus reflects also Thoreau's aim to relay not merely intellectual, but total experience, and it affords him the opportunity to exploit the common objects and actions that he can observe as he looks about him. *Walden* occasionally even shifts to the present tense, though its first chapter looks back at a distance of several years. In all these ways, it maintains without interruption a reference to present time and present experience, on as concrete a level as is ever established in any piece of fiction. An empirical foundation is laid for ideas, and these, it will be seen, concern the results of exploration.

Structure

Walden's first chapter, "Economy," is devoted to the question of how best to arrange the practical circumstances of one's life in order to exploit its possibilities to the limit: "that economy of living which is synonymous with philosophy." (*W*, II, 57) Philosophy, in Thoreau's usage, does not mean speculation or analysis of problems in thinking, but rather the intelligent shaping of one's way of life. What man seeks, he now says, is self-realization, and the main problem he faces is how to solve the practical problems that stand in his way. Since he must provide himself with food, clothing, and shelter, he must do it with simplicity and as little effort as possible, in order to allow a margin of leisure for the exploration of "reality." Man's whole moral life and the structure of his knowledge are built up from the primitive base of his practical dependence on nature; this is why Thoreau constantly uses the word "higher." His assumption of evolution has already been discussed. In man, it means the expansion of "spiritual" life, which always remains rooted in nature; he looks forward to his development as he looks backward to his source. "Spiritual" and "animal" are thus opposite directions, rather than a dualism. The point in returning to a more or less primitive condition in one's practical life is to clarify basic relations, to throw into relief the extent of one's ignorance and the distance he has travelled in his development. To become thus aware of who he is, where he stands and what direction is best for him to continue, is to awaken to conscious "spiritual" life, be renewed and invigorated. If man's actual condition, in contrast, seems to be largely one of ignorance, lethargy, sham, fear, and bad management, it is because he has not yet wakened to his possibilities. *Walden* begins with a practical plan for ordering one's life, concludes with an enthusiastic prediction of the results one may expect.

The dominant metaphors of inward spring and inward morning appear constantly in many forms, emphasizing this theme. In "Economy," for example, he sees a torpid half-thawed snake one spring day run into the water and lie quietly on the bottom: "It appeared to me that for a like reason men remain in their present low and primitive condition; but if they should feel the influence of the spring of springs arousing them, they would of necessity rise to a higher and more ethereal life"; (*W*, II, 46) "They were pleasant spring days, in which the winter of man's discontent was thawing as well as the earth . . ." (*W*, II, 45) In the next chapter, the famous "Where I Lived, and What I Lived For," the key image, on page after page, is that of the morning: "Morning is when I am awake and there is a dawn in me. Moral reform is the effort to throw off sleep." (*W*, II, 100) The book as a whole, as has already been pointed out, reflects in its sequence of seasons the basic symbol of spring as man's spiritual awakening; "Spring" in fact asks, "What is man but a mass of thawing clay?" (*W*, II, 339)

The statement of intention comes at the beginning of *Walden*, and what follows may be called practical demonstration. The double face of life is no longer "truth" and "fact" but rather "reality" and "sham." "Shams and delusions are esteemed for soundest truths, while reality is fabulous." (*W*, II, 106) The latter distinction does not differentiate between two kinds of knowing, but instead, degrees of knowing. There is still the insistence that knowledge not be indiscriminate or acquired simply for its own sake; it must have some point. The fact which was to flower out into a truth does so in a figurative sense, in *Walden*. "Truth" is very nearly a pragmatic concept for Thoreau: the study of fact must have results, must "flower out," in one's life. To be in contact with "reality" is to have established one's life on the basis of discovered truths. The explorer who intensively studies the life around him, as though it were the strangest land, is seeking the bed-rock of reality:

Let us settle ourselves, and work and wedge our feet downward through the mud and slush of opinion, and prejudice, and tradition, and appearance . . . till we come to a hard bottom and rocks in place, which we can call *reality*, and say, This is, and no mistake. . . . (*W*, II, 108) Be it life or death, men crave only reality. (*W*, II, 109)

It is important that Thoreau emphasizes man's ignorance, and the difficulty with which he wrests from nature "truths" that will satisfy his craving for reality. The idealist invariably assumes an a priori known structure. Thoreau adheres to the empirical approach:

If we knew all the laws of Nature, we should need only one fact, or the description of one actual phenomenon, to infer all the results at that point. Now we know only a few laws, and our result is vitiated, not, of course, by any confusion or irregularity in Nature, but by our ignorance of essential elements in the calculation. (*W*, II, 320)

Walden, then, is a study of relations, a study in orientation, an effort to explore relations so as to bring them into exact focus, and to establish them on the soundest basis that they may be as rich and fruitful as possible. "Reality" is definable not in an absolute sense; it depends on the nature of one's relationships. But before relationships can be aligned for results, even before one can ascertain what they are, there is an important step in one's education:

. . . not till we are completely lost, or turned around,—for a man needs only to be turned around once with his eyes shut in this world to be lost,—do we appreciate the vastness and strangeness of Nature. Every man has to learn the points of the compass again as often as he awakes, whether from sleep or any abstraction. Not till we are lost, in other words, not till we have lost the world, do we begin to find ourselves, and realize where we are and the infinite extent of our relations. (*W*, II, 189)

This is the pattern for exploration that constitutes the structure of *Walden*. The emphasis on the winter months, which is obvious even from a survey of titles—"Former Inhabitants; and Winter Visitors," "Winter Animals," "The Pond in Winter,"—serves more than to contrast with "Spring." Winter, with its dying down, retraction of life and freezing over, is the larger symbol of spiritual sleep, or loss, from which one awakens to the discovery of himself and the "infinite extent" of his relations. "Spring" announces that

"Walden was dead and is alive again." (*W*, II, 344) The concluding chapter's vitality and assertion of wakefulness, renewal and joy depend entirely on the preceding period of self-discovery.

The first two chapters, "Economy" and "Where I Lived, and What I Lived For," are introductory, concerning the techniques and specific aims of a purposeful mode of living. The following chapters represent stages in the year's adventures. It is interesting that Thoreau should begin these with "Reading." But then this chapter turns out to be not a discussion of authors, but rather of intellectual education, which concerns all men, not merely readers: "With a little more deliberation in the choice of pursuits, all men would perhaps become essentially students and observers . . ." (*W*, II, 110) The classics are those books which have the most to say about "reality," and hence are perennially fresh. The same scale of judgment described above is applied also to books: good books record the vital insights of the race, and are therefore companions in Thoreau's own venture. The classics are contrasted with newspapers and popular novels, which are produced and consumed on the surface. The important books are written by philosophers, in Thoreau's sense, and help teach us how to live.

> There are probably words addressed to our own condition exactly, which, if we could really hear and understand, would be more salutary than the morning or the spring to our lives, and possibly put a new aspect on the face of things for us. (*W*, II, 119)

Books, in this sense, are useful, and the real material for cultural improvement. This chapter concludes with a call for an expansion of schools and libraries—"It is time that villages were universities" (*W*, II, 121)—in order that we may "throw one arch at least over the darker gulf of ignorance which surrounds us." (*W*, II, 122)

Perhaps the main reason for the appearance of this chapter early in the book is that Thoreau is aiming to write just such a classic as he describes. One reads *Walden* with the author's own orientation toward books, with the relation in mind that he sees between books and the vital problem of living that he is to investigate.

The step from "Reading" to "Sounds" is that from the language of men to the "language" of things, from what can be said *about* nature, to nature itself:

> But while we are confined to books, though the most select and classic, and read only particular written languages, which are themselves

but dialects and provincial, we are in danger of forgetting the language which all things and events speak without metaphor, which alone is copious and standard. (*W*, II, 123)

In final contrast to Emerson, Thoreau asserts that things "speak without metaphor." To say that nature has a language, is itself a metaphor. Metaphor as Thoreau speaks of it always defines human experience, within human bounds.

This chapter is roughly held together by the depiction of a typical day of sounds, from early morning, through the afternoon, with its freight train, to the evening, and night, with its famous owls and frogs. This is actually the formal introduction to life at Walden Pond, the first primarily narrative episode. In its concluding discussion of the cock-crow—a domestic sound which Thoreau did not hear at Walden—it returns to the theme of morning, and imagines the crow of the wild cock in the original Indian forests:

It would put nations on the alert. Who would not be early to rise, and rise earlier and earlier every successive day of his life, till he became unspeakably healthy, wealthy, and wise? (*W*, II, 141)

The final exuberant statement of wildness and isolation that ends the chapter is the first definite assertion of the severance of ties and the facing into the unsubdued and unknown in nature, which are the conditions for exploration: "Instead of no path to the front-yard gate in the Great Snow,—no gate—no front yard,—and no path to the civilized world." (*W*, II, 142)

As *Walden* progresses, the focus settles on the uncivilized. It is in the early chapters (roughly the first six, through "Visitors"), that Thoreau is especially concerned with social relations; and these are measured from the perspective of self-sufficiency. "Solitude" and "Visitors" analyze communication, rejecting, again, what seems superficial and profane in the light of the sincerity and impartiality that one can learn from nature. Loneliness and fear are products of society and disappear from relationships disciplined by contact with nature. One is never alone if he is aware of his non-human relationships. "Shall I not have intelligence with the earth? Am I not partly leaves and vegetable mould myself?" (*W*, II, 153) "Solitude" is an affirmation of trust in the "indescribable innocence and beneficence of Nature." (*W*, II, 153) It is this which provides the scale against which social relations can be judged; "The value of a man is not in his skin, that we should touch him." (*W*, II, 151) "Real" distance, failure to communicate, Thoreau contrasts with his apparent distance, with its more intense contacts. "Visitors" is structurally the second half of "Solitude," and continues the exploration of human contacts.

"The Bean-Field" and "The Village," which follow next, do not suggest by their titles a further step into what is wild or unknown. But the beans are approved because "They attached me to the earth, and so I got strength like Antaeus." (*W*, II, 171) Beans are, after all, only another kind of weed:

> We are wont to forget that the sun looks on our cultivated fields and on the prairies and forests without distinction . . . In his view the earth is all equally cultivated like a garden . . . This broad field which I have looked at so long looks not to me as the principal culti-vator, but away from me to influences more genial to it, which water and make it green. (*W*, II, 183)

The cultivation of beans introduces one to the prodigality, magna-nimity, and impartiality of nature; it is the soundest basis for trust and freedom from anxiety. Planted grain is a symbol of hope; nature feeds herself very adequately, and may be depended on. It is im-portant for Thoreau to establish the fundamental attitude of trust, since it is this which makes fruitful the deliberate freezing in and getting lost. The next chapter, "The Village," is less concerned with society than with getting lost from it, its roads and landmarks. "In our most trivial walks, we are constantly, though unconsciously, steering like pilots by certain well-known beacons and head-lands . . ." (*W*, II, 189) The dominant symbolism of *Walden* ap-pears again here: one is most easily lost in a snow-storm, which covers the roads; "By night, of course, the perplexity is infinitely greater." (*W*, II, 189)

As important as the winter-spring and night-morning imagery in *Walden* is the considerable use of imagery drawn from measure-ment: fixed known points, relative distances, depths, maps and charts, geometry, astronomy. *Walden* is above all concerned with the adjustment of relations, and this is most evident in these images. "Economy" asserts that "It is by a mathematical point only that we are wise, as the sailor or the fugitive slave keeps the pole-star in his eye; but that is sufficient guidance for all our life." (*W*, II, 79) Thoreau quotes, "I am monarch of all I *survey* . . ."; (*W*, II, 92) the italics are his. Human relations are measured in terms of distance. Walden woods offer him the *"point d'appui"* at which to set up his "Realometer." (*W*, II, 109) This ingrained habit of vision in terms of measurement doubtless reflects his experience as a surveyor; but it is an important index to his thought as well. No measurement is absolute, since it is significant only by relation. Landmarks define one's position and direction; the unknown defines one's knowledge. A point is all one needs as center, since what one discovers is significant by reference to it. This explains the paradox of *Walden's* strategic metaphor, the explorer who examines the ground he lives on. "There are no larger fields than these . . .": (*W*, II, 230) the conditions for exploration are present wherever one is, and learning may progress more intensively where one's center of reference is most deeply established.

The metaphor in *Walden* usually combines the small specific fact and an enormous one: "Every nail driven should be as another rivet in the machine of the universe, you carrying on the work." (*W*, II, 364) This is evident also in the many examples already quoted. It expresses the relative importance of the specific act or discovery which on its small scale is equally definitive with what looms large to man's perception.

The end result of relations explored, clarified, and established from a focal point, is self-realization. To know one's relations is to know one's self. "Know" is scarcely an adequate word, however, unless taken in some active sense, since the objective is a fruitful and conscious adjustment, not simply passive insight.

Chapter IX, "The Ponds," following "The Village," identifies Walden Pond as that vital center: "It is earth's eye; looking into which the beholder measures the depth of his own nature." (*W*, II, 206) This figure is not fully exploited until near the end of *Walden*, when the bottom of the pond is sounded and measured in the dead of winter. The gradual shift from examining human relations to ascertaining one's relations to the larger natural world has already been pointed out. It is part of the process of working down to "rocks in place"; since the ultimate foundations of all human enterprise, whether morals, art, thought, or practical living, are in natural fact. As winter deepens, we shall see the focus on Walden intensified, and relations examined in their most primitive character.

"Baker Farm" describes an unforeseen adventure, due to a rainstorm which interrupts Thoreau's fishing. Though it is only a meeting with a poor Irish workman's family in the neighborhood, it is the pattern for any adventure and meeting with strangers, and

"Baker Farm" is another country than one's own. "We should come home from far, from adventures, and perils, and discoveries every day, with new experience and character." (*W*, II, 231)

"Higher Laws" is largely about eating, a human activity that presents a good index to morals. This chapter relies less on metaphor, more on direct statement, than any other in *Walden*. It seems at first that it could be cited as evidence of a dualism, "spiritual" and "animal," in Thoreau's thought, a contradiction of his other views. However, his "reverence" for primitive instincts begins to qualify what appears to be a bifurcation of nature, and what is "higher" is clearly laid out in a scale that graduates downward. The "animal" is characterized by unrestrained appetite and predatory practices. The moral scale measures development—"even in civilized communities, the embryo man passes through the hunter stage of development." (*W*, II, 236) This is true also of the growth of the race: "There is a period in the history of the individual, as of the race, when the hunters are the 'best men' . . ." (*W*, II, 235) The spiritual life—"as it is named" (*W*, II, 132)—is nothing absolute, but a direction away from the carnivorous and predatory. The hunter is something of a child, and the "mass of men are still and always children in this respect." (*W*, II, 235) Thoreau finds the hunter in himself dying out: "It is a faint intimation, but so are the first streaks of morning." (*W*, II, 235) This is an important linkage with the key symbolism of *Walden*, and establishes the continuity he sees between the "higher" and the "animal." Thoreau rejects humanitarianism as grounds for ceasing to prey on "other animals," (*W*, II, 238) and says only:

It may be vain to ask why the imagination will not be reconciled to flesh and fat. I am satisfied that it will not. (*W*, II, 238)

"Higher" morals he sees as the discipline of the animal in man, of his self-indulgent appetite, slothfulness and sensuality. Through self-discipline man enters conscious spiritual development. There is an emphasis on "purity" and "chastity" in these passages that strikes the twentieth century ear as excessively Puritanical; "Nature is hard to overcome, but she must be overcome." (*W*, II, 244) At this point there seems to develop a conflicting view. The reverence Thoreau has for the animal in himself fades before the strenuous task of self-purification. But while calling for the animal to be overcome, he has his misgivings, and admits that perhaps we may withdraw from the "animal in us" but "never change its nature." (*W*, II, 242) Indeed,

> The other day I picked up the lower jaw of a hog, with white and sound teeth and tusks, which suggested that there was an animal health and vigor distinct from the spiritual. This creature succeeded by other means than temperance and purity. (*W*, II, 242)

He shifts then to a compromise, sublimation of the sexual drive; the same energy, according to its direction, can be unclean or inspiring and invigorating, and Thoreau attributes all great "spiritual" achievements of the race to chastity.

There are at least two suggestions as to what he may mean by "Higher Laws." First, that natural law supports the development of the spiritual man: ". . . the laws of the universe are not indifferent, but are forever on the side of the most sensitive. Listen to every zephyr for some reproof, for it is surely there, and he is unfortunate who does not hear it." (*W*, II, 242) Or second, that "Laws" mean self-regulations according to the moral principles that rise from the "suggestions of his genius," (*W*, II, 239) which man must respect. Probably these are meant to be in some sense identical, as expressing trust of both external nature and one's self. In any case, he does not assert that there is a realm of "higher laws" separate from natural law, or that nature itself is moral. The conclusion one is forced to draw is that Thoreau does not work out an articulate view of the foundations of human morality in nature. He is most consistent in attributing to morality a natural sense of direction, in relating it to development and justifying moral practices by the results they have in terms of imagination and feeling.

This chapter has been dwelt upon because of its rather clear evidence of the proto-naturalistic character of Thoreau's thought. It has less continuity with the narrative of *Walden* than any other chapter, and is not given as emphatic a position as the introductory and concluding chapters, which also generalize more than others. It is followed by "Brute Neighbors," one of the most specific records of observation in the book, and this is the clue to the structural function of "Higher Laws." It would seem to have been intentionally imbedded among the chapters that center increasingly on primitive natural fact; it is essentially an attempt, though not fully successful, to analyze the relations between the "spiritual" in man, and nature.

"Brute Neighbors," to judge by the emphatic contrast of its title, is deliberately set next to "Higher Laws." But it begins with a curious dialogue between a "Hermit" and a "Poet," who, though unidentified, may possibly represent in caricature Thoreau and his friend Channing. It is undoubtedly meant to be humorous, since Thoreau has claimed earlier that he is "naturally no hermit, but might possibly sit out the sturdiest frequenter of the bar-room, if my business called me thither." (*W*, II, 155) This Hermit is a pure Oriental, contemplating a New England landscape and the unsatisfactory modes of life it presents. The Poet approaching through the bushes is suspected at first of being a lost pig, and when he appears he gushes over the beauty of the day, comparing it favorably with old paintings and the more picturesque scenes of Europe; "That's a true Mediterranean sky." (*W*, II, 248) When the Poet withdraws to dig worms for fishing, the Hermit tries to recover his interrupted meditation: "I was as near being resolved into the essence of things as ever I was in my life"; (*W*, II, 249) "I will just try these three sentences of Con-fut-see; they may fetch that state about again." (*W*, II, 249) The Hermit, however, has been considering in this exaggerated fashion the essentials of Thoreau's own philosophy, and is as much a caricature as the frivolous and superficial Poet, whose thoughts are as far from the "essence of things" as the Hermit's are presumably near, and who is not even aware that he has disturbed the Hermit's meditations.

This introduction precedes a chapter that is otherwise almost purely matter-of-fact observation, with some humorous commentary. This satire on himself follows, one remembers, the very serious speculation of "Higher Laws." The paragraph with which "Brute Neighbors" properly begins needs to be quoted in full; although obscure, it is almost the only key to interpreting the subsequent series of descriptions that seem to be otherwise unexploited as metaphor.

> Why do precisely these objects which we behold make a world? Why has man just these species of animals for his neighbors; as if nothing but a mouse could have filled this crevice? I suspect that Pilpay and Co. have put animals to their best use, for they are all beasts of burden, in a sense, made to carry some portion of our thoughts. (*W*, II, 249)

The first animal observed in close detail is a mouse, implying an answer to Thoreau's question. It is not one of "the common ones, which are said to be introduced into the country, but a wild native kind not found in the village." (*W*, II, 250) The selection of animals for this series of reports are all, likewise, to a degree unusual, or even rare, although mainly because they are rarely seen by human beings. "It is remarkable how many creatures live wild and free though secret in the woods, and still sustain themselves in the neighborhood of towns, suspected by hunters only." (*W*, II, 252) But even the most secret of animals will show themselves if waited for patiently. Thoreau seems less interested in what species fill the obvious crevices of the world than in what ones fill crevices that otherwise appear empty.

"Brute Neighbors" has considerable human content after all. Thoreau does not omit himself; one is likely to forget that the precision and objectivity of this reporting imply an attitude, a method of observation. In every case he describes his method of drawing close to the phenomenon that is rare or hides itself. The mouse learns to run on his arm and eat from his hand; he adjusts to the protective coloration of the young of the partridge, and he holds them in his hands; ants carry on their warfare under a tumbler as he watches with a magnifying glass; he maneuvers his canoe on the Pond to outwit the loon and get a glimpse of it at close range. There are a good many crevices of the world that have never been looked into; Thoreau's unknown in nature is always knowable, and our thoughts widen in range as we explore and discover new points and outposts. In this sense, and as this chapter demonstrates, animals carry some portion of those thoughts, when our perception is extended to reach them in their secrecy.

"House-Warming" is a title to be taken literally, since its theme is the approach of winter and the bringing of fire into the house. The description of the necessaries of life are translated in this chapter to animal terms. Like the animals, Thoreau gathers food to stock his burrow. Winter emphasizes the rootedness of man in the natural world; that is, the conditions and methods he shares with all other animals: "even the wildest animals love comfort and warmth as well as man, and they survive only because they are so careful to secure them." (*W*, II, 280) Civilization means only improved methods, which allow that valuable margin of leisure for development beyond the satisfaction of animal wants:

> The animal merely makes a bed, which he warms with his body, in a sheltered place; but man, having discovered fire, boxes up some air in a spacious apartment, and warms that, instead of robbing himself, makes that his bed, in which he can move about divested of more cumbrous clothing, maintain a kind of summer in the midst of winter,

and by means of windows even admit the light, and with a lamp lengthen out the day. Thus he goes a step or two beyond instinct, saves a little time for the fine arts. (*W*, II, 280)

Winter, by the limitations it imposes, sharpens our evaluation not only of the conditions whereby we live, but of the vital warmth of life itself, which continues on sufferance:

> . . . nor need we trouble ourselves to speculate how the human race may at last be destroyed. It would be easy to cut their threads with a little sharper blast from the north. We go on dating from Cold Fridays and Great Snows; but a little colder Friday, or a little greater snow would put a period to man's existence on the globe. (*W*, II, 280)

The increasing specificity of subject matter in *Walden* has already been pointed out. "Former Inhabitants; and Winter Visitors" and "Winter Animals" contain not a single reference to the thematic imagery of morning and awakening. There is even less exploration, and such as there is lacks the usual statement that would connect it with the explorer image. "Former Inhabitants; and Winter Visitors" continues indoors, as a natural sequence to "House-Warming"; but it is time spent in history and anecdote-telling, and there are now very few visitors. Thoreau waits for "the Visitor who never comes." (*W*, II, 298) "Winter Animals" is scarcely more than a résumé of observed fact, without comment or metaphorization. The deliberate low key of these chapters serves a function not appreciated until one comes upon the exuberant rise of spirits—and metaphor—in the concluding chapters, where spring arrives, and the weathering of snow-storms has a point which was not clear at the time.

The winter season does not end before Walden Pond is sounded, to "recover" its "long lost bottom." (*W*, II, 315) "The Pond in Winter" has three sections, the middle and longest one being devoted to the measurement of the Pond. The short introduction describes a psychological event:

> After a still winter night I awoke with the impression that some question had been put to me, which I had been endeavoring in vain to answer in my sleep, as what—how—when—where? But there was dawning Nature, in whom all creatures live, looking in at my broad windows with serene and satisfied face, and no question on *her* lips. I awoke to an answered question, to Nature and daylight . . . Nature puts no question and answers none which we mortals ask. (*W*, II, 312)

The explorer may look as hard as he wishes, but will never find some questions answered, which actually he has put to himself, and has not been asked. Thoreau's nature has no language. It only provides materials for use in working out answers to questions that arise from one's own life; anchoring points, landmarks, to serve what is developing in man. Thoreau's curiosity about the techniques of work and skilled trades, are definition enough of the kind of interrelatedness of man and nature that he sees.

The Pond satisfied for a long time the local credulousness that it might be really bottomless. In fact, men were so eager to believe in its fantastic depth that they ignored their own measuring line; "for while the 'fifty-six' was resting by the way, they were paying out the rope in the vain attempt to fathom their truly immeasurable capacity for marvelousness." (*W*, II, 316) Thoreau, willing to admit a bottom for Walden, made accurate measurements and thus brought an end to a fond legend. But Walden, he says, is still not too deep for the imagination. The Pond as a symbol for self-exploration must answer human nature, depth for depth.

> What if all ponds were shallow? Would it not react on the minds of men? I am thankful that this pond was made deep and pure for a symbol. While men believe in the infinite some ponds will be thought bottomless. (*W*, II, 316)

The figure is shifted to the measurement of man, and elaborately developed:

> . . . draw lines through the length and breadth of the aggregate of man's particular daily behaviors and waves of life into his coves and inlets, and where they intersect will be the height or depth of his character. (*W*, II, 321)

The strategic metaphor in *Walden* becomes the exploration of one's own life surroundings, because only here has one the centrality of focus from which to lay out measurements in all directions. One finds himself wherever he is by finding *where* he is. Walden Pond is only as deep as one's self, depending on the extent of its service to the imagination; for nature provides the only trustworthy measurement of man. The mind of man thrives and develops by meeting and coming to terms with the world he lives in. The metaphor in Thoreau's hands is shaped to express that relationship. Self-discovery is thus linked with discovery of fact outside one's self.

Walden concludes with the arrival of spring, and the invitation to enter a new season of self-exploration. The final chapter is a profusion of metaphor, reiterating the theme of reawakened spiritual life—the flooding river of our lives, the "strong and beautiful bug" (*W*, II, 366) that hatched to new life out of a table leaf, the unknown inner continent that still invites us to set foot upon it.

From *The American Adam*

by R. W. B. Lewis

"We have the Saint Vitus dance." This was Thoreau's view of the diversion of energies to material expansion and of the enthusiastic arithmetic by which expansion was constantly being measured. Miles of post roads and millions of tons of domestic export did not convince Thoreau that first principles ought to be overhauled; but a close interest in these matters did convince him that first principles had been abandoned. Probably nobody of his generation had a richer sense of the potentiality for a fresh, free, and uncluttered existence; certainly no one projected the need for the ritual burning of the past in more varied and captivating metaphors. This is what *Walden* is about; it is the most searching contemporary account of the desire for a new kind of life. But Thoreau's announcement of a spiritual moulting season (one of his favorite images) did not arise from a belief that the building of railroads was proof of the irrelevance of too-well-remembered doctrines. Long before Whitman, himself a devotee of the dazzling sum, attacked the extremes of commercialism in *Democratic Vistas*, Thoreau was insisting that the obsession with railroads did not demonstrate the hope for humanity, but tended to smother it.

> "Men think it is essential that the *Nation* have commerce, and export ice, and talk through a telegraph and ride thirty miles an hour, without a doubt, whether *they* do or not; but whether we should live like baboons or men is a little uncertain."

Watching the local railroad train as it passed near Walden Pond on the recently laid track between Fitchburg and Boston, Thoreau noticed that while the narrow little cars moved eastward along the

From *The American Adam: Innocence, Tragedy, and Tradition in the Nineteenth Century*, by R. W. B. Lewis, pp. 20-27. Copyright 1955 by The University of Chicago Press. Reprinted by permission.

ground, the engine smoke drifted skyward, broadening out as it rose. The picture (it occurs in the chapter called "Sounds") provided him with a meaningful glimpse of that wholeness, of interrelated doubleness, which was for Thoreau the required shape of the life that was genuinely lived. The trouble with railroads—he said it, in fancy, to the scores of workmen he saw starting up in protest against him—was that so few persons who rode on them were heading in any definite direction or were aware of a better direction than Boston; quite a few persons were simply run over, while the building of railroads crushed the heart and life out of the builders. The trouble, in general, with expending one's strength on "internal improvements" was that the achievement, like the aim, was partial: there was nothing internal about them. The opportunity that Thoreau looked out upon from his hut at Walden was for no such superficial accomplishment, but for a wholeness of spirit realized in a direct experience of the whole of nature. The words "nature" and "wholeness" have been overworked and devitalized (Thoreau and Emerson are partly to blame), and now they are suspect; but they glow with health in the imaginatively ordered prose of Henry Thoreau.

The narrator of *Walden* is a witness to a truly new world which the speaker alone has visited, from which he has just returned, and which he is sure every individual ought to visit at least once—not the visible world around Walden Pond, but an inner world which the Walden experience allowed him to explore. Thoreau liked to pretend that his book was a purely personal act of private communion. But that was part of his rhetoric, and *Walden* is a profoundly rhetorical book, emerging unmistakably from the long New England preaching tradition; though here the trumpet call announces the best imaginable news rather than apocalyptic warnings. Thoreau, in *Walden,* is a man who has come back down into the cave to tell the residents there that they are really in chains, suffering fantastic punishments they have imposed on themselves, seeing by a light that is reflected and derivative. A major test of the visionary hero must always be the way he can put his experience to work for the benefit of mankind; he demonstrates his freedom in the liberation of others. Thoreau prescribes the following cure: the total renunciation of the traditional, the conventional, the socially acceptable, the well-worn paths of conduct, and the total immersion in nature.

Everything associated with the past should be burned away. The past should be cast off like dead skin. Thoreau remembered with

sympathetic humor the pitiful efforts of one John Field, an Irish-
man living at near-by Baker Farm, to catch perch with shiners:
"thinking to live by some derivative old-country mode in this
primitive new country." "I look on England today," he wrote, "as an
old gentleman who is travelling with a great deal of baggage,
trumpery which has accumulated from long housekeeping, which he
has not the courage to burn." Thoreau recorded with approval and
some envy a Mexican purification rite practiced every fifty-two
years; and he added, "I have scarcely heard of a truer sacrament."
These periodic symbolic acts of refreshment, which whole societies
ought to perform in each generation ("One generation abandons
the enterprises of another like stranded vessels"), were valid exactly
because they were images of fundamental reality itself. Individuals
and groups should enact the rhythmic death and rebirth reflected
in the change of season from winter to spring, in the sequence of
night and day. "The phenomena of the year take place every day
in a pond on a small scale." These were some of the essential facts
discovered by Thoreau when he fronted them at Walden; and the
experience to which he was to become a witness took its shape, in
act and in description, from a desire to live in accordance with these
facts. So it was that he refused the offer of a door-mat, lest he should
form the habit of shaking it every morning; and, instead, every
morning "I got up early and bathed in the pond; that was a religious exercise, and one of the best things which I did."

The language tells us everything, as Thoreau meant it to. He had
his own sacramental system, his own rite of baptism. But his use of
the word "nature" indicates that the function of sacraments was to
expose the individual again to the currents flowing through nature,
rather than to the grace flowing down from supernature. The ritual
of purification was no less for Thoreau than for St. Paul a dying
into life; but Thoreau marched to the music he heard; it was the
music of the age; and he marched in a direction *opposite* to St. Paul.
His familiar witticism, "One world at a time" (made on his deathbed to an eager abolitionist named Pillsbury, who looked for some
illumination of the future life from the dying seer) was a fair summary of his position: with this addition, that poetry traditionally
taken as hints about what could be seen through a glass darkly
about the next world was taken by Thoreau as what had been seen
by genius, face to face with this one. He was among the first to see
Christian literature as only the purest and most inspiring of the
fables about the relation of man to nature and about the infinite
capacities of the unaided human spirit. The Bible (Thoreau referred

to it simply as "an old book") was the finest poem which had ever been written; it was the same in substance as Homeric or Hindu mythology, but it was richer in metaphor. The Bible spoke more sharply to the human condition. This was why Thoreau, like Whitman, could employ the most traditional of religious phrases and invest them with an unexpected and dynamic new life.

It is not surprising that transcendentalism was Puritanism turned upside down, as a number of critics have pointed out; historically, it could hardly have been anything else. Transcendentalism drew on the vocabularies of European romanticism and Oriental mysticism; but the only available local vocabulary was the one that the hopeful were so anxious to escape from, and a very effective way to discredit its inherited meaning was to serve it up in an unfamiliar context. There was something gratifyingly shocking in such a use of words: "What demon possessed me that I behaved so well?" Thoreau spoke as frequently as he could, therefore, about a *sacrament,* a sacred mystery, such as baptism: in order to define the cleansing, not of St. Paul's natural man, but of the conventional or traditional man; in order, precisely, to bring into being the natural man. For the new tensions out of which insights were drawn and moral choices provoked were no longer the relation of nature and grace, of man and God, but of the natural and the artificial, the new and the old, the individual and the social or conventional. Thoreau had, as he remarked in his other deathbed witticism, no quarrel with God; his concern was simply other.

His concern was with the strangulation of nature by convention. The trouble with conventions and traditions in the New World was that they had come first; they had come from abroad and from a very long way back; and they had been superimposed upon nature. They had to be washed away, like sin, so that the natural could reveal itself again and could be permitted to create its own organic conventions. They had to be renounced, as the first phase of the ritual; and if renunciation was, as Emily Dickinson thought, a piercing virtue, it was not because it made possible an experience of God in an infusion of grace, but because it made possible an experience of self in a bath of nature.

Thoreau had, of course, learned a good deal from Emerson, whose early energy was largely directed toward constructing "an original relation with the universe" and who reverted time and again to the same theme: "beware of tradition"; "forget historical Christianity"; "lop off all superfluity and tradition, and fall back on the nature of things." And what was this nature of things which men were en-

joined to fall back on? Lowell understood some of it, in one of the
better sentences of his querulous and uneven essay on Thoreau
(1865):

> There is only one thing better than tradition, and that is the original
> and eternal life out of which all tradition takes its rise. It was this life
> which the reformers demanded, with more or less clearness of con-
> sciousness and expression, life in politics, life in literature, life in
> religion.

But even in this moment of qualified approval, Lowell makes it
sound too pallid, soft, and ethereal. Nature was not merely the
mountains and the prairie, any more than it was merely the bees
and the flowers; but it was all of those things too, and it must
always include them. If nature was partly represented by "Higher
Laws," as the title of one chapter in *Walden* tells us, it was represented also by "Brute Neighbors," "Winter Animals," and a "Bean-
Field," as we know from the titles of other chapters. Thoreau's
nature is bounded by an irony which applies the phrase "Higher
Laws" to a chapter that, for all its idealism, talks at some length
about fried rats.

Irony too—the doubleness of things—Thoreau could learn from
Emerson, as each of them had learned from Coleridge and Plato.
"All the universe over," Emerson wrote in his journal (1842), "there
is just one thing, this old double." The old double, the ideal and the
actual, the higher law and the fried rat, required a double consciousness and found expression in a double criticism; nature could be
satisfied with nothing else. Emerson tramped in mud puddles, and
Thoreau, more adventurously, swam in Walden Pond; the puddle
and the pond were instances of unimpeded nature; but both men
searched, in their separate ways, for the spiritual analogues which
completed the doubleness of nature. Their ability to address themselves with very nearly equal fluency to both dimensions of consciousness gave later comfort to idealist and nominalists alike,
though neither group understood the Emersonian principle that
only the whole truth could be true at all. Bronson Alcott was the
most high-minded of the contemporary idealists, but Emerson
chided him for neglecting the value of the many in his rapture for
the one, and thought he had genius but no talent. "The philosophers of Fruitlands," Emerson said in 1843, naming Alcott's experimental community, "have such an image of virtue before their
eyes, that the poetry of man and nature they never see; the poetry
that is man's life, the poorest pastoral clownish life; the light that

shines on a man's hat, in a child's spoon." He was harder, of course
on those who saw only the hat and the spoon: the materialists and
the tradesmen whom he excoriated in many essays, and writers who
stuck too obstinately to the ordinary (Emerson would say, the
"vulgar") aspects of the visible world.

Thoreau's personal purification rite began with the renunciation
of old hats and old spoons and went forward to the moment—as he
describes himself in the opening paragraph of "Higher Laws"—
when the initiate stood fully alive in the midst of nature, eating a
woodchuck with his fingers, and supremely aware, at the same instant, of the higher law of virtue. "I love the wild not less than the
good," Thoreau admitted, announcing duplicity in his own peculiar
accent. The structure of *Walden* has a similar beginning and a
similar motion forward. The book starts amid the punishing conventions of Concord, departs from them to the pond and the forest,
explores the natural-surroundings, and exposes the natural myth of
the yearly cycle, to conclude with the arrival of spring, the full possession of life, and a representative anecdote about the sudden
bursting into life of a winged insect long buried in an old table of
apple-tree wood.[1]

Individual chapters are sometimes carried along to the same
rhythm. "Sounds," for example, starts with conventional signs and
then looks to nature for more authentic ones; it picks up the cycle or
the day, as Thoreau listens to sounds around the clock; and it concludes with a total surrender to the vitalizing power of unbounded
nature. Thoreau had been talking about his reading in the previous
chapter; now he reminds us: "While we are confined to books . . .
we are in danger of forgetting the language which all things and
events speak without metaphor." Sounds are elements of this natural
language: the sound of the trains passing in the morning; the
church bells from Lincoln, Bedford, or Concord; the lowing of
cows in the evening; "regularly at half-past seven," the vesper chant
of the whip-poor-wills; the "maniacal hooting of owls," which "represent the stark twilight and unsatisfied thoughts which all have";
"late in the evening . . . the distant rumbling of wagons over
bridges,—a sound heard farther than almost any other at night,—
the baying of dogs . . . the trump of bullfrogs"; and then at dawn
the morning song of the cockerel, the lusty call to awaken of the

[1] I am indebted here to the analysis of *Walden* as a rebirth ritual by Stanley
Hyman, "Henry Thoreau in Our Time," *Atlantic Monthly,* CLXXVIII (Novem-
ber, 1946), 137-46. Mr. Hyman acknowledges his own debt, which I share, to F. O.
Matthiessen's treatment of Thoreau in *American Renaissance* (New York, 1941).

chanticleer which Thoreau offered on the title-page as the symbol of the book. "To walk in a winter morning, in a wood where these birds abounded . . . think of it! It would put nations on the alert." Finally, in a morning mood, Thoreau closes his chapter rejoicing that his hut has no yard, no fence, but is part of unfenced nature itself.

It was with the ultimate aim of making such an experience possible—a life determined by nature and enriched by a total awareness —that Thoreau insisted so eloquently upon the baptismal or rebirth rite. What he was demanding was that individuals start life all over again, and that in the new world a fresh start was literally and immediately possible to anyone wide enough awake to attempt it. It was in this way that the experience could also appear as a return to childhood, to the scenes and the wonder of that time. In a particularly revealing moment, Thoreau reflected, while adrift on the lake in the moonlight and playing the flute for the fishes, on a boyhood adventure at that very place. "But now," he said, "I made my home by the shore." Thoreau reflected the curious but logical reverence of his age for children: "Children, who play life, discern its true law and relations more clearly than men, who fail to live it worthily." Children seemed for Thoreau to possess some secret which had been lost in the deadening process of growing up, some intimation (like Wordsworth's child) which had faded under the routine pressure of everyday life. Emerson found the new attitude of adults toward children the appropriate symbol with which to introduce his retrospective summary of the times (1867): "Children had been repressed and kept in the background; now they were considered, cosseted and pampered." Thoreau thought he knew why: because "every child begins the world again"; every child managed to achieve without conscious effort what the adult could achieve only by the strenuous, periodic act of refreshment. In this sense, the renewal of life was a kind of homecoming; the busks and the burnings were preparatory to recapturing the outlook of children.

Psychologists who have followed Jung's poetic elaboration and doctrinaire schematizing of the guarded suggestions of Freud could make a good deal of the impulse. They might describe it as an impulse to return to the womb; and some support could doubtless be found in the image-clusters of *Walden*: water, caves, shipwrecks, and the like. This approach might persuasively maintain that the end of the experience narrated by Thoreau was the reintegration of the personality. And since, according to Jung, "the lake in the valley is the unconscious," it is possible to hold that *Walden* enacts and urges the escape from the convention-ridden conscious and the release of the spontaneous energies of personality lying beneath the surface, toward a reuniting of the psychic "old double." An analysis of this sort can be helpful and even illuminating, and it could be applied to the entire program of the party of Hope, substituting terms associated with the unconscious for all the terms associated with Emerson's "Reason." A certain warrant for the psychological interpretation can be found in the novels of Dr. Holmes, and the methodological issue arises more sharply in that discussion. But we may also remind ourselves that the psychological vocabularly simply manipulates a set of metaphors other than those we normally use. Probably we do not need to go so far afield to grasp what Thoreau was seeking to explain; we may even suspect that he meant what he said. And what he said was that he went to the woods in order to live deliberately, "to front only the essential facts of life"; because human life and human expression were so burdened with unexamined habits, the voice of experience so muffled by an uninvestigated inheritance, that only by a total rejection of those habits and that inheritance and by a recovery of a childlike wonder and directness could anyone find out whether life were worth living at all.

Thoreau, like most other members of the hopeful party, understood dawn and birth better than he did night and death. He responded at once to the cockerel in the morning; the screech owls at night made him bookish and sentimental. And though their wailing spoke to him about "the low spirits and melancholy forebodings of fallen souls," the whole dark side of the world was no more than another guaranty of the inexhaustible variety of nature.[2] Thoreau knew not evil; his American busk would have fallen short, like the bonfire in Hawthorne's fantasy, of the profounder need for the purification of the human heart. He would have burned away the past as the accumulation of artifice, in the name of the natural and the essential. But if the natural looked to him so much more wholesome and so much more dependable than others have since thought it, his account of the recovery of nature was never less than noble: the noblest expression, in fact and in language, of the first great aspiration of the age.

[2] Thoreau goes on to say that the hooting of owls "is a sound admirably suited to swamps and twilight woods which no day illustrates, suggesting a vast and undeveloped nature which men have not yet recognized." The figurative language here is suggestive and may be surprising to anyone who supposes Thoreau unaware of the very existence of the cloacal regions of mind and nature.

A Fable of the Renewal of Life

by Sherman Paul

The knowledge of the seasons was the most important addition to Thoreau's thought after 1850. It made possible the metaphors of ripening and completion that give his last work a tone of acceptance and quiet satisfaction; and it also made possible the fable of the renewal of life in *Walden*. When "for convenience" Thoreau put the experience of his two years at the pond into one, when he saw that the narrative action might be related to the seasons, he had the "fable with a moral" with which to express the meaning he now gave to that period of his life. Unlike the fable of the *Week*, which made the day the unit of time and of inspiration, the fable of the seasons enabled Thoreau to be true to the trials, changes, and growth he had known—to actualize by means of his former life his present aspirations. "Some men's lives are but an aspiration, a yearning toward a higher state," he wrote in 1851, "and they are wholly misapprehended, until they are referred to, or traced through, all their metamorphoses." In the seasons of *Walden* he could trace his metamorphoses: the passage from servitude to liberation, and the self-transcendence of his transformation from impurity to purity—the rebirth of new life out of the old.

The day, of course, had its seasons; it was the epitome of the year: "The night is winter, the morning and evening are the spring and fall, and the noon is summer." The spiritual change from sleep to wakefulness—the prospect of the dawn that closes *Walden*—was proper to it; and the chapters nearest in fact to his ecstatic years employed it—"Where I Lived, and What I Lived For," with its morning philosophy, and "Sounds," with its account of his summer reverie, of a full day in Nature. He had used the day in the *Week* as the very possession of ecstasy, but now that he was earning it, he needed a longer cycle of time in order to participate in the organic processes of rebuilding and renewing his world. There had to be time to clear his land, build his hut, plant his seeds, and harvest his crop: time for that "something even in the lapse of time by which time recovers itself." Change, gradual transformation, now preoccupied him, and sleeping and waking, admirably fitted to the sudden advent of inspiration, were neither as adequate nor as rich in the details of change as the metaphors he now chose: ice-thaw-flux, seed-flower-fruit, grub-chrysalis-butterfly. These natural facts became the metaphors in terms of which he told of his desire to pass from a lower to a higher form of life, from fixity to fluidity (he would share again the "circulations" of Being), from the innocence of youth to the wisdom of maturity, from larval sensuality to aerial purity.

These transformations, moreover, were examples of change in obedience to the organic principle, by means of an inner expansion. In terms of Thoreau's personal life, their possibility was dramatized by his withdrawal from society to Nature, that is to say, from a condition fixed beyond growth (society for Thoreau was always a machine) to a condition permitting him to build his life from the inside out in obedience to his idea. "Our moulting season, like that of the fowls, must be the crisis of our lives," he explained. "The loon retires to solitary ponds to spend it. Thus also the snake casts its slough, and the caterpillar its wormy coat, by an internal industry and expansion. . . ." In society, however, he remained his old "scurvy self," and society, as he now used it in *Walden* to enclose his experiment in renewal, was the sum of all the anxieties and constraints and failures he wished to leave behind. Not only because he was preaching self-reform, but because he wanted to show what he had surmounted, he began *Walden* with the long social analysis of "Economy," setting up the emphatic polarities and perspectives that would awaken his readers to see their—and his—condition absolutely, from a vantage outside of society. As Emerson had done in *Nature,* he began with commodity before turning to spirit. But more fully than Emerson, whose treatise had its point-by-point parallels in *Walden,* he employed history, anthropology, books (even Scripture), paradox, humor, irony, ridicule, scorn, philological puns, parables, dramatization, utopian prospects, and every variety of symbolic statement to establish the contrasting values of surface and depth (appearance and reality), transient and permanent, complex and simple, disease and health, tradition and the uncommitted life, desperation and joy, spiritual emptiness and spiritual fullness. From externality and circumstance, he turned to the inner dominion of self-reliance, from collective "humanitarian" reform to self-discovery, from a world broken and in heaps to the cosmos he had made. Indeed, in dramatizing these changes from society and commodity to spirit and self, *Walden* worked inward from the circumferential to the central life, from the external to the real self, from extrinsic to intrinsic success.

Thoreau also began with "Economy" because it was the aspect of his experiment that had aroused the most curiosity. The life of quiet desperation that he so brilliantly anatomized, however, had been (or was) his own, and the economic anxieties merely pointed to deeper anxieties—those of a life gone stale, without savor or animating purpose. The economy he proposed, therefore, was to the end of getting and spending one's life, an economy of spirit his readers little expected, one that denied the Puritan necessity of working with the sweat of the brow, one that made work itself a joy and a pastime rather than a duty. The irony of his economy, given to the fraction of a cent, was that on so little, he had got so much, that he did not carry a house on his back or possess a corner of the world, but had all the landscape for his own, and time (which Franklin said was money) to read, to sit idle all day, to boat and fish, and to saunter at his ease and enjoy those bounties of Nature that were reserved for a "Lord of Creation." He had a self that he could hug, one that was not at society's beck and call or twisted and thwarted by relations, which, he had found by experiment, were customary rather than essential. And if the simplicity of his economy seemed Franklinian, he was not burning incense to the patron saint of State Street: the end of his economy was enrichment, not denial, and he spent lavishly. "Give me the poverty," he exclaimed when cursing Flint, "that enjoys true wealth." If anything, he was undermining the Franklinian virtues, replacing the *Autobiography* with a model for another kind of success—utilizing the very terminology of business to raise the uncomfortable question of whether possessions actually helped one possess life. This was the purpose of his reductiveness in treating the goods of the world, for the only good he wished to appropriate (and here he added his voice to the swelling clamor of American literature) was experience, the quality or bloom of life. The burden of "Economy," in fact, was that the way to wealth was not the way to health, but to lives of quiet desperation. When he wrote Blake, who was trying to use *Walden* as his guide, he said:

It is surprising how contented one can be with nothing definite,—
only a sense of existence. . . . O how I laugh when I think of my
vague, indefinite riches. No run on my bank can drain it, for my
wealth is not possession but enjoyment.

Standing in the way of this enjoyment, however, was the confusion concerning the means and ends of life which Thoreau had tried
to clarify by reducing his life to its simplest terms; and, accordingly,
the central issue to those who either rejected or accepted his life
was his doctrine of simplicity. He had reduced the means of life, of
course, not because he wanted to prove that he could go without
them, or to disclaim their value in enriching life, but because they
were usually factitious—they robbed one of life itself. And though,
like *Walden,* the "shallow meaning" of this economy was "but too
clear," the meaning it had for him was not. His economy, like his
withdrawal to Nature, was not an ultimate abdication from social
life; it was only the means of the self-emancipation, which many, accepting social bondage as the inevitable condition of life, did not
find necessary. Economy freed him from society, and Nature provided him the opportunity to share the recreative processes of life;
but this life in Nature was also a means, the goal being another, a
"higher" and an organic society, shaped by the same principles
whose efficacy Thoreau had demonstrated. To this end, rather than
to the renunciation of society, *Walden* was a social gospel.
He himself had adopted simplicity for many reasons. He believed, for example, that it would bring him nearer to those common influences in which Emerson had taught the poet to delight.
And as a social critic, he believed that the only honest or absolute
view required the detached prospect of "voluntary poverty." Considering his personal experiment, however, the most important reason was his need to clear away the obstacles that stood between him
and the "grand fact" of life. For in order to front the fact and recover reality, he had to reduce the problem of perception to its
simplest terms—self and Nature. Simplicity, then, was a discipline
and an ascetic, as necessary to his purification as the labor in the
beanfield or the dietary practices of "Higher Laws," and he often
hallowed it with religious associations by calling it "poverty." "By
poverty, *i.e.* simplicity of life and fewness of incidents," he wrote in
1857, bringing to the surface the sunken imagery of *Walden,* "I am
solidified and crystallized, as a vapor or liquid by cold. It is a
singular concentration of strength and energy and flavor. Chastity is

perpetual acquaintance with the All [In "Higher Laws" he said that "Chastity is the flowering of man. . . . Man flows at once to God when the channel of purity is open."]. . . . You think that I am impoverishing myself by withdrawing from men, but in my solitude I have woven for myself a silken web or *chrysalis,* and nymph-like, shall ere long burst forth a more perfect creature, fitted for a higher society. By simplicity . . . my life is concentrated and so becomes organized, or a Κόσμος [cosmos], which before was inorganic and lumpish."

When simplicity, finally, was associated with his life in the woods and his hunger for the wild, it raised another issue—that of primitivism *vs.* civilization. In espousing Nature, the transcendentalists, of course, had also glorified the primitive life. But having experienced the wilderness on his trips to the Maine woods in 1846 and 1853, Thoreau knew that his life at the pond and in Concord pastures was far from wild; and though he always maintained that the health of civilization needed the tonic of the wild, his experience had taught him that the pastoral landscape was the best setting for human life. On one level, in fact, he intended *Walden* for a modern epic of farming, and he had purposely begun his life from scratch in order to relive all history and test this mode of life against the achievements of civilization.

Had his problem been merely that of doing without society, it would have been easily solved; but his problem—the one that Lane had posed in *The Dial*—was what to do with it: how to join the values of urban and sylvan life. The paradox of civilization that Thoreau exploited (though it was hardly a paradox to one who recognized the enslavement to means) was that it did not civilize but barbarized most men, reducing them to a level of want below that of the savage. His own simple life, however, had been remarkably civil, and much of his satisfaction in it was due to the fact that it had provided the uncluttered and leisurely conditions of truly civilizing himself: savages, after all, did not read Homer or write books in the woods. His stance as a philosopher, moreover, made it clear that his demands on life were not simple or primitive, that only the self-sufficiency and adjustment of the Indians to the natural environment appealed to him—the style of their life rather than the "barren simplicity" of their elementary demands on it. "There are two kinds of simplicity," he had observed in the *Journal,* "one that is akin to foolishness, the other to wisdom. The philosopher's style of living is only outwardly simple, but inwardly complex. The savage's style is both outwardly and inwardly simple." The complex and refined life of society, however, did not necessarily yield a complex inner life. And when he proposed that the civilized man become a more experienced and wiser savage, he hoped that he would retain the physical simplicity of the one in order to achieve the complex goals of the other, that he would "spend as little time as possible in planting, weaving, building, etc." and devote his freedom to cultivating "the highest faculties." This could be done, he believed, as he had done it, not only by simplicity, but by making the organic communion of the sylvan the foundation of a higher life.

In showing the "positive hindrances" of civilization—that its means did not fit the ends of man—Thoreau used examples that also enabled him to develop the theory of organic functionalism so essential to his faith in the renewal of life. Everything—education, reform, clothing, shelter, and furniture—was tested by its fitness to living needs, by whether it answered to the inner necessities of man. Clothing, he found, for example, seldom fit the character of the wearer, in many cases did not even serve its basic function of preserving the "vital heat"; instead it was an outer covering worn in conformity to society. Houses, too, were "*exo*strious" [a pun on *indu*strious], a building from without, a more cumbersome clothing, indeed a "tomb" built by the "coffin-maker," as he called the carpenter, for the next generation. Fine houses, like fashionable clothes, he said, were not the expression or function of the indweller; they had not been built up from the "foundation" of "beautiful housekeeping and beautiful living." And furniture was *exuviae,* the cast skins of others, that cluttered the house, the spider's web of tradition that trapped the "gay butterfly." Accordingly, having by his withdrawal and simplicity divested himself of these impediments, he built his life from the inside out; and he proposed that others build in the same "Orphean fashion," that they "grow" their houses. "Let our houses first be lined with beauty," he said, "where they come in contact with our lives, like the tenement of the shellfish, and not overlaid with it." If he acknowledged that in building his hut he had built too heedlessly to build well, still he recommended that others consider "what foundation a door, a window, a cellar, a garret, have in the nature of man. . . ." For he knew that the circumstances that man creates also shape him, that "this frame," as he said of his hut, "was a sort of crystallization around me, and reacted on the builder."

These principles, as well as the prospectus of his hopes and the initial stages of his experiment, were placed in the intervals of the social analysis of "Economy." The contrast they provided, however, was immediately realized in "Where I Lived, and What I Lived For," for in his determination to adventure on life Thoreau was already reborn. When he went to the pond in March, 1845, he had already felt the influence of "the spring of springs"; he had overcome his "torpidity"; in the woods, as Emerson said in *Nature,* he had "cast off his skin, as a snake his slough," and had again become "a child." Though Thoreau buried this spring in "Economy," and deliberately began his account with summer, with his going to the pond to live on Independence Day, the imagery of the melting pond, the returning birds, and the stray goose were the same as in his second "Spring." This additional season made it possible for Thoreau to recapitulate the entire history of his life from youth to maturity: the first spring, the dewy, pure, auroral season of the Olympian life, was true to his youth, and the subsequent seasons and the second spring were the record of the growth of consciousness and of his conscious endeavor to earn the new world of his springtime again.

Thoreau most patently dramatized this process of organic growth and renewal by building his hut, the container of his vital heat and the symbol of the self, to meet the developing seasons of man and consciousness. The seasons of man, of course, corresponded to the seasons of Nature: summer representing the outdoor life, when man was alive in all his senses and Nature supplied his vital heat; autumn, the gathering of consciousness; and winter, the withdrawal inward to self-reflection. This development, moreover, had its counterpart in the seasons of history, for, as Emerson had noted, "The Greek was the age of observation; the Middle Age, that of fact and thought; ours, that of reflection and ideas." Thus, when Thoreau went to Walden, he found that "both place and time were changed and I dwelt nearer to those parts of the universe and to those eras in history which had most attracted me." Spring was the Golden Age, that morning time of heroic endeavor that he always associated with Greece; and this explained why his first spring was so full of allusions to Greece, why Homer was the proper scripture for his morning discipline, and why the second spring recalled his reading in Ovid's *Metamorphoses* and brought back the Golden Age. His year was the cycle of human history, and by renewing it he was trying to prove his proposition that the joys of life were not exhausted, that the counsel of despair of his elders, who believed that the whole ground of human life had already been gone over, was untrue.

The frame and foundation of Thoreau's hut came from Nature,

the boards or outer covering from a shanty Thoreau purchased from James Collins, an Irish laborer whose life, like his "dank, clammy, and aquish" dwelling, was the very sum of quiet desperation. Dismantling this hut, Thoreau bleached and warped the boards in the sun; he purified the materials of his life, as he did again the second-hand bricks he used for his chimney; and with the stuff of the old, for he knew that men must borrow from civilization, he built the new after an Orphean fashion. When he first occupied his house in the summer, it was "merely a defence against the rain, without plastering or chimney," with "wide chinks" between the boards, open, as he had been in the summer, to the influence of Nature. "I did not need to go out doors to take the air," he observed, "for the atmosphere within had lost none of its freshness." This was the time of his rich communion with Nature, when there were no barriers to the rapture he celebrated in "Sounds," when his solitude (which he defined in terms of his nearness to God) was a satisfaction his friends never suspected. As long as possible, therefore, he preferred to remain outdoors, warmed by these genial influences; but, anticipating the bleaker seasons, toward the end of summer he began to build his chimney and fireplace—"the most vital part of the house." The foundation had already been laid in the spring, and now in the cooler days of autumn, he carefully and slowly built his chimney a layer of bricks at a time. The chimney, of course, was his very self or "soul"—an "independent structure, standing on the ground and rising through the house to the heavens," and he built it deliberately because it "was calculated to endure for a long time." Finally, when the north wind came and the pond began to cool and he needed a fire to warm him, he first "inhabited" his house; he plastered and shingled, completely closing himself off from the elements—he internalized his life. "I withdrew yet farther into my shell," he wrote, "and endeavored to keep a bright fire both within my house and within my breast." In this season, as he told of it in "House-Warming," his chief employment was gathering wood for his fire: he was trying to keep alive, to maintain "a kind of summer in the midst of winter. . . ." For he found, during this "barren" season when he had only his heart to gnaw, that he began to grow torpid, that what he had gained in maturity by his self-confinement—by the change from outer to inner, from unconsciousness to consciousness—had brought with it an estrangement from Nature, the sense of "otherness" that bespoke his greatest loss.

If this development was true to Thoreau's life, so were the occupations or disciplines by which he hoped to burst the shell of his cocoon. His summer and morning work, for example, was cultivating beans, a discipline that was hardly consonant with the "fertile idleness" he had appropriately described in "Sounds" and "solitude." During the Walden period he had, of course, hoed beans, but solely for the purpose of paying his way; from the vantage of his later years, however, this labor became the discipline by means of which he participated in the natural process and renewed his intimacy with Nature. "They attached me to the earth," he said of his beans, "and so I got strength like Antæus." The value of farming, or of any unspecialized vocation in Nature, he also found, was that it helped one catch Nature unaware, that it restored unconsciousness and permitted one to see out of the side of the eye. He advised the American scholar to live by this manual labor, moreover, not only because it was honest and because it rooted one in the native soil, but because it taught one how to reason from the hands to the head: here was the very creative process that would instruct him in the symbolic use of things, that would make the concrete object yield its truth, and that, accordingly, would remove the "palaver" from his style. In his own case, he had been "a plastic artist in the dewy and crumbling sand" in order that his work might bear the "instant and immeasurable crop" of "tropes and expression." And the expression it yielded was the parable of the chapter itself: how to plant the seeds of "sincerity, truth, simplicity, faith, innocence, and the like," how by constant vigilance to make the "germ of virtue" bear, how by redeeming the "lean and effete" soil of Massachusetts—the "dust of my ancestors"—the seed of one man might bear the harvest of "a new generation of men." Here was a parable of both individual and social reform, of the kind of moral reform that went to the root of things and that could not fail because, as Thoreau pointed out in the case of the word "seed," its root was "spica," "spe," and "gerendo"—hope-bearing.

The most important result of this discipline was that it helped him "clothe that fabulous landscape of my infant dreams. . . ." At the beginning of "The Bean-Field" he told how he had first been brought to the pond in his childhood, and in "The Ponds" he told how the woodchoppers had since laid waste its shores. These alterations in the shore, he now realized, were the evidence of his own coarsened, actual self. For the pond itself, he discovered, was "the same water which my youthful eyes fell on," that "all the change," as he confessed, "is in me." The pond, then, was his own pristine, eternal self, and by cultivating beans, by discipline, he was chang-

ing the aspect of its shore, making it more agreeable to his imagination. If in his "decay" he lamented that the poet could not sing
because his groves were cut down, he was heartened now because,
he said, "one of the results of my presence and influence is seen
in these bean leaves, corn blades, and potato vines."

That the pond was his real or essential self and the shore his
actual self was made clear in "The Ponds." "It is no dream of
mine," he said of Walden. "I cannot come nearer to God and
Heaven/Than I live to Walden even./I am its stony shore. . . ."
In a variant of this verse, he wrote: "It is a part of me which I
have not profaned/I live by the shore of me detained." And he even
punned on its name—"*Walled-in* Pond." In "The Ponds," however, he did not linger over his shores, but lovingly related all the
details of the "crystal well" that he had once been made. There
he described the remarkable purity, depth, and transparency of the
pond, its coolness and constancy, the cerulean color that made it
a "Sky water," the "earth's eye," the very window of the soul. It
was the "distiller of celestial dews" whose seasonal tides and daily
evaporations kept it pure; it was alive with the motion imparted
by the "spirit" of the air, and its surface was "a perfect forest mir-
ror," reflecting all phenomena perfectly as an untarnished mind
should. Even its bottom was "pure sand," with only the sediment
of fallen leaves (Thoreau's autumnal decay); "a bright green weed,"
the token of life, could be found growing there in winter; and its
fish—its "ascetic fish"—were "cleaner, handsomer, and firmer." Having in his *Journal* thanked God for making "this pond deep and
pure for a symbol," Thoreau accounted for its creation with a
"myth" of the "old settler," the same old settler he had used to
explain why he was not lonely in "Solitude" and was to refer to
again in "Former Inhabitants; and Winter Visitors" to explain his
notion of society. "That ancient settler [God] . . . came here with
his divining-rod [pun]," he wrote, "saw a thin vapor rising from
the sward, and the hazel pointed steadily downward, and he concluded to dig a well here." Walden was " 'God's Drop.' " He also
gave it Edenic associations, describing its immemorial breaking up
in the imagery of his first and second springs, making the rebirth
this signified Adamic. Finally, having told of the ecstasy of his youth
upon its waters, he likened it to himself; for it was "the work of
a brave man," it lived "reserved and austere, like a hermit in the
woods," and like his life, which he had "deepened and clarified,"
it was "too pure to have a market value." And yet he "bequeathed
it to Concord," hoping that it would serve society as an example

of "greater steadfastness," that "this vision of serenity and purity" would "wash out State-street and the engine's soot."

"The Ponds" was a summer chapter, the record of the time when he floated on the bosom of Nature and even in the darkest night communicated with her by fishing her mysterious depths. Now, fishing, he explained in "Higher Laws," was the proper vocation of the Golden Age; with hunting, it was "the young man's introduction to the forest, and the most original part of himself." Following the inevitable cycle of the seasons, however, this youthful pursuit was soon over: "He goes thither at first as a hunter and fisher, until at last, if he has the seeds of a better life in him, he distinguishes his proper objects, as a poet or naturalist it may be. . . ." When unconscious communion was gone, showing him what his proper object was, the fisher angled instead (in "The Pond in Winter") for the pond itself, seeking the bottom or foundation "that will hold an anchor, that it may not drag."

But before this conscious exploration became necessary, Thoreau went afishing in the summer days. In "Baker Farm," he extolled the easy self-sufficiency of this uncommitted life in the wild and contrasted it with John Field's grubbing. Coming home with his string of fish, however, he turned to "Higher Laws," as if suddenly aware of the fact that in respect to diet at least he was as much in the larval condition as Field. Aware now that only discipline would help him continue his culture after manhood, that the instinct for the wild had been challenged by an instinct toward a higher or spiritual life, he repudiated his former mode of life and adopted the Oriental rituals of purification—bathing and diet and the conscious discipline of earnest labor. This resolution on purity, like the invocation to Hebe in "Solitude" and the martial vigilance of "The Bean-Field," betrayed an autumnal mood which Thoreau tried to dispel by the humorous dialogue that began "Brute Neighbors." There his going fishing was a breach of discipline that destroyed his "budding ecstasy"; but, having covered his loss by his self-protective humor, he nevertheless seriously explained the higher uses of Nature for which he was purifying himself. Nature, as Emerson said and as Thoreau first introduced this theme in "Sounds," was language. Thoreau's proper objects now were the correspondences of Nature; his brute neighbors were "beasts of burden . . . made to carry some portion of our thoughts." The partridge, for example, suggested "not merely the purity of infancy, but a wisdom clarified by experience." And the loon, whose return marked the advent of autumn, carried the heavy burden of his personal lapse.

Enacting the play of inspiration by chasing this deep-diving bird, Thoreau told the story of his decay: consciously trying to pursue it—"While he was thinking one thing in his brain, I was endeavoring to divine his thought in mine"—he was balked; and even his passivity would no longer help him. Always the loon, he said, raised its "demoniac" laugh "in derision of my efforts. . . ." Finally, he wrote, the east wind came and "filled the whole air with misty rain, and I was impressed as if it were the prayer of the loon answered, and his god was angry with me. . . ." Like the "tumultuous surface" of the pond, here were the signs that the serene communion of summer was over.

The chapters that followed—"House-Warming," "Former Inhabitants; and Winter Visitors," "Winter Animals," "The Pond in Winter"—recapitulated the themes of the summer chapters, taking up solitude, the resources of the natural scene, sounds, and the pond. With the change to the season of inwardness, however, the mood had changed: now was the time of Thoreau's greatest solitude, a sleepy time when life was reduced to routine and staying alive was a problem, a time when he retreated to memory and held communion with the former inhabitants whose lives suggested the possibility of failure. Every image, from the pond whooping as it turned in its sleep to the fox "seeking expression" and "struggling for light," conveyed a sense of impoverishment and spiritual restlessness, and the need for bravery under duress. Now he longed for the "Visitor" who never came, and turned to the spiritual necessity of friendship, recalling those days when the faithful Alcott had come and their discourse had summoned the "old settler" and "expanded and racked my little house. . . ." But if "moral reform," as he said, "was the effort to throw off sleep," and "to be awake is to be alive," he found that, like the pond, he could not escape his dormant season. "Every winter," he observed, "the liquid and trembling surface of the pond, which was so sensitive to every breath, and reflected every light and shadow, becomes solid to the depth of a foot or a foot and a half. . . . it closes its eyelids and becomes dormant for three months or more. . . . After a cold and snowy night it needed a divining rod to find it."

In the midst of his winter of discontent Thoreau began his intellectual search for faith. In "The Pond in Winter," he told of the question that he had tried to answer in his sleep, the question of "what—how—when—where?" which only dawning Nature, by her living presence, had answered for him. This awakening *to* life was the preparation for his rebirth, the beginning of the long proc-

ess of conscious penetration to the law of the "spring of springs."
This finally brought the rewards of "Spring," warranted his injunc-
tions on self-exploration, and provided the testimony of his "Conclusion"—"Only that day dawns to which we are awake." Now his
morning work was the "scientific" exploration of the bottom of
the pond; for he "was desirous," he said, "to recover the long-lost
bottom of Walden Pond," that "infinite" which its reputed bottomlessness suggested. In this survey he found that the fabulous pickerel
(fish and fishing, as early as the *Week,* were symbols of thought and
contemplation) still lived beneath the surface of the ice and that
the "bright sanded floor" of the pond was "the same as in summer."
And what was even more important for the foundation of his faith,
he discovered and verified by accurate measurement the spiritual
law of correspondences. The general regularity of the bottom—of
the unseen—conformed to the shores: the correspondence was so perfect that "a distant promontory betrayed itself in the soundings
quite across the pond, and its direction could be determined by
observing the opposite shore." This universal law, which he applied
to his own character, was also supported by the fact that "the line
of greatest length intersected the line of greatest breadth *exactly* at
the point of greatest depth. . . ." By these soundings he renewed
his faith in the transcendental method; and reading his own life
correspondentially, he found that the disciplines of his outer life
indicated the purity of his inner life. Though winter was the barren
season, it brought the compensation of "concentration"; in the
purity of the Walden ice he could see the symbol of his steadfastness. He could meet the priest of Brahma at his well—and the pure
Walden water could mingle with the sacred water of the Ganges—
because he had observed the purificatory disciplines, had bathed his
"intellect in the stupendous and cosmogonal philosophy of the
Bhagvat Geeta. . . ."

At the bottom of the pond he also found the "bright green weed"
that symbolized the everlasting life of organic Nature, the law of
life to which even the frozen pond undulated in its sleep, to which
it thundered "obedience . . . as surely as the buds expand in the
spring." Its booming, accordingly, was the sign of its awakening,
a morning phenomenon, when, responding to the sun, it "stretched
itself and yawned like a waking man. . . ." It sounded the signal
of spring, prefigured that irresistible thaw when "all things give way
to the impulse of expression." Indeed, with the warmer weather,
the snow and ice began to melt, the "circulations" began, and the
blood of winter was purged. Once more Nature supplied her "vital

heat" and, in the thawing clay of the railroad cut, gave way to the impulse of expression—to the impulse of life.

The most brilliant passage in "Spring," Thoreau's description of the thaw was a myth of creation as expression. This elaborate metaphor of the organic process that proceeds from the inside out, that creates and shapes by means of the Idea—the process of Nature, art, moral reform, and social reform—was also for Thoreau the metaphor of his purification and rebirth. Not only did the "bursting out" of the "insides of the earth" and the unfolding of "the piled-up history" of geology prove that there was nothing inorganic and that life provided fresh materials for the fictile arts of man, it showed that "Nature has some bowels, and . . . is mother of humanity. . . ." The frost coming out of the ground was Spring, a newly delivered child; and the flowing clay was an analogy of the development of the human body. The shapes and forms it took in its passage reminded him of "brains or lungs or bowels, and excrements of all kinds," but, as he explained this process in terms of "sand-foliage," the leaf-like character not only appeared in liver and lungs, but in feathers and wings. This evolution from excrementitious to aerial forms was a process of purification: "You pass from the lumpish grub in the earth," he wrote, "to the airy and fluttering butterfly. The very globe continually transcends and translates itself, and becomes winged in its orbit."

If the thawing made him feel that he was "nearer to the vitals of the globe," its leaf-like forms also reminded him that he was in the presence of "the Artist who made the world. . . ." The Creator was still in his laboratory, "still at work, sporting on this bank, and with excess of energy strewing his fresh designs about." In this analogy to the creative process, the earth was laboring with "the idea inwardly" and expressing itself "outwardly in leaves. . . ." For, as he had learned from Goethe, the leaf was the unit-form of all creation, the simplest form of which the most complex, even the world, was composed. "This one hill side illustrated the principle of all the operations of Nature," he explained. "The Maker of this earth but patented a leaf." This process, of course, not only applied to art, but to all re-forming and shaping. It illustrated Emerson's belief that "Nature is not fixed but fluid. Spirit alters, moulds, makes it"—that not only poems and individual lives, but institutions were "plastic like clay in the hands of the potter." Hoeing beans, Thoreau had himself been a plastic artist making the earth—that granary of seeds—express itself in leaves; and of all the former inhabitants he had identified himself with Wyman the potter, whose fictile art pleased him. Moreover, unknown to his neighbors, he had practiced that fictile art himself—for himself and society. He was not the reformer, however, who broke things, but one whose method, like that of the thaw with its "gentle persuasion," melted things. By recasting his life he hoped that Nature again would try, with him "for a first settler." For he was a "Champollion," deciphering the hieroglyphics of Nature, that "we may turn over a new leaf at last."

As a symbol of ecstasy the thaw, even with its remarkable suddenness, was spoiled by the intellectual purposes Thoreau made it serve. Whatever ecstasy the passage conveyed was intellectual rather than spontaneous or unconscious; it followed from his long observation of Nature, and it showed that he had with his intellect riven into the "secret of things." The faith he had earned by this conscious endeavor, however, was rewarded, at least in the pages of *Walden*, by his long-awaited ecstasy. This "memorable crisis"— "seemingly instantaneous at last"—came with the melting of the pond, when he saw its "bare face . . . full of glee and youth, as if it spoke the joy of the fishes within it, and of the sands on its shore. . . ." For in the sparkling water, he realized the contrast between winter and spring: "Walden was dead," he said, "and is alive again." The change he had awaited—"the change from storm and winter to serene and mild weather, from dark and sluggish hours to bright and elastic ones"—was at hand. "Suddenly," he wrote, "an influx of light filled my house, though the evening was at hand, and the clouds of winter still overhung it, and the eaves were dripping with sleety rain. I looked out of my window, and lo! where yesterday was cold gray ice there lay the transparent pond already calm and full of hope as in a summer evening, reflecting a summer sky in its bosom, though none was visible overhead, as if it had intelligence with some remote horizon. I heard a robin in the distance, the first I had heard for many a thousand years . . . the same sweet and powerful song as of yore. . . . The pitch-pines and shrub-oaks about my house, which had so long drooped, suddenly resumed their several characters, looked brighter, greener, and more erect and alive, as if effectually cleansed and restored by the rain. . . . As it grew darker, I was startled by the *honking* of geese. . . . Standing at my door, I could hear the rush of their wings. . . . they suddenly spied my light, and with hushed clamor wheeled and settled in the pond. So I came in, and shut the door, and passed my first spring night in the woods."

With the coming of spring, with renewal and rebirth, had come "the creation of Cosmos out of Chaos and the realization of the Golden Age." Like Ovid, Thoreau was ready to tell of bodies changed by the gods into new forms, even glad, in the presence of this alchemy, to accept the life in Nature—served though it was by death—as the grand fact. Once again he lived in the eternal present, reborn to innocence, with an overwhelming sense of freedom, release, hope, and pardon. But even though he had regained the Golden Age before the fall of man, his metamorphosis took the form of the hawk rather than that of the butterfly; for having won his renewal by lonely heroism, he saw his transcendence in the soaring, solitary hawk, the bird he associated with nobleness and knightly courage. The hawk, he wrote in his *Journal,* soared so loftily and circled so steadily and without effort because it had "earned this power by faithfully creeping on the ground as a reptile in a former state of existence." It symbolized his ultimate liberation, the emancipation from the senses. At last, as he copied from *The Harivansa,* he was "free in this world, as birds in the air, disengaged from every kind of chain."

As the logic of his metaphors demanded, Thoreau closed his book with the fable of the beautiful bug that had come out of the dry leaf of an old apple-wood table. This fable recapitulated his themes:

> Who knows what beautiful and winged life, whose egg has been buried for ages under many concentric layers of woodenness in the dead dry life of society, deposited at first in the alburnum of the green and living tree, which has been gradually converted into the semblance of its well-seasoned tomb . . . may unexpectedly come forth from amidst society's most trivial and handselled furniture, to enjoy its perfect summer life at last!

This was the fable of organic renewal. But the fable of the creative enterprise that made it possible—the transparent parable of his own life and vocation—was that of the artist of the city of Kouroo. This artist, Thoreau wrote, "was disposed to strive after perfection." Determined to make a staff, he went to the woods to select the proper materials, rejecting stick after stick, until "his friends gradually deserted him. . . ." In his striving, however, he lived in the eternal now of inspiration which made the passing of dynasties, even eras, an illusion. Finally, in fashioning his staff, merely by minding his destiny and his art, he discovered that he had "made a new system . . . a world with full and fair proportions. . . ."

And because "the material was pure, and his art was pure," the result, Thoreau knew, could not be "other than wonderful." *Walden* was that staff, that fuller and fairer and supremely organic world, because it was, by Thoreau's own test of sincerity, the form and expression of the life he had lived in the desire to live. But it was also—for in it he had enacted the process of creating scripture—the kind of heroic book that was worthy of morning discipline, a book so true "to our condition" that reading it might date a new era in our lives.

Wayside Challenger: Some Remarks on the Politics of Henry David Thoreau

by Heinz Eulau

Modern American Liberalism prides itself on being critical in spirit and pragmatic in method. Yet, if it has inherited anything from a less enlightened past, it is an attitude of self-righteous indignation which can see good only as good and bad only as bad. The logic of this morality is simple enough, but its consequences are paradoxical. Instead of fostering its central value, respect for the uniqueness and personality of the individual, liberalism succumbs to an ethical absolutism. Devoid of imaginative sympathy, it cannot understand that other creeds may have values at least comparable to its own. Liberalism then tends to become an affair of mere pronunciamento and simple magic formula. It seeks to counter the truths and perfections of its enemies by furnishing its own set of truths and perfections.

This paradox is due, I believe, to liberalism's failure to come to grips with the distinction between morality and moral realism. Moral realism, as here used, does not mean knowledge of good and bad, but knowledge of the ambiguities and anomalies of living the moral life. In contrast to morality, moral realism is aware of the possibility of good or bad consequences not as polar opposites, but of the possibility of "good-and-bad" consequences as ambivalent unities. Inasmuch as liberalism derives its values from moral realism, it has to accept ambivalence as necessary.

It is symptomatic of this dilemma, if a dilemma it is, that liberalism allows itself to be challenged by the metaphysical notion of individual moral conscience as a valid axiom of democratic politics.

"Wayside Challenger: Some Remarks on the Politics of Henry David Thoreau" by Heinz Eulau. From *The Antioch Review,* IX (Winter 1949-1950), 509-522. Copyright 1950 by *The Antioch Review.* Reprinted by permission.

It suggests, in part at least, why Henry David Thoreau, though standing pretty much by the wayside of American life, is as germane today as he ever was in the development of political thought. The one hundredth anniversary of his essay, "Civil Disobedience," is therefore only a fortuitous occasion to write about him. More pertinent, it seems, are the critical implications of his political ideas, absurd and inconsistent as they may appear.

It is unfair, perhaps, to judge Thoreau's political philosophy by present-day standards. Yet, it is necessary to do so because some recent interpreters have tried, in vain I think, to make Thoreau palatable to liberalism by reading their own preferences into his writings. But even if they seek to strike a balance, the end effect of their expositions is tortuous. Max Lerner, for instance, writes inaccurately, I believe, that Thoreau's individualism should be seen as part of "a rebellion against the oversocialized New England town, in which the individual was being submerged. . . . He was not so limited as to believe that the individual could by his own action stem the heedless onrush of American life, or succeed wholly in rechanneling it." Similarly, Townsend Scudder states that "though so intense an individualist, Thoreau favored the ideal of communal living as in keeping with the spirit of America." Significantly, Lerner, Scudder as well as F. O. Mathiessen repeat, by way of evidence, a single passage from Thoreau's *Walden*—"to act collectively is according to the spirit of our institutions." The bulk of proof is, in fact, on the other side. Even Vernon Parrington, whose progressivist bias is rarely concealed, recognized that Thoreau "could not adopt the cooperative solution." Thoreau refused to join Brook Farm because, in his own words, he "would rather keep a bachelor's hall in hell than go to board in heaven."

Thoreau does not give much comfort to those who seek to prove a point. But it should be remembered that *Walden*, his most famous and widely read book, does not alone represent his ideas. For an understanding of his politics, "Civil Disobedience" as well as the less-known and less-read essays, "Slavery in Massachusetts" (1854) and "A Plea for Captain John Brown" (1859), are of at least equal importance. They leave little doubt that Thoreau's whole political philosophy was based on the theoretical premise of individual conscience as the only true criterion of what is politically right and just. It was the very perfection of his belief in the veracity of each man's soul and conscience as harbingers of some truth highter than human fiat that made inconsistency in his theory inevitable. Action from principle, he wrote in a prophetic sentence in "Civil Disobedience," "not only divides states and churches, it divides families; ay, it divides the *individual,* separating the diabolical in him from the divine." Within the short span of ten years, Thoreau, though holding to the same premise, would draw conclusions as opposite as passive resistance and violent action. Obviously, both his personality and ideas were complex. Any attempt to reduce them to simple, and hence simpleton, propositions is futile.

2

While the subsequent essays are significant because they prove, better than critical argument, that "action from principle" is a politically dangerous concept, "Civil Disobedience" is the most complete theoretical statement of Thoreau's basic assumptions. Because it expounded a queer doctrine, unlikely to make much of an impression on his contemporaries, Thoreau apparently elaborated his political premise more fully in "Civil Disobedience" than in the subsequent essays.

His starting point is the half-mocking, half-serious observation that if Jefferson's motto—"that government is best which governs least"—were carried out, it would amount to "that government is best which governs not at all." Does this mean, as has been suggested, that Thoreau brought Jefferson's ideas to their logical conclusion? By no means. In placing the individual "above" the state, Jefferson attacked the autocratic state, not the democratic state which he did so much to bring about. If Thoreau went at all beyond Jefferson, it consisted in his attack on democracy. But, paradoxically, he attacked democracy not because it was strong; on the contrary, because it was weak. The American government, he wrote, "has not the vitality and force of a single living man; for a single man can bend it to his will." He refused to vote because he considered the democratic ballot an ineffective political instrument. His own contact with the government being limited to the annual *tête-a-tête* with the tax collector, his refusal to pay the poll tax loses some of its bravado. He did not really sacrifice much when he declared, somewhat grandiloquently, that he should not like to think he would ever have to rely on the protection of the state. Basically, Thoreau was the very opposite of Jefferson; he was as unpolitical as Jefferson was political. It is simply not conceivable to hear Jefferson say, as Thoreau said, "the government does not concern me much, and I shall bestow the fewest possible thoughts on it."

If Thoreau had let the matter rest at this point, his position would have been consistent. But as if he needed to test his own propositions, he would suddenly speak "practically and as a citizen, unlike those who call themselves no-government men." And as a citizen Thoreau demanded "not at once no government, but *at once* better government." Such a government would anticipate and provide for reform, cherish its "wise minority" and encourage its citizens "to be on the alert to point out its faults."

It appears that Thoreau could not fully discern that his metaphysical assumptions had to lead, almost necessarily, to ambiguous consequences when subjected to the test of practical politics. The essential weakness of the metaphysical premise is that it is absolutist as long as it deals with abstractions, just as it is relativistic when applied to unique and observable situations. Like his fellow idealists, Thoreau was incapable of recognizing those distinctions of degree which are politically decisive. He could not recognize them because he fell back, again and again, on the principle of individual conscience as the sole valid guide in political action. He realized only faintly that this principle was inherently deficient for political purposes, as when he said that while "all men recognize the right of revolution . . . , almost all say that such is not the case now." Individual conscience as a political principle was too obviously in conflict with the democratic principle of majority rule, even for Thoreau. But the rather dogmatic assertion, "there is but little virtue in the masses of men," was too hazardous in view of the manifest strength of the democratic faith of most men in his time. Thoreau's only way out was, once more, a paradox: "Any man more right than his neighbors constitutes a majority of one already."

Consequently, Thoreau had to postulate a (by democratic standards) curious distinction between law and right, with the explanation that one has to have faith in man, that each man can determine for himself what is right and just. Hence, no conflict is possible, so the argument goes, because law is law only if identical with right. Thoreau could not demonstrate, however, that there is, in case the majority is wrong, an objective criterion for assaying the correctness of an individual's or a minority's judgment.

He was content, therefore, with declaring war on the state in his own fashion:

It is not a man's duty as a matter of course, to devote himself to the eradication of any, even the most enormous wrong; he may still properly have other concerns to engage him; but it is his duty, at least, to wash his hands of it, and, if he gives it no thought longer, not to give it practically his support.

Great as his hurry seemed in "Civil Disobedience," Thoreau remained, in fact, unpolitical. Actually, he did not wish to be bothered at all with the obnoxious phenomenon of slavery. He had other affairs to attend to. "I came into this world," he concluded, "not chiefly to make this a good place to live in, but to live in it, be it good or bad." Joseph Wood Krutch has aptly described this kind of reasoning as Thoreau's "sometimes desperate casuistry."

3

The ideas expressed in "Civil Disobedience" fell into the Walden period (1845-1847) and are, to some extent, an early reaction to Thoreau's own dim sense of failure as a recluse from society. Existence at Walden Pond was an experiment for the purpose of finding reality. But subjectively real as life at Walden may have been, to judge from his famous report, it came to be unreal, apparently, when Thoreau was forced to compare it with the objective reality of the impending Mexican War which he encountered on his almost daily visits to town. There he would see his neighbors getting ready for what seemed to him a hateful and stupid enterprise. Its effect could only be the extension of the unjust institution of slavery and of the slaveholders' power. Thoreau felt a deep personal disgrace in being associated with a government which was the slaves' government also. So deeply did he feel on the issue that he was ready to warn that "this people must cease to hold slaves, and to make war on Mexico, though it cost them their existence as a people." So great seemed the evil that there was no time to change the laws except by breaking them. Refusal to pay taxes was, in Thoreau's mind, "the definition of a peaceful revolution, if any such is possible." Otherwise, he continued, the conscience is wounded: "Through this wound a man's real manhood and immortality flow out, and he bleeds to an everlasting death. I see this blood flowing now."

All his protestations about "signing off" from human institutions to the contrary, "Civil Disobedience," in contrast to *Walden,* was a first indication of Thoreau's theoretical difficulties. It contained the seeds of its own denial, seeds which were fertilized by the untenable metaphysical premise of individual conscience as a criterion of collective action. In the very act of counseling and practicing individual resistance to and renunciation of government was implicit a growing sense of social responsibility which the hermit of Walden Pond could scarcely disclaim.

Thoreau was not, therefore, as *Walden* might suggest and some critics have said, an American exponent of the Rousseauist doctrine of the natural rights of man. His philosophy certainly lacked the liberating drive which Rousseau's individualism had in the eighteenth-century French context. Thoreau's individualism was, most interpreters agree, an inspired protest against the modern cult of progress, materialism and efficiency, with its deteriorating effect on the individual. But it was essentially out of date. Because it renounced industrialism rather than seeking to bring it under social control, Thoreau's individualism could not possibly find practical application. The moral and the morally real were at odds.

"Civil Disobedience" differed from *Walden* in another respect. *Walden* was the report of a highly personalized experience. And in spite of its persuasiveness, its almost egocentric individualism made communication difficult. Only the most liberal imagination can perceive it for what it was: namely, the attempt of a sensitive spirit to discover his own integrity and convey this discovery, not to be imitated literally—a mistake against which Thoreau himself explicitly warned, but to serve as a symbolic expression of man's need for finding his own integrity in whatever fashion seemed best. "I desire," he wrote, "that there be as many different persons in the world as possible; but I would have each one be very careful to find out and pursue *his own* way. . . ." As such, life at Walden Pond was a meaningful experiment, even though it was meaningless as a form of *social* living.

However, Thoreau's individualism was not simply, as Parrington remarked, "transcendental individualism translated into politics." His radicalism differed in more than degree from the innocuous, often opportunistic, politics of most Abolitionists. Their humanitarianism seemed all too sanguine to him. Were they not actually giving aid and comfort to the enemy by refusing to withdraw from political society altogether? In asking this question it must be admitted that Thoreau himself remained on a largely rhetorical level throughout his political life. Certainly, his refusal to pay the poll tax and being jailed for it was a frankly ephemeral episode. But he found it increasingly necessary to communicate his ideas in a manner which would leave no doubt where he stood.

4

There is no better index of Thoreau's need to express himself unequivocally than the changing tenor of his humor. In "Civil Disobedience" it is of the most elusive variety. It was all too self-conscious and artificial to make it deeply personal and tragic as his human condition might have warranted. He shared his cell, "the whitest, most simply furnished, and probably the neatest apartment in town," with an alleged incendiary, "a first-rate fellow and a clever man." From the cell window, he reported, "I was an involuntary spectator and auditor of whatever was done and said in the kitchen of the adjacent village inn,—a wholly new and rare experience to me. It was a closer view of my native town. I was fairly inside of it." One cannot but feel that the atmosphere of mischief so created is more literary than political.

But the more Thoreau became involved in the slavery question in later years, the more his sense of frustration grew, the more scornful and vitriolic his humor would become. In "Slavery in Massachusetts" he would direct it at his Yankee audience. The soldier who lets himself be trained to return fugitive slaves to their masters "is a fool made conspicuous by a painted coat." Judges upholding the constitutionality of slavery "are merely inspectors of a pick-lock and murderer's tool." When he reads a newspaper defending the Fugitive Slave Law, he does it "with my cuffs turned up," and hears "the gurgling of the sewer through every column." It is a paper "picked out of the public gutters, the groggery, and the brothel, harmonizing with the gospel of the Merchants' Exchange."

Humor would finally give way to blasphemy in "A Plea for Captain John Brown." Though his counsel of passive, peaceful resistance had by then been replaced by the justification of violence, Thoreau's venom was that of a man close to despair. "Away with your broad and flat churches, and your narrow and tall churches," he cried; "take a step forward, and invent a new style of out-houses. Invent a salt that will save you, and defend your nostrils." He would excoriate the politicians as "office-seekers and speech-makers, who do not so much as lay an honest egg, but wear their breasts bare upon an egg of chalk."

Thoreau's desire to be understood by his fellow citizens is equally apparent if the symbols with which he appealed to his readers in "Civil Disobedience" are compared with those in "Slavery in Massachusetts." In the earlier essay he is preoccupied with Right, Truth and Justice. It is never quite clear whether he regarded passive resistance as a virtuous political goal, an end in itself, or whether he thought of it as the most effective means to abolish slavery. If the latter, he obscured his thinking pretty successfully. While a superb exposition of nonviolent resistance as a political instrument, the language used in "Civil Disobedience" does not indicate that Thoreau was particularly anxious to protest against the evil of slavery.

Indeed, it was not till the surrender by Massachusetts of the fugitive Negro Thomas Sims in 1851, an event which struck him as a "moral earthquake," and again of the Negro Anthony Burns in 1854, that Thoreau's anger was sufficiently aroused to make him abandon the convenient obscurantisms of the political idealists. No longer was the slavery issue a remote question which only incidentally annoyed him. His own state, Massachusetts, had violated a sacred trust when it returned these Negroes into slavery. Thoreau would now resort to patriotic sentiments in order to make his plea effective. "Every man in Massachusetts capable of the sentiment of patriotism," he wrote, must have had his own experience of "having suffered a vast and indefinite loss." And what was this loss which yesterday's anarchist felt so surprisingly? "At last it occurred to me that what I had lost was a country. . . . The remembrance of my country spoils my walk. My thoughts are murder to the State, and involuntarily go plotting against her."

This does not mean, of course, that Thoreau had abandoned his deep conviction that individual conscience is the safest guide in human affairs. It only means that, as time went on and the demands of politics required greater sophistication, Thoreau became somewhat more realistic. It was simply a matter of tactics if, as in "Slavery in Massachusetts," he identified individual conscience with the "laws of humanity," or, as in "A Plea for Captain John Brown," with "respect for the Constitution." Here he used catch-phrases which could be more easily grasped by the average citizen than metaphysical abstractions. But his attempt to make out of John Brown "a transcendentalist above all, a man of ideas and principles," did not quite come off. It merely showed that Thoreau knew as little about Brown as about slavery, and that he was projecting his metaphysical notions on a situation which hardly called for them.

5

As has been mentioned, in spite of the apparent urgency of his argument in "Civil Disobedience," Thoreau had experienced the Mexican War and its implications for the slavery question as a fairly remote conflict. But with the passage of the Fugitive Slave Law in 1850 it became evident, even to a political hermit like Thoreau, that continued detachment from affairs of state would not avert the threat to his personal liberty which the law implied. The state, he now discovered, "has fatally interfered with my lawful business." "Slavery in Massachusetts" was, therefore, as outspoken a piece of indignation as "Civil Disobedience" had been casual. He bade farewell to the pipedream of a state which would permit a few people, who so desired, to live aloof from it, "not meddling with it, nor embraced by it." He had never respected the government, he said, but "I had foolishly thought that I might manage to live here, minding my private affairs, and forget it." Thoreau now dropped the role of the bohemian anarchist who could wash his hands of society's "dirty institutions," as he had called them in *Walden*. Before, he admitted, he had dwelt in the illusion that "my life passed somewhere only *between* heaven and hell, but now I cannot persuade myself that I do not dwell *wholly* within hell."

Moreover, his rebellion was no longer a matter of denials alone. He still fulminated against majority rule, but a new line of thought occupied him. It would be too simple to say that a democratic faith emerged, but Thoreau's attack on existing institutions is certainly not that of the vociferous anti-democrat of "Civil Disobedience." As against judges deciding questions involving slaves, Thoreau would now "much rather trust the sentiment of the people. In their vote you would get something of value, at least, however small." It was no longer the state in the abstract, but the State of Massachusetts in the concrete which he attacked. He would recognize the possibility of a government which is worth fighting for. "Show me a free state, and a court truly of justice, and I will fight for them, if need be . . . ," he proclaimed; "it is not an era of repose. We have used up all our inherited freedom. If we would save our lives, we must fight for them."

"Slavery in Massachusetts" was not a theoretical exercise in political philosophy. It concentrated its verbal fire on an evil situation. But it is indicative of Thoreau's political immaturity that he now went so far as to join the militant abolitionists in advocating the secession of Massachusetts from the union with the slave states. He was apparently quite unaware of the possibility that the consequences of such action might accentuate the evil which he sought to remedy. That is, permit slavery to continue unopposed elsewhere. In addition, he still confused what seemed to him the iniquity of law with the legal process itself. And though he spoke of breaking the law, of boycotting proslavery newspapers, of ousting ignorant politicians and seceding from the Union, it remains unclear just what specific political means Thoreau considered appropriate to achieve his objectives. He had almost given up passive resistance, but he had not completely accepted majority rule.

With all its new affirmations, "Slavery in Massachusetts" did not answer the question which is central from the point of view of political theory—whether the practicality of political concepts can be assessed by any kind of objectively rational standard. It seems that Thoreau was neither willing nor able to develop such a criterion. Not even "truth" would serve that purpose. Truth, he wrote in "Civil Disobedience," "is always in harmony with herself, and is not concerned chiefly to reveal the justice that may consist with wrong-doing." In other words, the consequences of an act are separable and, indeed, must be separated from its nature. Even truth is thus reduced to being a matter of individual taste. Thoreau admitted the existence of other truths, but being altogether personal and private they did not permit contact or comparison with each other. As so many of his concepts, his truth is paradoxical. His moral absolutism, being so individualized, becomes relativistic. It is not surprising to find, therefore, that Thoreau envisaged various hierarchial levels of political evaluation. "Seen from a lower point of view," he wrote, "the Constitution, with all its faults, is very good; the law and the courts are very respectable; even this State and this American government are, in many respects, very admirable, and rare things, to be thankful for, such as a great many have described them; but seen from a point of view a little higher, they are what I have described them; seen from a higher still, and the highest, who shall say what they are, or that they are worth looking at or thinking of at all?"

Paradox may serve the purpose of literary construction. In political theory it is self-defeating. Inasmuch as Thoreau's anarchism followed from the doctrine of the individual's duty to his conscience alone, it should lead to at least some mutual tolerance as an avenue to human cooperation. But Thoreau would carry the matter to absurdity. In a sentence remindful of the vicarious a-moralism of the later social Darwinians he wrote:

> I am not responsible for the successful working of the machinery of society. . . . I perceive that, when an acorn and a chestnut fall side by side, the one does not remain inert to make way for the other, but both obey their own laws, and spring and grow and flourish as best they can, till one, perchance, overshadows and destroys the other. If a plant cannot live according to its nature, it dies; and so a man.

6

It is quite clear that Thoreau's mind was totally closed to the democratic conception of politics as a never-ending process of compromise and adjustment. As a matter of fact, if the politics of "action from principle," with its insistence on ends, is shorn of metaphysics, it appears as little more than the old and familiar doctrine that the end justifies the means. Comparison of "Civil Disobedience" and "A Plea for Captain John Brown" underlines the fact that in Thoreau's mind both passive resistance and violent action were *right* if employed toward the accomplishment of ends whose truth is predicated on the complete assumption of responsibility by the individual for his acts.

Just as nonviolent resistance as an instrument of politics is proper if the state interferes with an individual's principles, so violence can be justified. Given Thoreau's moral intransigence, it is not surprising to find that he would round out his basic position by eulogizing an event which only the most rabid Abolitionists supported as politically justifiable. John Brown, Thoreau came to believe, was not only right in holding that a man has "a perfect right to interfere by force with the slaveholder, in order to rescue the slave"; but the doctrine that the end justifies the means was given explicit expression: "I shall not be forward to think him mistaken in his method who quickest succeeds to liberate the slave." The decisive question, Thoreau finally felt, was not "about the weapon, but the spirit in which you use it." And he would write in his *Journals:* "I do not wish to kill nor to be killed, but I can foresee circumstances in which both these things would be by me unavoidable."

Actually, however, "A Plea for Captain John Brown" was concerned with the slavery issue only indirectly. Thoreau undoubtedly felt its iniquity and the urgency of its solution most intensely, but his primary concern was again with justice and injustice, with principle and expediency, with truth and falsehood. "A Plea for Captain John Brown" is therefore more closely related to "Civil Disobedience" than to "Slavery in Massachusetts." It differed, however, from his first political essay in that Thoreau had abandoned his earlier quietist position. Violence was in the air. Almost everywhere in the nation men were girding themselves for the great conflict which would soon disrupt the Union. While it may have been his intention merely to bring his disagreement with the moderate Abolitionists into sharper focus by advocating violence before the peaceful alternatives had been exhausted, the end effect of "A Plea for Captain John Brown" was the admission of an inveterate moralist that violence can only be combatted by violence.

It is symptomatic of his greater sense of realism that the government did not seem weak any longer as it had in "Civil Disobedience" ten years before. "When a government puts forth its strength on the side of injustice, as ours to maintain slavery and kill the liberators of the slave," he wrote, "it reveals itself a merely brute force, or worse, a demoniacal force. It is the head of the Plug-Uglies. It is more manifest than ever that tyranny rules. I see this government to be effectually allied with France and Austria in oppressing mankind." The government, he continued, is "a semi-human tiger or ox stalking over the earth, with its heart taken out and the top of its brain shot away."

Thoreau could no longer subscribe to the quietist doctrine of "Civil Disobedience" with its counsel of escape. He fiercely excoriated all those who adhered to a nonviolent solution of social conflict. "What sort of violence is that," he now asked, "which is encouraged, not by soldiers, but by peaceable citizens, not so much by laymen as by ministers of the Gospel, not so much by the fighting sects as by the Quakers, and not so much by the Quaker men as by the Quaker women?" Here Thoreau squarely faced the question of resistance by force which modern pacifism, confronted with the infamies of totalitarian terror and violence, slave labor and concentration camps, fails to answer. Here, in essence, he returned to the age-old concept of the "just war," which modern quietists refuse to acknowledge. John Brown would "never have anything to do with any war," Thoreau intimated, "unless it were a war for liberty," expressing an opinion since challenged by competent historians.

In John Brown, Thoreau had found the man of principle whom he had anticipated in "Civil Disobedience," the man "who is a *Man,* and, as my neighbor says, has a bone in his back which you cannot pass your hand through!" That this abstract man of principle had changed from the passive resister envisaged in 1849 into the violent and very real actionist of 1859 suggests that Thoreau had become aware of the futility of peaceful disobedience as much as he was oblivious of the dangers inherent in the idea of "action from principle."

Thoreau's conversion to violence as a legitimate means in the social conflict cannot be attributed to a purely rational thought process. The fervor of his eulogy betrays its emotional content. He identified himself with Brown so much that he experienced the latter's ordeal after the disastrous incident at Harpers Ferry as a personal tragedy. "I put a piece of paper and a pencil under my pillow," he wrote, "and when I could not sleep I wrote in the dark." Brown had the stuff heroes are made of. "No doubt," Thoreau postulated, "you can get more in your market for a quart of milk than for a quart of blood, but that is not the market that heroes carry their blood to." As if he felt a sense of personal guilt about his own irresponsibility in days gone by, Thoreau expressed his admiration for Brown because he "did not wait till he was personally interfered with or thwarted in some harmless business before he gave his life to the cause of the oppressed." And it is more than obvious that Thoreau rationalized the a-moral consequences of his new departure when he stated that people at most criticized Brown's tactics and then added: "Though you may not approve of his method or his principles, recognize his magnanimity."

Significantly, too, the eulogy in defense of John Brown was not characterized by so transitory a feeling as that which attended the experience of his own imprisonment. On being released from jail after having refused to pay the poll tax, he had joined a huckleberry party in the highest hills, where "the State was nowhere to be seen." Many weeks after his passionate plea, he noted in his *Journals* that it was hard for him to see the beauty of a remarkable sunset when his mind "was filled with Captain Brown. So great a wrong as his fate implied overshadowed all beauty in the world." Bronson Alcott reported in his *Journals* that Thoreau had called on him because he thought that "someone from the North should see Gov. Wise, or write concerning Capt. Brown's character and motives, to influence the Governor in his favor."

7

It has not been my intention to disparage Thoreau's reputation as the outstanding American spokesman for those human values which the empty materialism of our culture so readily relegates to the limbo of sanctimonious oratory. Criticism of his politcal theory cannot possibly deprive Thoreau's words of that immortality with which his moral sincerity, his spiritual courage and his sense of genuine inquiry have endowed it. His ideas are living ideas for the very reason that he lived them, day in and day out. The acidity of his attack and the persistence of his independence are admired and emulated by thousands who grope for a way to withstand the seemingly invincible force of personal and social maladjustments. As his friend and earliest biographer F. H. Sanborn has said, "The haughtiness of his independence kept him from a thousand temptations that beset men of less courage and self-denial."

But I also believe that those who neglect and even deny the ambiguities and paradoxes of Thoreau's moral intransigence misunderstand the real challenge of his politics. They overlook the essential assumptions underlying his advice of civil disobedience. Hence, they are at a loss in explaining his repudiation of his own advice and his justification of violent resistance.

Thoreau's philosophy should warn us of the dilemma into which he fell and from which he could not escape because he returned time and again, to individual conscience as the "ultimate reality." His thought was full of ambiguity and paradox, and he did not realize sufficiently how contradictory and, in fact, dangerous the moral can be. Granted, he had no fear of consequences in disregarding the law. But, as Pascal observed, "he who would act the angel acts the brute." There is no virtue in accepting the consequences of an act because the premise from which they flow might be essentially good. Thoreau's politics suggests that it is a small step, indeed, from insistence on the principle of morality to insistence on the principle of expediency.

An Evaluation of Thoreau's Poetry

by Henry W. Wells

Eighty-one years after the death of Henry Thoreau has appeared under the careful editorship of Carl Bode the first edition of Thoreau's verse to provide an adequate view of his poetical attainments. The story is, to say the least, unusual. One recalls that eighty years is more than twice the time required to give due appreciation to the lyric art of Emily Dickinson. At last we are able to arrive at a critical estimate of Thoreau's place in American poetry and to speculate upon how much influence his poems, now that they are fairly available, may exercise.

The long period of tepid praise or total silence has been occasioned not only by inadequate publicity but by inadequate criticism and understanding. He himself gradually yielded to the pressure of circumstances and, as years advanced, largely deserted verse for prose. His poems were commonly accused of rawness and lack of poetical refinement. Whatever their faults, they were not vulgar. The middle-class emotionalism and false optimism, monotonous rhythms and facile sentiments, found no place in his personally sincere, highly imaginative, and deeply expressive lines. His poetic prose the public accepted, but found his verse prosaic. It possessed sterner qualities discoverable only in the most vigorous schools of poetry and foreign not only to the effeminate phase of nineteenth-century taste but to the true comprehension of other leaders of American thought, such as Emerson and Lowell.

When a poet views his own lyrics casually, however carefully he may have produced them, sends few of them to his friends and to but one or two periodicals, and publishes them for the most part as appendages to his prose, his readers can scarcely be expected to weigh their intrinsic value as literature. Moreover, when such

"An Evaluation of Thoreau's Poetry" by Henry W. Wells. From *American Literature*, XVI (May 1944), 99-109. Copyright 1944 by The Duke University Press. Reprinted by permission.

poems do at last see print in a becoming form, they will at first almost inevitably be regarded a bit cavalierly. Even the editor in his Introduction scarcely ventures to check a natural impression that they were casual jottings left half finished or in a shape unsatisfying to their author and blithely discarded by him when he reached full maturity of authorship. This view is unhappily furthered by a wholly legitimate inclusion in the collected edition of some fifty or more items of a few lines each which are in truth trifles, abruptly broken off, lacking in their opening lines, or left palpably unrevised. To the enthusiast they may appear precious fragments but to the larger public they may well be the rotten apples which tend to spoil the entire barrel. They tempt us to miss the main point, which is that three quarters of the poems and some nine tenths of the total number of lines are of finished workmanship, so far, at least, as the author's taste and judgment admitted. No part of Thoreau's voluminous manuscripts shows such painstaking revision as his verse.

Almost all Thoreau's poetry may be regarded as the achievement of a conspicuously independent young man who resolutely declined to ape the popular fashions of his age. While Emily Dickinson quietly discarded much of the specious writing of her times and country, Thoreau displayed a more vigorous opposition. To a remarkable degree he turned away from the main streams of contemporary taste in poetry as directed by Wordsworth, Byron, and the younger British writers of his own day. To be sure, he loved Wordsworth, and his poetry betrays this love; but in its rugged, terse, and abrupt expression it shows an art fundamentally unlike Wordsworth's. Scarcely a single poem from his hand can be associated with American fashions soon to be securely established by Longfellow, Whittier, and Lowell. In short, he is unregenerately unorthodox so far as midnineteenth-century America is concerned. It is well known that his reading was very little in his contemporary fellow countrymen and widely disseminated among the English classics and the literatures of the world. His unusual grasp of Greek and Latin poetry and his exercises in the translation of classical verse, notably Pindar, at least indicate his scope. It is true that whatever he writes springs from his heart—the clearest evidence of his genuine poetic faculty. Yet one of the outstanding features of his work is this evidence of the fruits of his reading and prophetic insight. Of his major poems not a single specimen adheres narrowly to the norm of romantic verse at the time of its composition, although, as we shall see, some extraordinary variations on romantic themes are to be found. The American environment itself is clearly indicated by his art in only half a dozen pieces, which as least resemble though they do not entirely agree with Emerson's rugged, didactic manner. At least an equal number strongly suggest Horace and the pure classical vein itself. A few stand in a surprising relation to medieval thought, feeling, or verse patterns. Slightly more are in much the same style as the manly verse of the founder of British neoclassicism, Ben Jonson. The more mannered and pseudo-heroic eloquence of the English Augustans, as in James Thomson, is occasionally turned by Thoreau to his own purpose. A larger group of lyrics share the spiritual inwardness, lively imagination, and chaste exterior of the English seventeenth-century metaphysical poets, whom Thoreau read and grasped uncommonly well. The nervous vigor and high excitement of some of the spiritual or didactic poetry of the Revolutionary period, notably William Blake's, has striking analogues in the New England radical. Where his nature poetry and his expressions of exaggerated idealism, optimism, and enthusiasm most approximate the high romantic style, he still shows his characteristic independence in thought and feeling. Finally, the largest group of his most memorable poems, nearly a third of them, belongs when historically considered not so much with the past as with the future. Thoreau, like Emily Dickinson or Baudelaire, anticipates the bold symbolism, airy impressionism, stringent realism, and restless inconsistencies of twentieth-century poetry. In the art of poetry no less than in his metaphysics, the recluse of Walden made the world and its epochs his province.

> If with fancy unfurled
>   You leave your abode,
> You may go round the world
>   By the Old Marlborough Road.

Moreover, he is a spiritual cosmopolitan by virtue of his intuitive grasp of the poetic imagination of other periods than his own and not by any mere wealth of allusions which he plunders from abroad. None of Poe's exotic bric-a-brac glitters from his pages. He makes no display of his internationalism, for it is the most natural and instinctive thing about him. His allusions and images are drawn from common nature and from life as seen in the neighborhood of Concord. It is with the eye of the soul and not of the body that his art looks toward past, future, and the ultramontane world.

His classical studies left him, while still in his teens, with a sense of form sufficiently rare in the comparatively formless nineteenth century. His insight is suggested by a few quatrains with a shapeliness resembling the Greek Anthology. In speaking of Thoreau's epigrams Emerson not unnaturally referred to Simonides. A less derivative and more creative poet than Landor, Thoreau transports the classical form to the New England scene; the form is revitalized, the scene reinterpreted:

> Not unconcerned Wachusett rears his head
> Above the field, so late from nature won,
> With patient brow reserved, as one who read
> New annals in the history of man.

The long and impressive ode entitled "Let such pure hate still underprop" is clearly fashioned with the strict Horatian sense of proportion. One of his more romantic nature poems ends with an obvious recollection of Horace; the bare New England trees are pictured thus:

> Poor knights they are which bravely wait
> The charge of Winter's cavalry,
> Keeping a simple Roman state,
> Disencumbered of their Persian luxury.

It is worth notice that he refers to several of his poems as odes. Moreover, his lyrics are often classical in content as well as in form. He appropriately expresses Platonic doctrine in a poem of strict classical outline, "Rumors from an Aeolian Harp." Much of the classical morality of life appealed to him, especially in his later years when the extremes of his naturalistic romanticism wore thin. In "Manhood" he sees man and not nature as master of human fate. Man guides nature to do his will, as he might guide a horse. Experience teaches him a doctrine of ripe humanism:

> And it doth more assert man's eminence
> Above the happy level of the brute
> And more doth advertise me of the heights
> To which no natural path doth ever lead,
> No natural light can ever light our steps,
> But the far-piercing ray that shines
> From the recesses of a brave man's eye.

Traces of thought and art more or less deliberately derived from medieval sources may at first seem incongruous in a lover of the Maine woods, but they are present in no negligible degree. Thus a surprising poem entitled "The Virgin" reveals her place in the Catholic system midway between Heaven and Earth, the Old Law and the New. This paradoxical account of Mary resembles her praise as put into the mouth of Saint Bernard by Dante, yet Thoreau follows the spirit rather than the letter of medieval sources:

> With her calm, aspiring eyes
> She doth tempt the earth to rise,
> With humility over all,
> She doth tempt the sky to fall.
>
> In her place she still doth stand
> A pattern unto the firm land
> While revolving spheres come round
> To embrace her stable ground.

If this poem does not consciously refer to the Virgin Mary, it affords at least a remarkable coincidence. Much more usual in his poetry than theological reminiscences are inheritances, conscious or unconscious, from medieval verse patterns, possibly with aid from the German lyric tradition. Thoreau is a keen metrical experimenter, seeking exotic devices, both in rhyme and a free blank verse, to express his highly various moods. He revives Skeltonic measures, dimeter in general, and a dipodic verse typical of medieval poetry no less than of nursery rhymes. Metrically, and to some degree verbally, such a stanza as the following carries us back to the inspired doggerel of medieval mystery plays:

> The axe resounds,
> And bay of hounds
> And tinkling sounds
> Of wintry fame;
> The hunter's horn
> Awakes the dawn
> On field forlorn,
> And frights the game.

But to Thoreau the poetry and culture of the Middle Ages must indeed have seemed an interlude. To his ear as an English-speaking poet the classical manner which he loved was to be heard most forcibly rendered in English by Ben Jonson, father of English neo-classicism, and by Jonson's most intimate followers. Their simple and disciplined style leaves an unmistakable mark upon the wholly unaffected elegy, "Brother Where Dost Thou Dwell." The balanced and severely controlled style is crystallized in "Inspiration":

> I hearing get who had but ears,
>   And sight, who had but eyes before,
> I moments live who lived but years,
>   And truth discern who knew but learning's lore.

Also from the English seventeenth century Thoreau drew a poetic heritage still more congenial to him. Such lucidity and formality as are illustrated in the foregoing quotation, drawn ultimately from ancient models, were transformed by the "metaphysical" poets following Donne into a more sensitive and indigenous English verse, thus bestowing upon our poetry in general and upon Thoreau in particular the most charming of octosyllabic verse and a similarly fluid and controlled stanzaic structure. Marvell or some other poet of his times may be regarded as godfather to such a passage as the conclusion of "The River Swelleth More and More":

> Here Nature taught from year to year,
> When only red men came to hear;
> Methinks 'twas in this school of art
> Venice and Naples learned their part;
> But still their mistress, to my mind,
> Her young disciples leaves behind.

Marvell's school, with its metaphysical and subjective insight, also contributed an important part to the transcendental vision and lusty imagination of the New Englander. His inwardness appears notably in such a poem as "The Inward Morning." A highly fanciful symbolism ingeniously employed to express the mysteries of consciousness appears very much after the pattern of the "metaphysicals" in "Farewell," "Poverty," and "On Ponkawtasset, Since, We Took Our Way." The New Englander, with a realism exceeding Vaughan's, uses in "Upon This Bank at Early Dawn" the same bold and spiritualized image of the cock which Vaughan employs in his memorable "Cock-Crowing." The rigid architecture of the typ-

ical metaphysical poem also leaves an imprint on Thoreau's art,
as may be seen in "I Knew a Man by Sight," with its stanzas in the
most logical sequence possible. In one of the most nearly imitative
of all his truly successful pieces, "I Am a Parcel of Vain Strivings
Tied," he comes strikingly close to the verse forms of Herbert:

> I am a parcel of vain strivings tied
>   By a chance bond together,
> Dangling this way and that, their links
>   Were made so loose and wide,
>   Methinks,
>   For milder weather.

He became sensible to the charms of the baroque neoclassical
rhetoric of the age and school of James Thomson and William
Cowper. The poet who in one lyric employs the simplest and most
colloquial manner, in another assumes for gravity's sake the full
panoply of Augustan artifice and eloquence. He uses a heroic or
an epic diction in treating subjects where such a diction seems far
from inevitable. Yet here his warmth of feeling proves his salva-
tion. There is something genuinely poetic and instinctively noble
in his style, so that his poetry is seldom frozen into the rhetorical
frigidities which occasionally deface not only Lowell but Emerson.
"The Sluggish Smoke Curls up from Some Deep Dell" is a piece
by Thoreau in this pseudo-epic manner. Augustan robes, though
worn lightly, are still perceptible. This is his description of smoke
at dawn rising from a farmer's chimney.

> It has gone down the glen with the light wind,
> And o'er the plain unfurled its venturous wreath,
> Draped the tree tops, loitered upon the hill,
> And warmed the pinions of the early bird;
> And now, perchance, high in the crispy air,
> Has caught sight of the day o'er the earth's edge,
> And greets its master's eye at his low door,
> As some refulgent cloud in the upper sky.

Thoreau was kindled from the spiritual fires struck by the violence of the French Revolution upon the sterner and more mascu-
line of English minds, such as Blake's. The revolutionary temper,
so strong in Thoreau, found in the language of these earlier revo-

lutionaries an inspiration for his own poetic speech. There are revolutionary explosives in the defiant poem which begins:

> The Good how can we trust?
> Only the Wise are just.

Several of his more reflective quatrains strike with an energy very similar to that of Blake. Again, in their faith and enthusiasm some of his most vigorous transcendental verses, as the superb lyric "All Things Are Current Found," bear the accent of spiritual assertion belonging to the more spiritual discoveries of the pioneers of the romantic movement.

Although Thoreau is never a strictly representative figure of either the earlier or later phases of romanticism, he naturally participates to a considerable degree in some of its major trends. An imagery finely descriptive of nature, a power in this imagery to beget a mood rich in emotion and vague in intellectual definition, as well as an audacious idealism show him a cousin, though not quite a brother, to the leading popular romantic poets in America and Europe. Thus while his remarkable poems on smoke and clouds bear the strongest marks of his own genius, they obviously stem from the main body of romantic nature verse. Notable in the same connection is his romantic fondness for autumn, almost as marked as in Corot. He wrote a cheerful nature lyric, "May Morning," Wordsworthian in its general intention though hardly in its execution, while the lines, "My Books I'd Fain Cast Off," praising nature above books, are also Wordsworthian in content though not in style. In "Walden" he dreams of nature before and after the Age of Man. The ethical phase of romanticism also affects him. One of his most notable flights of romantic idealism may be seen in the strongly imaginative lyric with the rather unfortunate first line, "Away! Away! Away! Away!"

Thoreau also participated in the rugged but somewhat strident didacticism which entered American poetry with Emerson and his immediate associates; and once more he reflected a movement without in any way losing his own individuality. Since he most nearly resembles Emerson yet differs from him notably, it becomes a nice test of Thoreau's art to place beside his own pieces Emerson's poems on like themes. Each poet, for example, wrote a fairly long ode on Mount Monadnock, alike not only in much of their imagery but in their ideas, language and, to a rather less degree, in rhythm. Yet the differences afford an excellent measurement of the general distinction between the two poets. Emerson's poem is clearer in meaning and nearer to the usual practices of the times in metre, symbol, texture, and total effect. A Yankee practicality in his verse withholds it from the more catholic and liberated imagination conspicuous in all Thoreau's best lyrics. To his contemporaries Thoreau's poem must certainly have appeared rough and raw. To us it seems less regular in its beauty, subtler, more meditative and, in the very delicacy and elusiveness of its symbolism, so much the more poetic. Thoreau's picture of mountains as ships pioneering on strange seas possesses a poetic scope and a richness of imagination of which Emerson proved incapable.

Thoreau as a poet flourished more in spiritual contact with past and future than with his own present. Hence the largest single group into which his chief poems fall, when considered historically, is that showing him in various ways anticipating the mind of the twentieth century. He touches the poetry of our own times closely largely in terms of its acute tensions. His verse, for example, often directly expresses the abrupt and vivid experience of the moment. Monuments to such sharp and intense experience appear in such pieces as "Music," "The Cliffs and Springs," and that unique poem on the imaginative import of unmusical sounds:

> They who prepare my evening meal below
> Carelessly hit the kettle as they go
> With tongs or shovel,
> And ringing round and round,
> Out of this hovel
> It makes an eastern temple by the sound.

A typical abruptness of phrase and boldness in sound connotative imagery may be seen in the first line of one of his lyrics, "Dong, sounds the brass in the East." The close and astringent conjunction of the concrete and the elusive, so much sought after in the poetry of the present age, may be seen in a poem comprised of six short lines:

> The waves slowly beat,
> Just to keep the noon sweet,
> And no sound is floated o'er,
> Save the mallet on shore,

> Which echoing on high
> Seems a-calking the sky.

As in much twentieth-century verse, nature imagery is first used to produce a mood and then suddenly surprises us by unveiling an imaginative idea, as when, in the lyric "Where Gleaming Fields of Haze," the "ancient" sound of the name "Souhegan" abruptly leads to thoughts of the Xanthus and Meander. The nervous heightening in subjectivity so keenly felt in much poetry of the twentieth century appears foreshadowed in the startling couplet at the end of "I Am the Autumnal Sun":

> And the rustling of the withered leaf
> Is the constant music of my grief.

Some less drastic features of modern verse making it appear more rugged than its nineteenth-century predecessor also give nerve and vigor to Thoreau's lines. These may be seen in bits of light but effective verse where humor comes to the support of idealism, or a homely realism to the aid of a lofty transcendentalism. "My Boots" and "Tall Ambrosia" offer instances. Finally, Thoreau's drastic and startling realistic satire in such highly acid poems as "For Though the Caves Were Rabitted" and "I Am the Little Irish Boy" resembles in a broad way the forthright manner of the brilliant satires of Yeats.

These powerful projections into the poetic mood of a restless age still almost a century in advance should free the scholar poet from any suspicion that he is merely imitative, overderivative, or immature. It is obviously true that as a young man he revolted from most contemporary fashions in letters as well as in life and gave himself to a devoted study of our heritage from Greece and Rome and from all the periods of the English literary record. But his scholarly habits were vitalizing habits, which happily added strength to his strongly creative mind and in no way fettered his creative faculties in chains of pedantic imitation. His scholarship is merely the outward sign of his universality as poet. His occasional lapses owing to bad taste may generally be ascribed to the limitations of his age, from which even so pronounced an individualist as he could not entirely escape. The refinements of his art, on the contrary, may best be discerned in his highly varied and modulated rhythms, his uncommonly flexible vocabulary and his many unclassifiable nuances. His strength is most intimately associated with his breadth. Thoreau found all schools of poetry his teachers, none his master. The publication at the present time is no accident. Thoreau's breadth of vision is precisely what our own age, tragically seeking a new consolidation of mankind, most of all requires.

The Red Face of Man

by Edwin S. Fussell

> I have not decided whether I had better publish my experience in
> searching for arrowheads in three volumes, with plates and an index,
> or try to compress it into one.

According to legend and Ellery Channing, Thoreau's last words
were "moose" and "Indian." Perhaps he was only delirious and
his mind wandered backward along the trail of his beloved excursions to the Maine woods; or perhaps, as has also been conjectured,
and as I should prefer to believe, his mind wandered forward, and
thus bore final witness to his long-standing determination to write
a great book about the natives of America. The book itself, unquestionably, remained unwritten at his untimely death, though he
had labored toward its composition for at least twelve years—and
probably much longer—collecting in the process over 2800 pages
of notes and excerpts from other writers on the subject. Unfortunately, these "Indian Notebooks" reveal little about his literary
intentions, except as their bulk and doggedness convince us he
meant business. Most of the entries are factual and bare; most of
the excerpts direct quotation, close paraphrase, or careful translation. Only a few pencilled notes (added later) represent the first
stirrings of an organizing impulse, and a couple of references to
the *Journals* the rudiments of a correlating instinct. From this
evidence, his critics have tended to derive certain debatable inferences: Thoreau was written out after *Walden,* or was increasingly
succumbing to the desperate collection of meaningless data, or the
Indian as a literary problem was insoluble. None of these inferences
is provable or even probable. Thoreau's later writing will not support any theory of creative exhaustion. There is an inherent absurdity in charging with an abject surrender to data the man of
the age most sensitive to that particular disaster of the spirit (and

who regularly guarded himself against it by thinking of the Indian).

In any case, Thoreau's customary processes of composition almost automatically rule out any possibility of reconstructing his literary intentions through a study of the Indian Notebooks. These are only raw material; not proximate but initial sources. Doubtless their contents were continuously passing into his *Journals* as they were assimilated by his literary intelligence. Doubtless they would have passed through many another stage, now impossible to reconstruct, both before and after their appearance in the *Journals*. In fact, there was no earthly reason why Thoreau should have entered in these Indian Notebooks indications of attitude toward his subject or speculations concerning the general nature of the book he meant to write. The first were in his mind always; the second would emerge, organically, as his images took shape. He was not gathering data in the hope that he might ultimately discover their meaning, nor in the wilder hope that they might of themselves "compose"—to say so is utterly to miss the point of what "inspiration" meant, in a purely practical sense, to a writer of Thoreau's particular bent—but collecting further evidence to underwrite and embody convictions he already possessed.

What would Thoreau's Indian book have been like? That question can only be answered by reference to what he had already written. His *Journals,* and his published writings from *A Week on the Concord and Merrimack Rivers* to *The Maine Woods,* are full of passages about the Indian. From this material, it is not only possible but relatively easy to project the unborn soul of the book itself. "The future reader of history will associate this generation with the red man in his thoughts," he wrote in an 1839 diary, "and give it credit for some sympathy with his race. Our history will have some copper tints and reflections at least." That was the ambition, considerably antedating his first public appearance as a serious writer. From the outset he recognized the extent of the challenge: "The Indian has vanished as completely as if trodden into the earth; absolutely forgotten but by a few persevering poets." [1] As another persevering poet of the copper-tinted generation had already written: "The habits and sentiments of that departed people were too distinct from those of their successors to find much real sympathy" (Hawthorne in "Sketches From Memory"). He was required to attain an almost unattainable empathy by means of—not by avoidance of—the facts of the case; in short,

[1] *The First and Last Journeys of Thoreau,* ed. Franklin B. Sanborn (Boston, 1905), I, 36.

the usual business of the poet, only in this instance aggravated, to engender the poetic image from the coupling of accurate knowledge and rectitude of heart. Negatively, Thoreau had to divest himself of parochial prejudices—a few of them personal, many of them national; from some of his youthful utterances, it seems he had much to learn. Fortunately, he was a diligent scholar.

Thus he resolutely went to school to Cartier, Champlain, the compilers of the Jesuit *Relations,* Gookin, Lewis and Clark, Heckewelder, Schoolcraft, and the countless other authorities in whom he sought particularities for the incarnation of his personal response to the idea of the Indian. His remarks in the *Week* on Alexander Henry's *Travels and Adventures* must represent his attitude toward them all: "It reads like the argument to a great poem on the primitive state of the country and its inhabitants, and the reader imagines what in each case, with the invocation of the Muse, might be sung, and leaves off with suspended interest, as if the full account were to follow . . ." (*W,* I, 231). Thoreau as poet was to invoke the Muse, supply the song; the full account would follow perforce. He worked at it all his life, for the great poem he was writing (and of which *Walden* is the most impressive part he was permitted to finish) must be envisaged as nothing less than the epic of the New World, the same epic that all the major writers of the age were in their various ways approaching.

The crucial step in cultivating a sense of Thoreau's unconsummated masterpiece is taken the minute we begin to perceive how regularly his remarks about the Indian group themselves into a small number of surprisingly clear and closely connected categories. In the terminology of Emerson's *Nature,* we may say that Thoreau apprehended the Indian according to one or another of five "uses." Merely to run through them, understanding by them what Thoreau understood, is to fill the mind with the richest awareness of what possibilities in form and development awaited only the stylistic cunning of that inveterately cunning hand.

The Indian as the Past Facing the problem of the Indian, the representative man of the New World inevitably confronted his deepest historical necessity and sternest historical challenge. "What happened here before I arrived?" The answer to that question would plainly affect the answer to the question perpetually posed by the West (for all the persevering poets): "What shall I be tomorrow?" Thoreau especially was a narrowly vertical historian, an ecologist of the human condition passionately committed to the vision of one place through all time, past, present, and future.

Despite the romantic extravagances of "Walking," he was basically indifferent to man's Westward migrations from a European past; rather, to seek the past of where he lived was increasingly what he lived for.

Yet he was also unusually aware how new and raw his country was, how much it lacked in lacking all that the ancient and medieval worlds had deposited on European soil. He set himself the task of supplying their nearest equivalent, knowledge of what was in those far-off times actually going on in the Western Hemisphere. After all, his favorite idea of *strata* applied to man, and to his history, quite as well as to nature; in either realm, what was wanted was a sense of something firm under foot, a solid ground formed by the contributions of the dead past. The plowing up of bones was no ghoulish satisfaction for Thoreau, but the necessary reassurance that he was currently at home where other men had made themselves at home.

But it was extraordinarily difficult for Thoreau or anyone else to achieve this sense of a continuous human community extending indefinitely backward, partly for want of historical records, partly for want of a dependable channel of sympathy. As conceived by the vertical ecologist, American history was by no means the relatively single development of a Western Europe, but a story broken in the middle by the conflict of two races, two forms of human consciousness and sensibility and culture, opposing faces of man— in one light the same, in other lights tragically disjunct. In order to write the natural and human history of the New World, Thoreau must himself become something of an Indian. As he said, "there is only so much of Indian America left as there is of the American Indian in the character of this generation" (*J*, I, 338). How deliberately Thoreau cultivated the Indian character is impossible to tell; but even before the Walden experiment, Hawthorne in his *American Notebooks* instinctively reached for precisely this comparison in attempting to define his friend's peculiar behavior.

Even the contemporary Indian was sufficiently bewildering. No matter what he asked, Thoreau was answered "out of that strange remoteness in which the Indian ever dwells to the white man" (*W*, III, 175). A number of anecdotes in *The Maine Woods* illustrate this point. Much more overwhelming was the difficulty of acquiring accurate knowledge of the Indian in his proper state, before contact with Europeans ruined his type. Speaking in the *Week* of Lovewell's Flight and other early frontier skirmishes, Thoreau indirectly defined his problem as a writer: "I think that posterity will doubt if such things ever were—if our bold ancestors who settled this land were not struggling rather with the forest shadows, and not with a copper-colored race of men. They were vapors, fever and ague of the unsettled woods. . . . In the Pelasgic, the Etruscan, or the British story, there is nothing so shadowy and unreal" (*W*, I, 176). Obviously, this unreality is the historian's or poet's special experience of "unreality"—not an inherent quality of the object but a symptom of his present inability to lay his hands on the object. Of course, there were minor compensations: if the Indian's past was as obscure as all that, then Thoreau could easily supply the Americans their wistfully desired "antiquity," and even arm them with an ancient world more primitive, more mythical, more "shadowy and unreal" than anything the upstart Europeans could boast. Yet even though the New World's antiquity thus happily managed to straggle down to the present moment, Thoreau to the end despaired of grasping it fully. The Indian, he said, "lives three thousand years deep into time, an age not yet described by poets," by implication permitting himself to antedate even his favorite Homer. But only if he could realize the phantom, "dim and misty to me, obscured by the aeons that lie between the bark canoe and the batteau. . . . He glides up the Millinocket and is lost to my sight, as a more distant and misty cloud is seen flitting by behind a nearer, and is lost in space. So he goes about his destiny, the red face of man" (*W*, III, 87-88). I am far from thinking the Indian's elusiveness would have prevented Thoreau's writing about him; in dozens of passages like these, he is already doing so, and as well as he ever wrote. On the other hand, the Indian as literary subject would clearly have imposed certain tones, and among them paradox. The Indian was all paradox. But in Thoreau he would have met his master.

"Wherever I go, I tread in the tracks of the Indian," he wrote in an early meditation (*J*, I, 337), before he knew how far that track was to lead or how difficult to follow. As he learned these things, he increasingly cultivated the retrospective glance. In one remarkable vision, the sort of passage that might well have formed an imaginative node in the Indian books, as comparably imagined passages do in *Walden,* he even persuaded time to reverse itself, turning the civilized landscape of his own day backward, stage after stage, until at last the Indian reappeared, true to life, in his unspoiled habitat:

At first, perchance, there would be an abundant crop of rank garden weeds and grasses in the cultivated land,—and rankest of all in the cellar-holes,—and of pinweed, hardhack, sumach, blackberry, thimbleberry, raspberry, etc., in the fields and pastures. Elm, ash, maples, etc., would grow vigorously along old garden limits and main streets. Garden weeds and grasses would soon disappear. Huckleberry and blueberry bushes, lambkill, hazel, sweet-fern. . . . Finally the pines, hemlock, spruce, larch, shrub oak, oaks, chestnut, beech, and walnuts would occupy the site of Concord once more. The apple and perhaps all exotic trees and shrubs and a great part of the indigenous ones named above would have disappeared, and the laurel and yew would to some extent be an underwood here, and perchance the red man once more thread his way through the mossy, swamp-like, primitive wood. (*J,* XIV, 262-263)

Who will have the heart (or nerve) to call this an idle fantasy? Such visions are never the result of idle hours, as the remarkable list of plants—so cautiously ordered along a scale from domestic to wild—sufficiently indicates. Or if fantasy, then the historical poet's necessary fantasy, his ritual, magical, quasi-literal, initiating reversion through the dark concrete recesses of the temporal . . .

Thoreau's ability to render the Indian—and the literary situations involving the Indian—in metaphor is our best warrant for thinking him readier to compose his vaunted book than some of his more skeptical readers are willing to allow. "Another species of mortal men," begins another of these desperately successful attempts at figurative definition and embodiment, "but little less wild to me than the musquash they hunted. Strange spirits, daemons, whose eyes could never meet mine; with another nature and another fate than mine. The crows flew over the edge of the woods, and, wheeling over my head, seemed to rebuke, as dark-winged spirits more akin to the Indian than I. Perhaps only the present disguise of the Indian. If the new has a meaning, so has the old" (*J,* I, 337). Once again—but not this time by way of paradox—Thoreau's humility in the face of the inscrutable leads him straight to the mark. The image of the wheeling crows (perhaps only the Indian himself in disguise) flying over the boundary of the woods (that inescapably Western emblem) summons up nearly everything he most wished to say of the Indian: his dark elusiveness, his daemonic sympathy with nature, his contiguity with and discreteness from the white man's life, his eternal presence in nature as warning and inspiration.

Thoreau sought more than arrowheads in his constant rummaging around the fields of Concord. Again and again, on those walks which were the source and structure of all he wished to be, to know, and to write about, his eye would light on an arrowhead or pot shard, which his companion almost as invariably failed to notice. He even developed a personal *mystique*—the same as for the finding of rare plants—to account for his luck. But of course he perfectly well understood, and was sometimes willing to explain, that these wonderful discoveries depended on his incredibly close knowledge of local conditions and Indian habits. He knew upon what kind of ground they customarily encamped, what kinds of soil and site they selected for crops, as he also knew at what time of year and in what climate the relics were likely to rise to the surface. The quest for arrowheads was not literal but mimetic, a representative action exactly analogous to the quest of the historian, so curiously blended of active search and a habit of patience. In *Walden* Thoreau wished to anticipate if possible nature herself. But in his passion for Indian relics he desired to anticipate something altogether more wraith-like, the emergent presence of the past, the imaginative return of the dead. It must have been a little like the descent into Hades; except that Thoreau sat at the edge of the fosse, with his eyes wide open, until the shades rose. He was chanticleer only when occasion demanded, as in *Walden;* otherwise, it was more and more the past he tried to recapture. For this attempt, he was remarkably gifted, though receiving little enough credit for it; had he lived to complete the Indian book, he would probably have been remembered as (among other things) the greatest historian of the age.

Because he was free of prejudice, rhetoric, and melodrama, depending instead upon poetry, or the exact imitation of real life in the right images, he would have written more useful history than Prescott or Parkman. He was always chiding his contemporaries for their indifference to the evidence (not only arrowheads) lying before their eyes: "On the sandy slope of the cut . . . I notice the chips which some Indian fletcher has made. Yet our poets and philosophers regret that we have no antiquities in America, no ruins to remind us of the past" (*J*, XI, 212). Only fourteen months later, in the *Marble Faun* preface, Hawthorne would be complaining again that America lacked relics. But he was still abroad, and probably unaware how Thoreau's collections (not only arrowheads) were flourishing. Or perhaps he had lost his sense of ancient and gloomy wrong. Increasingly that was Thoreau's business, along with snowstorms and huckleberries.

Ruins would find a second life through form and style—in the perfect present of art—as in such passages as this:

> As I drew a still fresher soil about the rows [of beans] with my hoe, I disturbed the ashes of unchronicled nations who in primeval years lived under these heavens, and their small implements of war and hunting were brought to the light of this modern day. They lay mingled with other natural stones, some of which bore the marks of having been burned by Indian fires, and some by the sun, and also bits of pottery and glass brought hither by the recent cultivators of the soil. When my hoe tinkled against the stones, that music echoed to the woods and the sky, and was an accompaniment to my labor which yielded an instant and immeasurable crop. It was no longer beans that I hoed, nor I that hoed beans. . . . (*W*, II, 175)

Thus in *Walden* Thoreau cultivated timelessness; not, as his fellow Transcendentalists were prone to do, by asserting a childish independence of history, but by incorporating so much of the essential past, so much of the essential future in his present consciousness that history ceased to matter. It ceased to matter when it became real. Insofar as history became real, Thoreau might save his own soul and thereby gain the whole New World. Unavoidably, then, the Indian book would have owed much to Thoreau's special sense of the past and his specific identification of the Indian with the American past. The sense of the past would also have furnished the underlying structure of the book; that structure would have been integral, thematic, pervasive, and compelling.

The Indian as Fundamental Man   This use of the Indian is less uniquely Thoreau's than his vision of him as the past, but comes closer to representing that aspect of his attitude shared with the other major writers, notably Cooper and Melville. It is to be understood in all three as primarily the ironic consequence of regarding the Indian from a fundamentally Christian point of view—that is, with both realism and charity—in a fundamentally non-Christian society. To most nineteenth-century Americans, the savage and heathen Indian was outside the purview of their ordinary religious obligation, too different from themselves to afflict the conscience. The way to deal with Indians was to root them out, and then bewail their disappearance in neurotic plays and novels. Cooper, Thoreau, and Melville insistently declared that if the Indian was different, he was also the same. Doubtless they meant to irritate; they were all of them moralists. Their attitudes also entailed striking literary consequences: witness the outraged cry that Cooper's Indians were "idealized." What hurt was their being human.

According to the prevailing idealism of mid-nineteenth-century American thought, such a phrase as "The Indian as Fundamental Man" might mean either the Indian as one of several specific expressions of the general idea of humanity (as in Thoreau's superb phrase, "the red face of man"), or the essence of humanity, common to all, but more conspicuous in primitive man, whose basic nature is not yet overlaid with civilization (as when Thoreau says: "Inside the civilized man stands the savage still in the place of honor") (*W*, I, 368). Thus the Indian might suggest, alternately or concurrently, the richly various possibilities of human life, or, more simply, humanity itself (or even "reality," as in *The Confidence-Man*). Either way, Thoreau was further encouraged to express the Indian through metamorphosis or metaphorical action, the Indian suddenly erupting into the present, the spirit of the past entering and animating the heavy body of the contemporary: "In the musquash-hunters I see the Almouchicois still pushing swiftly over the dark stream in their canoes. These aboriginal men cannot be repressed, but under some guise or other they survive and reappear continually" (*J*, XI, 424-425). If the American thought he was replacing the Indian, he was wrong. Dispossession was a reciprocal process, and more complicated than anyone but poets suspected. The Indian was not gone, but had merely taken another form.

There is no question of the humility and decency with which the author of *Walden* approached the Indian, nor that these qualities would have informed every page of this even more ambitious book. Naturally, he thought most American historians on this subject as contemptible as they obviously thought the Indian. In a crucial *Journal* passage, he worked out a careful indictment of their inhumanity and proposed an alternative frame of mind:

> Some have spoken slightingly of the Indians, as a race possessing so little skill and wit, so low in the scale of humanity, and so brutish that they hardly deserved to be remembered,—using only the terms "miserable," "wretched," "pitiful," and the like. In writing their histories of this country they have so hastily disposed of this refuse of humanity (as they might have called it) which littered and defiled the shore and the interior. But even the indigenous animals are inexhaustibly interesting to us. How much more, then, the indigenous man of America! If wild men, so much more like ourselves than they are

unlike, have inhabited these shores before us, we wish to know particularly what manner of men they were, how they lived here, their
relation to nature, their arts and their customs, their fancies and
superstitions.

In short, the questions Thoreau would ask about the Indian,
thereby eliciting an altogether novel kind of American history (still
unwritten), are precisely the questions he asked about himself and
his countrymen in *Walden*.

Continuing his indictment of "historians," Thoreau proceeds to
define their activity through a comparison even more suggestive
to the student of American culture: "It frequently happens that
the historian, though he professes more humanity than the trapper,
mountain man, or gold-digger, who shoots one as a wild beast,
really exhibits and practices a similar inhumanity to him, wielding
a pen instead of a rifle." This observation is dated February 3, 1859.
The central episode of *The Confidence-Man*—whose American edition was published on April Fools' Day, 1857—is a radical attack
on the frontier attitude of "Indian-hating," defined there and
elsewhere in Melville as hunting one's fellow man as if he were
a beast; this crime against humanity is ultimately attributed, not
directly to the pioneers themselves, but indirectly to writers, and
specifically to that popular chronicler of the West, James Hall. Of
course, it makes little difference whether Thoreau read *The Confidence-Man* and was "influenced" by it. For us, the important
point is the obvious meeting of minds, and the way it supplies
another lively perspective on the potentialities inherent in Thoreau's unwritten book. At any moment, it might have veered in the
direction of Melville.

The passage about historians concludes more broadly and affirmatively: "It is the spirit of humanity, that which animates both
so-called savages and civilized nations, working through a man, and
not the man expressing himself, that interests us most. The thought
of a so-called savage tribe is generally far more just than that of a
single civilized man" (*J*, XI, 437-438). To such a state of humility
had the youthful egotist arrived, doubtless instructed by his perpetually difficult meditation on the Indian. For all their apparent
difference and disjunction in time and culture, that Indian was
only another man like himself. Thoreau's simplest insight into the
life of the Indian is also the most extraordinary. Surely it promised
well for his literary ambitions, which were capacious and just beyond the comprehension of all except a small handful of other

writers. But Thoreau had one advantage over them: he had learned
the hard way what he was talking about, whereas Cooper and
Melville, for all their magnanimity, were only guessing.

  The Indian as Nature   That the Indian's contact with nature
was closer than ours scarcely needs arguing; that this was a fact
of central importance to Thoreau scarcely needs discussing. Like
Melville—but with less ambiguity of attitude and a more accom-
plished control of image—Thoreau persistently sees the Indian as
an emanation of nature. Such a vision is hard to put into words—
both for them and for me—but is easy enough to trace to the habit
of making metaphors between the Indian and his environment in
which the terms of comparison practically coalesce. "They seem
like a race who have exhausted the secrets of nature, tanned with
age. . . . Their memory is in harmony with the russet hue of the
fall of the year" (*J*, I, 444). In that image the Indian and the autumn foliage are almost indistinguishable. The memory of the Indian (his memory, and perhaps also our memory of him) resembles
the russet leaves because he, like they, is "tanned with age"; tanned
with nature, too, for in exhausting her secrets he has taken on her
color. A much later notation repeats substantially the same image:
"Many trunks old and hollow, in which wild beasts den. Hawks
nesting in the dense tops, and deer glancing between the trunks,
and occasionally the Indian with a face the color of the faded
oak leaf" (*J*, XIV, 231). (Deer and Indian additionally fused in
"glancing.") Alternatively, Thoreau's comparisons show the natural
object gradually turning into a red man: "The pine stands in the
woods like an Indian,—untamed, with a fantastic wildness about
it, even in the clearings. If an Indian warrior were well painted,
with pines in the background, he would seem to blend with the
trees, and make a harmonious expression. The pitch pines are
the ghosts of Philip and Massasoit. The white pine has the smoother
features of the squaw" (*J*, I, 258). These metaphors rest upon close
correspondence between significant visual aspects of Indian life
and details from nature observed with equal accuracy; nearly always they also insinuate a more general point, most frequently
the Indian's harmonious identification with his environment.

  The Indian was the *native*—a word of terrible force in Thoreau—
of the New World. After a list of indigenous animals threatened
with extinction, he adds: "With these, of course, is to be associated
the Indian" (*J*, III, 72). If he were to be associated historically
and realistically with nature, the Indian could consequently be as-

sociated with nature in metaphor. Then Thoreau could disregard as basically irrelevant his immediate annoyance with Indians who lived in town, got drunk, accumulated property, and went to church on Sunday. Some of the images I have been quoting are early and some are late; in every one, Thoreau is obviously trying to reduce his response to the Indian to manageable poetic status. The idea he had all the time; for example, in 1841: "The charm of the Indian to me is that he stands free and unconstrained in Nature, is her inhabitant and not her guest, and wears her easily and gracefully. But the civilized man has the habits of the house. His house is a prison" (*J*, I, 253). If in *Walden* Thoreau imitated the pioneer, he was also imitating the Indian whom in history the pioneer imitated. Nature-Indian-pioneer-poet, poet-pioneer-Indian-nature: that is the reversible series of terms organizing the single poem Thoreau spent his life preparing to write. The reversible series is essentially the social stages of history theory, with poet replacing merchant as final term. None of Thoreau's subversions of American assumption was more radical, none more prophetic.

The Indian's "use" as nature sufficiently explains Thoreau's distaste for the idea of "civilizing" him. "We talk of civilizing the Indian, but that is not the name for his improvement. By the wary independence and aloofness of his dim forest life he preserves his intercourse with his native gods, and is admitted from time to time to a rare and peculiar society with Nature. He has glances of starry recognition to which our saloons are strangers." Then to the main point, how would Thoreau himself use the Indian for poetry: "There are other, savager and more primeval aspects of nature than our poets have sung. It is only white man's poetry. . . . If we could listen but for an instant to the chant of the Indian muse, we should understand why he will not exchange his savageness for civilization. Nations are not whimsical. Steel and blankets are strong temptations; but the Indian does well to continue Indian" (*W*, I, 55-56). Thoreau likewise did well to continue Thoreau, for the essential paradox was that he (who must fight his way back to nature) was a poet, and the Indian (who was nearly nature herself) was not. By sympathetic communion with the Indian, Thoreau might some day escape the bounds of "white man's poetry" and realize an art wholly appropriate to this New World. But poetry was the expression of civilization, and would only be written by civilized man.

The Indian as Language   Naturally, the Indian as language was

also a crucial concern to the writer intending to use him for substance and style in an epic about nature and man in the New
World. To know the Indian's language was to know what he knew;
to know what he knew was to know how to say it in words of one's
own. In this respect, as in others, Thoreau conceived the two races
as complements: the Indian remembered what the white man had
forgotten, spoke what the white man could no longer comprehend.
To master the whole meaning of life on this continent, Thoreau
must join, in the mind, by means of poetic images, what the course
of history (and maybe the will of God) had put asunder.

Especially as a point of entry into that primitive past he longed to
penetrate, the Indian's language was so central to Thoreau's poetic
problem that the mere sound of it was enough to evoke all his
deepest responses. "It took me by surprise," he reported, "though I
had found so many arrowheads, and convinced me that the Indian
was not the invention of historians and poets. It was a purely wild
and primitive American sound. . . . These were the sounds that
issued from the wigwams of this country before Columbus was
born. . . . I felt that I stood, or rather lay, as near to the primitive
man of America, that night, as any of its discoverers ever did" (*W*,
III, 151). Wildness, remoteness, mystery, simplicity, purity—these
were the tones of voice Thoreau was always listening for, in the
hope of modulating the language he inherited. The English of *his*
past was the English of another place, however estimable, and must
needs accommodate itself to the new life; how better than by contact
with the Indian, whose language was not only the language of the
past, and thus the speech of the fundamental man (miraculously
surviving into the present), but the very language of nature in these
parts? To discover and assimilate some of its meaning and manner
would be indispensable, but not easy. Nor in a literal way were
Thoreau's accomplishments in "Indian" remarkable. But a literal
command of the language was not what he required.

The main thing about the Indian's way with words—as with
things—was its organic quality, the sympathetic closeness to nature,
reality. As he worried it out in the privacy of his study:

> We would fain know something more about these animals and stones
> and trees around us. We are ready to skin the animals alive to come
> at them. Our scientific names convey a very partial information only;
> they suggest certain thoughts only. . . . How much more conversant
> was the Indian with any wild animal or plant than we are, and in his
> language is implied all that intimacy. . . . It was a new light when

> my guide gave me Indian names for things for which I had only
> scientific ones before. In proportion as I understood the language, I
> saw them from a new point of view. (*J*, X, 294-295)

Few expository passages in Thoreau indicate more clearly the directions he was intending to go. Still, it is not exposition that will
seriously advance our understanding of what this extraordinary man
was projecting. The perpetually pertinent questions are, could he
have realized such ideas in poetry, and how? Once again, the
answers are "yes," and "the way he had always done," of which the
little narrative concluding his observations for July 24 in "The
Allegash and East Branch" (*W*, III, 196-201) affords an altogether
satisfying example. As usual in Thoreau, it is *multum ex parvo*,
realistic, lyric, witty, devout, nocturnal, prophetic, and passionate.

The story opens quietly with Thoreau's simple narration of the
fact that his Indian guide "cut some large logs of damp and rotten
hard wood to smoulder and keep fire through the night." (But in
Thoreau's writing, the simplest fact turns figurative as soon as we
look at it.) Thoreau rises in the middle of the night, to find the
fire out, but the logs still shining in "a perfectly regular elliptical
ring of light." He decides this must be phosphorescent wood, which
he has heard about but never seen. "It could hardly have thrilled me
more," he tells us, revealingly moving from science to significance,
"if it had taken the form of letters, or of the human face." The
literary importance is further emphasized by his receiving next
morning from his favorite guide Joe Polis the Indian word for the
phenomenon, together with the information that Indians frequently
see this and like sights. ("Nature must have made a thousand revela-
tions to them which are still secrets to us.")

Consequently Thoreau transforms this anecdote into a parable for
the acquisition of a more important kind of knowing than white
man's "science." ("I let science slide, and rejoiced in that light as if
it had been a fellow creature.") Merely the possibility of such
knowledge renews the world, by re-creating the world as sentience:

> I believed that the woods were not tenantless, but choke-full of honest
> spirits as good as myself any day,—not an empty chamber, in which
> chemistry was left to work alone, but an inhabited house,—and for
> a few moments I enjoyed fellowship with them. . . . It suggested, too,
> that the same experience always gives birth to the same sort of belief
> or religion. One revelation has been made to the Indian, another
> to the white man. . . . [But now both have been made to Thoreau.]

Long enough I had heard of irrelevant things; now at length I was glad to make acquaintance with the light that dwells in rotten wood. Where is all your knowledge gone to? It evaporates completely, for it has no depth.

But not Thoreau's kind of knowledge, which is solidly grounded, like the Indian's, in the accurate apprehension of apprehensible things. Recognizing the necessary transience of this particular kind of "thing," Thoreau with a final flourish "destroys" it, thereby putting it forever beyond the temptations of overstatement or undue perpetuation: "I kept those little chips and wet them again the next night, but they emitted no light."

The Indian as the Frontier Apart from those occasions when he thinks of the Indian in his original state, Thoreau likes best to conceive him at the exact point of contact with white civilization. At the risk of imperiling his other views of the Indian, Thoreau is drawn by the common obsession of the age to that traditional, enchanted neutral ground, "the meeting point between savagery and civilization" (Frederick Jackson Turner's definition), thereupon to arrange a mutual and presumably beneficent confrontation of white man and red. Yet that mutual confrontation having been in history so cruelly destructive, so apparently without benefit to either party, it is not at first easy to imagine how he would have achieved those affirmative resolutions of contradiction which the shape and purpose of the frontier—as conceived by nineteenth-century Americans—imperiously demanded. One solution was to concentrate on those moments in history where exception denied the rule's necessity; in the narrative of phosphorescent wood, we find the following reflections about Joe Polis:

> His singing carried me back to the period of the discovery of America, to San Salvador and the Incas, when Europeans first encountered the simple faith of the Indian. There was, indeed, a beautiful simplicity about it; nothing of the dark and savage, only the mild and infantile.

That Thoreau is thinking of the point of meeting between Indian and European—not of the Indian in his primeval state—is confirmed by his guess that the song "probably was taught his tribe long ago by the Catholic missionaries." That they necessarily concentrated on the first encounters of Europeans and Indians, but in a rare spirit of charity, explains why the Jesuit *Relations* were Thoreau's favorite source for Indian materials.

Another solution was to envisage Indian and white man as complements within a harmony large enough to reduce realistic anomaly to the status of local detail. Within that comprehensive frame, Thoreau might also conceive the Indian as mediating the major contradiction of human life in the New World (not so much between white man and Indian as between man and nature). Thus he argued the case of the Indian against Alcott's simplistic (and genteel) plea for "civilization": "Thoreau defends the Indian from the doctrine of being lost or exterminated, and thinks he holds a place between civilized man and nature, and must hold it." [2] *He must hold it* because the most urgent need of the American writer and people then and always was the reconciliation of a world split in two in nearly every conceivable direction (Indian and European, past and future, nature and culture, not to mention the multitude of epistemological and aesthetic dualisms that harassed the American Romantic). The point of meeting between these various antitheses is the Indian himself. The frontier is the Indian, the Indian is the frontier. Whenever Thoreau, the civilized poet, turns to nature—his best word for the Being he needed to propitiate—he finds a personal intercessor, the American Indian.

Hence the anxiety of his excursions to the Maine woods, the all-importance of securing the right Indian guides, and, especially after the third journey, the happy conclusion (often reiterated): "I have now returned, and think I have had a quite profitable journey, chiefly from associating with an intelligent Indian." [3] It was wonderful that Joe Polis should be so unspoiled by civilization; it was even better that he should so marvellously combine "civilized" and "savage" virtues. Thoreau concludes an account of Polis's hunting prowess with the triumphant assertion:

> Thus you have an Indian availing himself cunningly of the advantages of civilization, without losing any of his woodcraft, but proving himself the more successful hunter for it. (*W*, III, 222)

That was the Indian on whose trail Thoreau had been following so long. If we follow it far enough, we come to Cooper's *Leatherstocking Tales* and then to the basic conditions of American civilization lying behind them.

[2] *The Journals of Bronson Alcott*, ed. Odell Shepard (Boston, 1938), p. 525.

[3] *The Correspondence of Henry David Thoreau*, ed. Walter Harding and Carl Bode (New York, 1958), p. 491. In the same letter: "I have made a short excursion into the new world which the Indian dwells in, or is. He begins where we leave off."

But this idealized description could never be final. Thoreau's story must also be tragic, or at least elegaic. Somehow he would have to explain the fate of this red man who was the oldest inhabitant of the Western Hemisphere, the common element in the species man, the *confidant* of nature in the New World, the potential source of a renewed poetic language, and the primary human fact confronting the European in America—and who was, for all that, plainly dying. The easiest answer was fatalistic, as when Thoreau condescendingly generalizes: "There is always a slight haze or mist on the brow of the Indian. The white man's brow is clear and distinct" (*J*, X, 77). Such a view, however, met neither the facts nor Thoreau's sentiments. Or he might "explain" Indian decline in terms of the social stages of history hypothesis: "If he would not be pushed into the Pacific, he must seize hold of a plowtail and let go his bow and arrow." (Hunters are always superseded by farmers, in the social stages theory.) Unfortunately, an Indian so saved was hardly worth saving. A few paragraphs later, Thoreau is saying: "The Indian, perchance, has not made up his mind to some things which the white man has consented to; he has not, in all respects, stooped so low" (*J*, I, 444-45). The Indian was of value only so long as he remained true to his nature; remaining true to his nature, he guaranteed his destruction. Paradox, elegy, irony: these are the literary tones that would have contributed most to the shaping of Thoreau's poem. Imagining the various "uses" under which his responses to the Indian were organically arranged, formed and styled by these predominant and inherent tones, we perhaps come closest to a sound guess as to the probable nature of the prospective work.

One consideration would have controlled all the rest. The book about the Indian would have been a work of art, and specifically (apart from mechanics) a poem. It is entirely predictable, then, that Thoreau should finally have explained the decline of the Indian in terms of his wanting art. The central point of view must needs have been something like this: Thoreau, the writer, the highest expression of civilized value, confronting the Indian, in order to derive from his experience whatever was most required by civilized men, together with the realization, urgent and ironic, that it is the Indian's inability to express himself in art that has caused his extinction and at the same time necessitated this poem, which is now the only way he can be saved. Thoreau must do for the Indian what he cannot do for himself—leave his mark—by means of the civilized attribute, art, or the ability of the mind to affect nature, which the Indian lacks, yet the very lack of which strangely constitutes his value for us. As the preartistic, the Indian is the primary challenge of the poet in the New World.

So in his effort to redeem the Indian, if in memory only, Thoreau was always searching for evidence of an aesthetic sensibility which, sufficiently developed, might have saved the race; but was for the most part compelled to believe that the Indian's response to nature was utilitarian, inadequately conscious (a judgment containing pleasant implications for his compatriots). His most important evaluation of the Indian's fate it thus centrally stated in a summary passage about relics:

> As long as I find traces of works of convenience merely, however much skill they show, I am not so much affected as when I discover works which evince the exercise of fancy and taste, however rude. It is a great step to find a pestle whose handle is ornamented with a bird's-head knob. It brings the maker still nearer to the races which so ornament their umbrella and cane handles. I have, then, evidence in stone that men lived here who had fancies to be pleased, and in whom the first steps toward a complete culture were taken. It implies so many more thoughts such as I have. The arrowhead, too, suggests a bird, but a relation to it not in the least godlike. But here an Indian has patiently sat and fashioned a stone into the likeness of a bird, and added some pure beauty to that pure utility, and so far begun to leave behind him war, and even hunting, and to redeem himself from the savage state. In this he was leaving off to be savage. Enough of this would have saved him from extermination. (*J*, V, 526)

That, or something like it, might well have been Thoreau's final word on the subject. He would be talking of himself still, about that best part of himself, which is also one of the best parts of human nature, the compulsive passion to create a truthful image of the self in its world. He too was patiently sitting, fashioning a stone into the likeness of a bird; but was cut off before he had a chance to set that lovely artifact before the eyes of men, for their admiration and improvement.

Therefore I have tried to sketch for the modern reader some outline sense of what that bird might have looked like. Partly for Thoreau's sake: I am convinced too few of us have yet realized the scope of his ambition, nor how tragic was his death at forty-four. (No wonder he died babbling of Indians and moose.) Partly for our sake: America is not yet so overrun with literary masterpieces that we can afford to forego the opportunity of acquainting ourselves with one, even if the acquaintance be almost purely speculative, and the bird in question only stone.

Introduction

by Laurence Stapleton

"Says I to myself"[1]: this, Thoreau resolved, should be the motto of his journal. And he understood that the journal must, therefore, excel in some respects his other writing. By it the sap ascended; in it he grew newness of thought and feeling, and shook off inspiration ill-disposed.

Thoreau's life was an intuitive speaking, a testimony such as we have witnessed in Gandhi or in Schweitzer. How such men live instructs us, even that another individual could not repeat their choices. But while Thoreau could make a simple action suggest a parable, he knew that his calling was that of a writer. To make the discipline of the writer not only a theme but a celebration: for this he kept his journal.

The journal is Thoreau's principal, if not his greatest work. It provided the motif and much of the substance of his books. Yet we must prefer *A Week on the Concord and the Merrimack,* and *Walden,* to any section of the journal with which they may be compared. The significance of the journal is that in it Thoreau practiced: practiced his ways of observing, his laments, his methods of composition, and his sentences.

To be fully aware of the unique worth of the journal we must read it slowly, over a period of time, and read consecutively. A true selection will induce the thoughtful and responsive reader to proceed to an acquaintance with the whole. To learn from Thoreau as a writer, to hear his prophecy—neither identical with nor in conflict with his art—we must be in his company as often as he permits.

From *A Writer's Journal,* by H. D. Thoreau (New York: Dover Publications, Inc., 1960), pp. ix-xxix. Reprinted by permission of Dover Publications, Inc., New York 14, New York and William Heinemann Ltd. of London.

[1] Bradford Torrey and Francis H. Allen (ed.), *The Journal of Henry D. Thoreau* (Boston: Houghton Mifflin Company, 1906), III, 107. Hereafter only the volume and page number will be cited.

Thus we may obtain his thought even on those walks when he would allow no companion.

It is time to emancipate Thoreau from transcendentalism and from the concerns he shared with his contemporaries—whether with Emerson, the younger Channing, Alcott, or John Brown. The co-existence of these men speaks to us powerfully and we benefit because their association made a difference to the outcome of their lives. But Thoreau has, in addition to these, other affiliations, which connect him with writers since his time—with Virginia Woolf, for instance, or Gerard Manley Hopkins. And the nature of his commitment to his art, the resolve that he would speak first to himself, stands to the modern writer an incorruptible revelation.

Few have so sharply considered the economy of the writer. By the economy of the writer, I mean not merely how he gets a living, but what he decides about the uses of his time when he is not writing. Thoreau perceived early that there were certain uses of his time that he could not afford—either for the sake of money or of being more affable with his neighbors. "In my experience nothing is so opposed to poetry—not crime—as business" (IV, 162). He often wryly commented on the seemingly industrious villagers who thought his sauntering by the river margins or through the woodlots an idle thing. For in these "true paths to perception and enjoyment" (X, 146) his highest energy was employed. "How much, what infinite leisure it requires . . . to appreciate a single phenomenon. You must camp down beside it as if for life, . . . and give yourself wholly to it" (IV, 433). Both the day's excursion and his recording of it braced his mind to overcome the dissipation of attention caused by trivial persons and events (III, 5) of whom there were, and always will be, many. He walked "to return to his senses" (II, 110).

Thoreau lived in the way that enabled him to write what he was best fitted to write. The force of his example lies not in the specific solution he achieved for himself, but in the manner of his deciding. Every true writer has both to learn his own discipline, and to learn to live with what he lacks of it. Thoreau was entitled to say to himself, "By poverty I am crystallized" (IX, 246); yet with as much nobility, Emerson could have witnessed, "I am improved by some prosperity." It is not the being poor, or prosperous, that diminishes creative power, but the irrelevant choice or incongruous necessity of either.

Thoreau had chosen relevantly and had no need to doubt. He was not unaware of the cost of having been, "by the want of pecuniary

wealth, . . . nailed down to [his] native region so long and steadily"
(V, 496-97). He did not conceal his disappointment that his townsmen placed a higher value on what was second-best in him—his
surveyor's skill—than on his prophetic teaching. They showed little
desire to hear him at the Lyceum. Although he would not have
written in order to earn his living as a writer, he would have preferred to have had more manuscripts accepted, to have had sold
more than 200 copies of the small edition of his first book. But
although he understood, as well as anyone ever can, that the activities of getting a living, so consecrated in our present society, must be
secondary to the purpose of a whole human life, he neither failed
to support himself nor overlooked the indubitable value to the
writer of some task other than writing.

Of the occupations to which at various times he set himself—
teaching, handyman extraordinary, pencil manufacturer—that of
surveyor proved best. It kept him outdoors where he meant to be.
If it compelled him to abandon his lean diet, and eat coarse meals
in the usually unrewarding company of farmers, it brought him
across the trail of hunters, fishers, tramps, and loafers, in meetings
he often prized. Most of all, surveying reinforced the deep, concentrated, instinctive nature of his observation. "The man who is bent
upon his work is frequently in the best attitude to observe what is
irrelevant to his work" (III, 123). After a long day's surveying in
Lincoln and a wait of an hour and a half at the depot for the "cars,"
Thoreau recorded:

> . . . it is when I have been intently, and it may be laboriously at
> work, and am somewhat listless or abandoned after it, reposing, that
> the muse visits me. . . . It is from out the shadow of my toil that I
> look into the light. (VI, 194)

Here, as respects the glance from one space of sense and feeling
into another, Thoreau expresses an essential principle of his habits
of observing, as he might read a level of his inner life. In his philosophy of seeing, no law of the excluded middle impedes his in-
tuitionist logic. The observer is required to be wholly respectful of
outward fact, while aware that his presence and the state of his
belief impart identity to what he sees.

The veracity of the fact to be ascertained is the primary value
not only of that fact but of its successors, to which it is the clue. "If
you make the least correct observation of nature this year, you will

have occasion to repeat it with illustrations the next, and the season
and life itself is prolonged." Observation, like nature itself, is
generative, and begins with simply seeing.

> The woman who sits in the house and *sees* is a match for a stirring
> captain. Those still piercing eyes, as faithfully exercised on their talent,
> will keep her even with Alexander or Shakespeare. . . . We are as
> much as we see. Faith is sight and knowledge. . . . The farthest blue
> streak in the horizon I can see, I may reach before many sunsets. What
> I saw alters not. . . . (I, 247-48)

As this passage reveals, seeing is an inclusive name for what is far
more than any purely optical phenomenon. Thoreau could have
said to himself, as Virginia Woolf does to herself, "The look of
things has a great power over me." [2] Yet the power of seeing has its
own conditions:

> Many an object is not seen, though it falls within the range of our
> visual ray, because it does not come within the range of our intel-
> lectual ray, i.e., we are not looking for it. (IX, 466)

Thus, although what exists to be known does not alter, the discovery
of it needs some precedent favour.

> The scarlet oak must, in a sense, be in your eye when you go forth.
> . . . In my botanical rambles I find that first the idea, or image of a
> plant occupies my thoughts, though it may at first seem very foreign
> to this locality, and for some weeks or months I go thinking of it and
> expecting it unconsciously, and at length I surely see it, and it is
> henceforth an actual neighbor of mine. This is the history of my
> finding a score . . . of rare plants. . . . (XI, 285-86)

Thoreau convinces us that it is not by chance, but by an intention
of his mind to the object, his bringing it into the "intellectual ray,"
that he finds his rarities. Nevertheless, good observation must not be
governed by an intent that is set or mechanical or self-willed. A
respect for the actual is synonymous with acknowledgment of its
mystery. For this reason, I think, Thoreau emphasizes to himself,
repeatedly, that it is best to saunter to his task. As, from out the
shadow of his toil, he looked into the light, he found that a walk
of which little was expected, a walk that had some necessary pur-

---

[2] Virginia Woolf, *A Writer's Diary* (New York: Harcourt, Brace & Co., 1954),
p. 131.

pose, might turn out best. To be receptive to his truest sense of things, the observer looks from a detached perspective, both of space and of time—waits for himself, as it were. "So in my botanizing or natural history walks, going for one thing, I get another thing." Many of Thoreau's fulminations against organized research or the habits of the laboratory worker sound callow enough. But at the root of all of them, lies his refusal to allow a utilitarian aim, or even such an attitude, to distort his impressions.

The task, then, as incidental to the observation—the discovery to be foreseen, but not commanded, these are the conditions of attention heeded by Thoreau; and when he had in any interval been distracted from them, he recreated them in his earliest moment of freedom. Observation that is too deliberate disappoints him, and he frequently reminds himself of the advantage to the poet or philosopher or naturalist "of pursuing from time to time some other business than his chosen one,—seeing with the side of the eye" (VIII, 314).

For a similar reason, Thoreau loved certain states of weather as witnessing the never-ceasing individuality of the world. Mist, snow, dew, moonlight, he welcomed not only for themselves, but because they summon the senses to new perception, perception from another point of view. Herein he paid respect to the reserve of nature:

Man cannot afford . . . to look at Nature directly, but only with the side of his eye. He must look through her and beyond her. To look at her is fatal as to look at the head of Medusa. It turns the man of science to stone. (V, 45)

All these means of seeing "with the side of the eye" might be termed modes of reflection; and reflection interested Thoreau greatly, so much so that he found in it the principle of composition itself. The difference between a hillside seen looking straight on, and its reflection, exhibits different angles; when one sees the reflection of a tree, different pieces of sky appear between the branches. Thus Nature avoids repetition. For

the reflection is never a true copy or repetition of its substance, but a new composition, and this may be the source of its novelty and attractiveness . . . I doubt if you can ever get Nature to repeat herself exactly. (X, 97)

Reflection then (or a modulation of it, the landscape seen in fog or haze), reveals the infinite variability of nature. Looking at the image

of button bushes, in the river, Thoreau sees them appearing against
the sky, whereas when they are looked at directly only the meadow
or hill stands behind them.

> . . . at twilight [we] dream that the light has gone down into the
> bosom of the waters; for in the reflection the sky comes up to the
> very shore or edge and appears to extend under it. . . . *In the
> reflection you have an infinite number of eyes to see for you and re-
> port the aspect of things each from its own point of view.* (XI, 213,
> italics added)

In the observation itself we must find a means to realize the in-
finitude of relations that constitute actuality. Reflection is such a
means to observe the seemingly familiar in "unsuspected lights and
relations" (XI, 293). It is like a rhyme, or metaphor, in nature itself. It impresses us "with a sense of harmony and symmetry, as
when you fold a blotted paper and produce regular figures—a
dualism which nature loves. What you commonly see is but half"
(III, 51).

An interval in time may produce a similar effect. By making two
distinct reports of the same event at different times, by recurring
to an experience after a day or two, he apprehends it more significantly. "I begin to see such an object when I cease to understand it."
Writing itself can be improved by distancing oneself from it in time
—even by planning revision without the manuscript at hand:

> I find that I can criticise my composition best when I stand at a little
> distance from it,—when I do not see it, for instance. I make a little
> chapter of contents which enables me to recall it page by page to my
> mind. . . . The distraction of surveying enables me rapidly to take
> new points of view. A day or two surveying is equal to a journey.
> (VI, 190)

A re-flection, then, or second image in time of the life contained in
the composition, afforded a chance of novelty, the possibility of
sentences "which do not merely report an old, but make a new,
impression . . . not mere repetition, but creation." (II, 418-19).

Thoreau instinctively relished small appearances, for example,
the study of lichens—so seemingly minimal and marginal in their
existence, as to be informative of "Nature in her everyday mood and
dress." The lichenist "has the appetite of the worm that never dies";
he is fitted for the "barrenest and rockiest experience." On a wet day
—best for this study—the effect of the lichens is a minor phenom-

enon of reflection; thus "a little moisture, a fog, or rain, or melted snow makes his wilderness to blossom like the rose" (XI, 440). And a day of low mist in the woods may be counted on to be a good lichen day, since the confined view "compels [the] attention to near objects" (III, 166).

Ice or snow wrote new legends. When a fine rain begins to freeze on twig or culm, Thoreau remarks "a white glaze (reflecting the snow or sky), rhyming with the vegetable core" (XI, 372). Ice is "graphic" (XI, 430) in its structuring. It makes the heavens a road for man; we walk upon the sky. In effect, it reminds us of correspondences in time, as in vision:

> How few are aware that in winter, when the earth is covered with snow and ice, . . . the sunset sky is double. The winter is coming when I shall walk the sky. . . . There is an annual light in the darkness of the winter night. (XIII, 141-42)

The love of correspondence here, the interest in reflections, haze, fog, ice, as conditions for scanning the variations that "rhyme" with their precursors, or with more frequently seen, sunlit vistas—has nothing in common with the Platonizing theory of correspondences of which Emerson is the exponent. Thoreau did, like Emerson, have an affinity with seventeenth century writers whose intuitions were magnetized by reading in the "Book of Nature" the hieroglyphics of invisible things. This literary and temperamental filiation has been honored by Mr. Matthiessen's unwinding of it in *American Renaissance.* But in observing the ever-new, the "other half" of any substance shown in its rhymed appearances, reflected in water or apparelled in ice, differently related to surrounding objects in moonlight or in haze, Thoreau is not in search of the idea or archetype of these phenomena. Even more than those seventeenth century writers he most resembles—Henry Vaughan and Sir Thomas Browne —his interest not merely begins with but stays with the particular, the minute, the unseen or unnoticed resemblances or differences among concrete objects. He is a veritable seeker of *thisness;* the individual, unduplicatable object can be discerned in its uniqueness when any seeming repetition of it shows it slightly changed.

Herein Thoreau parts company with Emerson in a way that has been little understood. Emerson's mind passes rapidly from perception to abstraction. He thinks philosophically, though not with a philosopher's purpose; he *feels* as a man would who believed throughout his nature what Plato taught. With Emerson the divining of the idea in the concrete fact is not an outcome of the process of dialectic. It is, rather, the *terra firma* of his temperament, the ground he starts from. To Thoreau, as genius of the wood, such assumptions were of course familiar, and it would seem, from some vague acknowledgments of the "ideal," were not uncongenial. But Thoreau's business was with relatedness: of lichen to rock, disintegrated rock to soil, soil to tree, tree to sky, and himself, a man, to each of these in each phase of change. Individuality is significant alone, it needs analogy to identify it, does not itself merely serve to provide an analogy for themes more abstract.

Here is a major difference in emphasis between Emerson and Thoreau. Thoreau had learned so much from Emerson that he could advance on his own path emancipated from much that might have impeded him. Both men, sensitive to and respectful of realities that evade recognition, use some of the same shorthand terms: especially *Nature*. But in the direction and quality of his observation, intent on thisness, *haecceitas*, Thoreau is more akin to Gerard Manley Hopkins. "Let me not be in haste to detect the *universal law*, let me see more clearly a particular instance of it!" (III, 157). Nature depends upon and favours the individual thing, "strews her nuts and flowers broadcast, and never collects them into heaps." He follows this statement by a comment that "A man does not tell us all he has thought upon truth or beauty at a sitting." This might seem like a neo-Platonist train of thought, but is not: Thoreau is emphasizing for the thinking man his discovery of truth at individual moments of time. Essentially, then, the second statement reinforces the first. And in one of a number of passages contrasting Nature and Man (counterpoint to his other theme, that "Nature must be viewed humanly to be viewed at all"), he praises Nature

> *because* she is not man. . . . None of his institutions control or pervade her. . . . He makes me wish for another world. *She makes me content with this.* (IV, 445, last italics added)

In his ardent pursuit of the uniqueness, particularity, to be observed in every changing phase, Thoreau markedly resembles Hopkins. An inevitable difference lies between them—temperamental and artistic. The descriptions of clouds, trees, shadows, river lights, in Hopkins' *Note-Books* have, as compared with any similar descriptions in Thoreau's *Journal,* an effect that is at once more static, more specialized. But in allowing for dissimilarities of conviction, habit, and opportunity between the two men, we shall find them to be like explorers of the same terrain, explorers approaching from different directions and on tangential lines. On November 17, 1869, Hopkins relates that after a damp fog

> . . . the trees being drenched with wet a sharp frost that followed in the night candied them with ice. Before the sun . . . melted the ice . . . I looked at the cedar on the left of the portico and found every needle edged with a blade of ice made of fine horizontal bars of spars all pointing one way, N. and S. . . . There was also an edging of frost in the clematis . . . and . . . the little bars of which the blades or pieces of frost were made up though they lay all along the hairy threads with which the seed vessels of the clematis are set did not turn with their turnings but lay all in parallels N. and S.[3]

Looking at a lunar halo, Hopkins' eye is alert to a composition of light that he records in language strikingly similar to passages in Thoreau's journal:

> The halo was not quite round, . . . what is more it fell in on the nether left hand side to rhyme the moon itself, which was not quite at full. I could not but strongly feel in my fancy the odd instress of this, the moon leaning on her side, as if fallen back, in the cheerful light floor within the ring, after with magical rightness and success tracing round her . . . the steady copy of her own outline.[4]

Hopkins' notion of "instress" or of "inscape" is more strict and more restricted than Thoreau's freer search for form in his study of reflections, of the rhyming of appearances, and of parallel facts or moments. But where in an occasional entry Hopkins treats inscape casually, one is struck by the closeness of intention:

> The chestnuts . . . were a beautiful sight: each spike had its own pitch, yet each followed in its place in the sweep with a deeper and deeper stoop. When the wind tossed them they plunged and crossed one another without losing their inscape. (Observe that motion multiplies inscape only when inscape is discovered . . .)[5]

Words come into Hopkins' mind in figures of sound even when he is writing prose: "in the sweep, with a deeper and deeper stoop . . .

[3] Humphry House (ed.), *The Note-Books and Papers of Gerard Manley Hopkins* (New York: Oxford University Press, 1937), p. 125.
[4] *Ibid.*, p. 158.
[5] *Ibid.*, p. 133. Cf. also his observations on freezing ice crystals in wind, etc. (p. 136), the "idiom" of snow (p. 128), and the reflection in the sky of planets (p. 125).

tossed and crossed." In language as in seeing he has this innate sense
for the *sake* of it, "the sake of things, the being a thing has outside
itself, . . . a voice by its echo . . . a body by its shadow." [6] In the
structure of verse, that which constitutes it, and lacking which
poetry is absent, Hopkins found the fundamental principle to be
parallelism:

> But what the character of poetry is will best be found by looking at
> the structure of verse. The artificial part of poetry, perhaps we shall
> be right to say all artifice, reduces itself to the principle of parallelism.
> Only the first kind, that of marked parallelism, is concerned with the
> structure of verse—in rhythm, the recurrence of a certain sequence of
> syllables, . . . in alliteration, in assonance and in rhyme. Now the
> force of this recurrence is to beget a . . . parallelism answering to it
> in the words or thought. . . . To the marked or abrupt kind of
> parallelism belong metaphor, simile, parable, and so on, where the
> effect is sought in likeness of things, and antithesis, contrast, . . .
> where it is sought in unlikeness.[7]

To the astute generalizing of this principle as a foundation for
poetics Thoreau could not have attained; he seemingly did not
comprehend the possible structures of verse, or the verse he wrote
would have been somewhat better. But his choice of a similar principle as providing, in essence, a transition from nature to art—
essential both to the veracity of observation and to the veracity of
the statement of it, the "report," puts him on a track going in the
same direction. Both were observers of things in their "beautiful
changes." [8]

The insight into individuality possessed by both Thoreau and
Hopkins is the faith that "Nature is never spent." The form of
Hopkins' religion would have been antipathetic to Thoreau, for
whom religion is "that which is never spoken" (XI, 113). But as
students of all that is not man, all that lies before him, that "shines
out, like the shining of shook foil," they are prophets of a concept
of nature with which man's freedom is linked. For nature, all the
more because not man, reflects him. A true knowledge of Nature is
not obtained inhumanely—as by killing a snake (VI, 311). Respect
for the freedom of other men enters our awareness of nature too;
and if that freedom is injured, we cannot absent ourselves from

[6] Claude Colleer Abbott (ed.), *Letters of Gerard Manley Hopkins to Robert
Bridges* (London: Oxford University Press, 1935), p. 83.
[7] Hopkins, *op. cit.,* pp. 92-93.
[8] *Ibid.,* p. 140.

knowledge of the loss, and desire to repair it. Although Thoreau wrote that he would not so soon despair of the world for the fragrance of the white water-lily, "notwithstanding slavery, and the cowardice and want of principle in the North" (VI, 352), he looked sternly at such evils when they were in the foreground. "There was a remarkable sunset, I think the 25th of October," he wrote in his journal some three weeks later. "But it was hard for me to see its beauty then, when my mind was filled with Capt. Brown" (XII, 443).

Ultimately, the relation between man and nature is reciprocal. An injury done to man impairs his relation to nature; and an injury done to nature lessens the scope of man. Rarely is it granted to the writer to be a prophet in his art; yet on this theme the writing of Thoreau has prophetic meaning for all Americans today, all others. Where we see daily the bulldozers and earthmovers invading the woodlands and meadows, with no thought taken for the best preservation of the natural contours of the land, we must learn again "to love the crust of earth on which [we] dwell" (X, 258). Many fine lines of the incantations necessary for our new learning are in Hopkins: "Long live the weeds and the wilderness yet!" ("Inversnaid"). But Thoreau is the composer of chorales in their honor. Every town should have a park, he directed, or rather a primitive forest, of five hundred or a thousand acres,

> where a stick should never be cut for fuel, a common possession forever, for instruction and recreation. . . . Let us keep the New World *new*, preserve all the advantages of living in the country. (XII, 387)

In the age of the supermarket, superhighway, and the bestuccoed acres of superbungalows called ranch houses, these are words of revolutionary comfort and counsel. For in the banishing of the wilderness, the destruction of the country, Thoreau saw human destruction, the diminution of consciousness. This realization prompted his careful notes on the oaks and chestnuts, in the last volumes of his journal, notes on the oldest trees, the trees it takes longest to produce, but which often are first to be destroyed or to become extinct. A man who is contemporary with an oak that has been growing a hundred years, shares some of its past, some of its future. Sometimes the cutting of a tree, he said, "lays waste the air for two centuries" (III, 162-64).

Because he would live in antiquity as well as in the present, in order to sound eternity in the present moment, he would preserve

for the future some at least of the woods that were here before the
country was discovered. And not at a distance, not remote from our
daily living. What makes a township handsome? He answers, "A
river, with its waterfalls and meadows, a lake, a hill, a cliff or individual rocks, a forest, and ancient trees standing singly. . . . I do
not think him fit to be the founder of a state or even a town who
does not foresee the use of these things" (XIV, 304). And, in proclaiming that the top of Mt. Washington should not be private
property, Thoreau explained that parts of the land should be forever unappropriated, for modesty and for reverence's sake, "or if
only to suggest that earth has higher uses than we put her to" (XIV,
305).

Children have a right to know the trees and revel in their color.

> Blaze away! . . . A village is not complete unless it has these trees
> to mark the season. . . . Such a village will not . . . work well. . . .
> Let us have willows for spring, elms for summer, maples and walnuts
> and tupelos for autumn, evergreens for winter, and oaks for all sea-
> sons. An avenue of elms as large as our largest . . . would seem to
> lead to some admirable place, though only Concord were at the end
> of it. (XI, 220-21)

Only Concord! Although it had taken him forty years and more
to know its six square miles and, as he says, thereby to "acquire his
language" (XI, 137), Thoreau did not sentimentalize Concord. He
invested it with a universal significance, because he had taken its
soundings in time, because he knew it better than its selectmen or
census takers, understood how to be a stranger there.

One of Thoreau's most mysterious, indispensable themes is the
prehension of time. In bringing the works of antiquity to the test of
the present, he seeks the living words that abolish distances in time.
But the consideration of antiquity as a whole—of what has disappeared from ken as well as what remains to view—strikes him as
melancholy, because "we forget that it had any other future than
our present. As if it were not as near to the future as ourselves" (I,
294-95). A modern metaphysician pondering time's complexities,
and possible infinities of outcome—a Meade, a McTaggart, or an
Alexander—would not have to be dissatisfied with this: Thoreau's
contemplation of the multiple futures existing for any slice of the
past—and finally the glimpse that they have not all been realized.

In hunting for arrowheads ("one of the regular pursuits of the
spring"), he imagines this crop as dragon seed that are to create a
race—if from the past, no less new to modern man.

Like the dragon's teeth, which bore a crop of soldiers, these bear crops of philosophers and poets. . . . Each one yields me a thought. . . . It is humanity inscribed on the face of the earth. . . . The Indian arrowhead will balk [Time's] efforts and Eternity will have to come to his aid. . . . I would fain know that I am on the trail of mind. . . . When I see these signs I know that the subtle spirits that made them are not far off. . . . The footprint, the mind-print of the oldest men. (XII, 90-92)

Time, and the past, are balked by eternity, which the Indian arrowhead, found in a present moment, reveals. "The immortals are swift,"—that is to say, each present moment brings to the alert observer an untold immensity of content.

Nature never lost a day, nor a moment. . . . In the moment, in the aeon, well employed, time ever advances with this rapidity. . . . The plant that waited a whole year, and then blossomed the instant it was ready and the earth was ready for it, . . . was rapid. (IV, 350)

In his frequent, unaffected sorties into a past that unwittingly liberates this instant, as well as in his concentration on the intensity of life within it, Thoreau greatly resembles Virginia Woolf.

The window was all sky without color. The house had lost its shelter. It was night before roads were made, or houses. It was the night that dwellers in caves had watched from some high place among rocks.[9]

And Mrs. Swithin reads, "Once there was a sea . . . between us and the continent. . . . There were rhododendrons in the Strand, and mammoths in Piccadilly."[10] This is not incidental illustration; it is an extension of feeling essential to the book as a whole. Just as in *Jacob's Room*, the sunrise moving from Greece to London provides in the context a stratification of time as well as spatial omnipresence:

But the wind was rolling the darkness through the streets of Athens. . . . All faces—Greek, Levantine, Turkish, English—would have looked much the same in that darkness. At length the columns and the temples whiten, turn rose; and the Pyramids and St. Peter's arise, and at last sluggish St. Paul's looms up.[11]

[9] Virginia Woolf, *Between the Acts* (New York: Harcourt, Brace & Co., 1941), p. 219.
[10] *Ibid.*, p. 38.
[11] Virginia Woolf, *Jacob's Room* (New York: Harcourt, Brace & Co., 1922), p 276.

This awareness of the past, of antiquity, ancient time, America before it was discovered, prehistory, in Thoreau as in Virginia Woolf backs up an intense love of life. "Life like some gay pavilion" —the phrase is Thoreau's (I, 224)—but it would not be a surprise to find it in *Mrs. Dalloway*. Like Thoreau, Mrs. Woolf noted in her diary the stimulating power of dissatisfaction as of enjoyment: "If I never felt these extraordinary pervasive strains—of unrest or rest or happiness or discomfort—I should sink down into acquiescence." [12] The selection from her journals that has been published provides remarkable evidence of the discipline that she, like Thoreau, evolved for herself, to win or conscript truthful impressions. She notes that she marked "Henry James' sentence: observe perpetually." [13] Yet, as Thoreau discovered, this should not be a method too methodical; the "true paths to perception and enjoyment" lie in the direction of freedom of attention. Hence Thoreau commanded:

> Obey the spur of the moment. These accumulated it is that make the impulse and the impetus of the life of genius. . . . Let the spurs of countless moments goad us incessantly into life. I feel the spur of the moment thrust deep into my side. . . . My life as essentially belongs to the present at that of a willow tree in the spring. (III, 231-32)

"More and more," said Mrs. Woolf to herself, "do I repeat my own version of Montaigne—'It's life that matters.' " [14]

> I don't often trouble now to describe cornfields and groups of harvesting women in loose blues and reds, and little staring yellow-frocked girls. But . . . coming back the other evening from Charleston, again all my nerves stood upright, flushed, electrified (what's the word) with the sheer beauty . . . astounding and super-abounding.
> . . . And I don't describe encounters with herds of Alderneys any more—. . . how they barked and belled like stags round Grizzle; and how I waved my stick and stood at bay; and thought of Homer as they came flourishing and trampling towards me; some mimic battle. . . . Ajax? That Greek, for all my ignorance, has worked its way into me. [15]

I know knothing that so much resembles the first part of this passage as Thoreau's description of himself, in a similar moment of

[12] Virginia Woolf, *A Writer's Diary*, pp. 147-48.
[13] *Ibid.*, p. 365.
[14] *Ibid.*, p. 72.
[15] *Ibid.*, pp. 65-66.

entire perception: "At sight of this my spirit is like a lit tree" (X, 205). Or more like the second, than his description of the thrush's singing:

> This thrush's song is a *ranz des vaches* to me . . . where the hours are early morning ones, . . . and the day is forever unproved. . . . I would go after the cows, I would watch the flocks of Admetus there forever, only for my board and clothes. (V, 293)

At another moment of exhilaration in the present, as he watches a pine tree waving like a feather in the gale, the light flashing upward incessantly from its base, he wrote, "I feel somewhat like the young Astyanax at sight of his father's flashing crest" (XII, 64). The ancient past backs up the present, identifies its immediacy, the mythological figure lively in the new scene.

Emerson rightly advised (in his "Biographical Sketch") that Thoreau did not systematize or define what he represented to himself by the term, Nature. Thoreau confirms this: "I do not know where to find in any literature, whether ancient or modern, any adequate account of that Nature with which I am acquainted. Mythology comes nearest to it of any" (II, 152). For this reason Thoreau as artist (though not always as thinker) is free of any limiting moral perspective. In lamenting the limited existence of so many of his fellow townsmen, the prejudices of the farmers and pretences of the merchants, the tyranny of money-grubbing, money-seeking, and money-prizing that destroyed the finer promise of America, Thoreau's message deserves our hearing. But it reflects a less accurate appreciation of the inclinations, successes, and defeats of the individual human life than is indispensable to a great imaginative writer. Thoreau himself was not deceived about this: "The best thought is not only without sombreness, but even without morality" (I, 265). "The artist must work with indifference" (I, 349); he must let "Repentance and Co." go (XII, 344). One reason, he decides, that farmers are less interesting than sportsmen and loafers is that "for society a man must not be too *good* or well-disposed, to spoil his natural disposition. The bad are frequently good enough to let you see how bad they are" (VI, 21). Not among the lawyers or learned ones of Concord did Thoreau find the features of nature in men, but in those sportsmen and loafers, the musquash hunters, or in a little Irish boy like Johnny Riordan, who "revives . . . the worthies of antiquity" (III, 149).

If Thoreau had had time to write another book, it would have been very different, I believe, from any he had hitherto composed.

The latter volumes of his *Journal* are full of the raw material for
his book on Concord—a Concord mythology—it would have become. Everything about the inhabitants—from human beings to
frogs, mosquitoes, kinds of fish, mice, birds, trees, weeds, and special
grasses—would have had its place in a scheme of relatedness. For
whether the man acknowledged it or the frog, Henry Thoreau who
had been auditor to both recognized the difference it made to each
that the other lived nearby. As to the people, I venture the guess
that a directory of Concord in Thoreau's time would list few names
about which there is not some note—however seemingly insignificant the fact put down—in the volumes of the journal. Hall, the
telegraph operator, or Ferrar, the blacksmith, Lewis, the blind man,
Ai Hale and his dog—we do not meet them in the pages of Emerson's journal, but Thoreau wished to record some event of each
one's life.

What form this Concord book might have taken we cannot determine. But human scenes with the intensity of life, "like some gay
pavilion," could not have failed to include the sportsmen and
loafers, woodchoppers and musquash hunters.

> Now that the Indian is gone, [the woodchopper] stands nearest to
> nature. Who has written the history of his day? . . . Homer refers
> to the progress of the woodcutter's work, to mark the time of day on
> the plains of Troy. . . . (III, 245)

Minott, "the most poetical farmer," got out his own wood, and
knew the history of every stump on his lot, and the age of every
sapling. He was one of the worthies. Another farmer, Cyrus Hubbard, was a potential character in Thoreau's Concord mythology.

> I see the old pale-faced farmer out again on his sled now for the five-
> thousandth time . . . a man of a certain New England probity . . .
> immortal and natural. . . . He rides on the sled drawn by oxen,
> world-wise, yet comparatively so young . . . He does not melt the
> snow where he treads. . . . Moderate, natural, true, as if he were made
> of earth, stone, wood, snow. I thus meet in this Universe kindred of
> mine, composed of these elements. I see men like frogs; their peeping
> I partially understand. (IX, 144-45)

Thus, in the journal at least, Cyrus Hubbard's sketch resolves into a
metamorphosis. At another time, Thoreau, sailing on the river towards night, sees the fisherman, John Goodwin, loading driftwood
into his cart,

. . . and that man's employment, so simple and direct,—though he is
regarded by most as a vicious character,—. . . charmed me unspeakably. So much do we love actions that are simple. They are all poetic.
(V, 444-46)

Elsewhere, Thoreau christens John Goodwin "the one-eyed Ajax."
Melvin, the hunter, is always accompanied by his dog:

Saw Melvin's lank bluish-white-black-spotted hound, and Melvin with
his gun near. . . . He follows hunting . . . as regularly . . . as the
farmers follow farming. . . . How I . . . thank him for [it]. . . .
Few know how to take the census. I thank my stars for Melvin . . .
awkward, gawky, loose-hung, dragging his legs after him. He is my
contemporary and neighbor. He is one tribe, I am another, and we are
not at war. (IX, 148)

Few know how to take the census! Thoreau had expressed his desire
for a book of worthies, a more intelligible directory of men worth
seeing, than had been provided. Increasingly his journal contained
sections in which the census of the woodcutter, the poetical farmer,
the fisherman, and hunter is put together with the census of frogs
and mice, buds and sprouts. Not only might Thoreau perceive these
worthies in, or perceive in them, a metamorphosis, but sometimes
such a man could verily produce one himself, such a man as Minott,
who, Thoreau noted,

. . . adorns whatever part of nature he touches. . . . If a common
man speaks of Walden Pond to me, I see only a shallow, dull-coloured
body of water . . . but if Minott speaks of it, I see the green water
and reflected hills at once, for he *has been* there. I hear the rustle of
the leaves from woods which he goes through. (X, 168)

But above all, the coming of the musquash hunters excites Thoreau s
admiration, as if a more primitive race appeared in the spring:

The musquash hunter (last night), with his . . . powder and shot and
boat turned up . . . even he, dark, dull, and battered flint that he is,
is an inspired man to his extent now . . . and the Musquetaquid
meadows cannot spare him. . . . [The hunters] keep up their fires by
means unknown to me. . . . I know them wild and ready to risk all
when their muse invites. . . . I meet these gods of the river and woods
with sparkling faces (like Apollo's) late from the house of correction,
it may be carrying whatever mystic and forbidden bottles concealed.
. . What care I to see galleries full of representatives of heathen

gods, when I can see natural living ones. . . . These aboriginal men
cannot be repressed, but under some guise or other they survive and
reappear continually. (XI, 423-25)

Such passages suggest a work in prose, somewhat like the *Georgics*
—for if Thoreau's notes in the journal are any guide, the human
figures when they appear serve not merely their own purposes but to
set the leaves rustling, alert the muskrat who is as immortal as the
hunters. They provide incidents he finds allegorical, "like myths or
passages in a myth" (V, 203). The relation of one such happening,
the hunter Melvin's reluctantly leading Thoreau to the site of the
rare azalea which he has kept secret for many years, is one of the
most high-spirited and amusing passages in the *Journal*.

Thoreau, it is clear, used the journal for books he was writing or
about to write (as Leonard Woolf says of Mrs. Woolf's use of her
diary), although he never talks as directly about the planning of a
book, or his way of working on it as distinct from keeping his
journal. Like Mrs. Woolf, he found that "writing for my own eye
only is good practice." [16] Necessarily much in it would be unfinished.
But the context, thought allied to thought as in life, less arbitrarily
connected than in the framework of an essay, gave it to him a
unique character.

> Perhaps this is the main value of . . . keeping a journal. . . . Having
> by chance recorded a few disconnected thoughts and then brought
> them into juxtaposition, they suggest a whole new field in which
> . . . to labor and to think. Thought begat thought. (III, 217)

A Herculean task he found it: no exercise could be more vigorous
than "joining thought to thought," than to "think a thought about
this life and then get it expressed" (X, 405).

While it is hardly possible to exaggerate the value of Thoreau's
journal, he did himself tend to overestimate the general value of
this form of writing—thinking for example that had Shakespeare
kept a journal it would excel his plays and poetry. Here Thoreau
the warrior vaunting his own prowess interferes with Thoreau the
writer—as, for the same reason, when he claims that "one man shall
derive from the fisherman's story more than the fisherman has got
who tells it" (X, 404). Only a writer of Shakespeare's potential
power of sympathy with so many kinds of men, could see that the
fisherman who tells the story has precisely as much—no more and

---

[16] *Ibid.*, p. 13.

no less—of life than the best recreator of his story. Unless he knows this, the writer must be allegorist, essayist, pastoral poet. The other kind of writer, the true novelist or dramatist, must disappear into his work; and the more perfectly that transformation occurs, the more completely does he fulfill Thoreau's highest counsel, "Say the thing with which you labor" (III, 144).

But as Thoreau, if we taxed him, would, I think, admit, each kind of writing has its own necessities. His is the very best of its kind we have; his limitations were necessary to it. They are transcended on those remarkable pages when he realizes that not awe, but the intensity of life gives true relatedness (IX, 377). Not "natural history," but the history of true relatedness is the motif of all his Concord explorations, the minute appearances of buds and sprouts as well as the larger scenes of the musquash hunters gathering in the dark. At last to find one hitherto unknown species of pickerel in Walden Pond: of what moment? Because it had been there all the while, without anyone's awareness: "And all these years I have known Walden, these striped breams have skulked in it without my knowledge!" (XI, 351). His becoming conscious of a relation with this aboriginal, first-found creature altered, if ever so slightly, the nexus of relationship with all other Concord beings. In the new relatedness, the intensity; in the intensity, the true relatedness: thus to report life "tried out of the fat of my experience and joy" (IX, 195). And these unique moments, facts, occasions, that he conferred with and confederated, he rescued from the lapse of time because he made his first report to himself. Unmistakably, his is a writer's journal.

Letter from a Distant Land

by Philip Booth

*I, on my side, require of every writer, first or last, a simple
and sincere account of his own life . . . some such account
as he would send to his kindred from a distant land; for if
he has lived sincerely, it must have been in a distant land
to me.*

Henry, my distant kin,
                I live halfway,
halfway between an airfield and your pond,
halfway within the house I moved to buy
by borrowing. On transcendental ground,
come south from colder hills and early dusk,
we claim two acres of uneven land.
Alone now, sitting at my birch-plank desk,
I see an acre out these wide new windows:
my wife cuts brush, two small girls both risk
a foot in appletrees. Across the meadows,
the alder swamp, an ash grove not yet green,
a deafening pair of jets outrace their shadows.
We do not look up. A grosbeak in the pine
pecks under wing, the shy hen pheasant leaves
her nibbled sumac for our scattered grain.
With rabbits, too, we share uncertain lives;
not quiet or desperate, we measure man
by how he lives and what he most believes.
I am half teacher, half-week chopping blow-down
for our fire, half-time professing words
to warm new minds with what my heart has known.

My classes are good failures. Afterwards,
I change clothes, moult my partial self,
and walk completed through the open woods.
Behind the grillwork branches where I half
confess, the chapel that I most attend
is choired by migratory birds; I loaf
within the absolution of the wind.
My thought is swiftest when my feet are slow,
but far abroad I own a spendthrift mind.
My Spanish grandfather, a tall man, knew
his knighthood from a book. So, pastoral
beside a fire, do I come slowly to know
you, odd Uncle of my wakeful, still,
and secret dawns. My least experiments
with seed, like yours with a dried apple, fail:
the weeds, slugs, borers, grow as dense
as crows. I own a herd dog, but no sheep;
my cultivation is, like learning, chance.
Slack puritan I am, I let my garden shape
itself with skunks. I am halfway, I tell you;
there are midnights when I do not sleep.

*

The quick night-fighters' sudden thunder shakes
this house awake. I know no metaphor
for them except to say they are great sharks
with silver fins that plane the ocean air.
Propelled by jets of flame fired through their vents,
they school a noisy mile Northeast of here,
guided by blind pilots, and by governments.
A war ago, I flew myself. Now, bound
to these two acres, I owe the several debts
a lonely conscience knows. I love this land
by the good sweat it costs to own it whole.
My birthday was a bucksaw, I still defend
the new growth with an ax; the trees I fell
need cutting to let the hardwood grow. I chop
at the lush swamp, hack down the summer jungle
rich with flies. You know how fires earned chip
by chip are warmest. Still, you could not guess
the shapes of proved destruction. Chain saws rape
a virgin stand to stumps. Raw foremen boss

more horsepower in a fleet of airfield trucks
than Concord ever stabled. Machines as murderous
as mad bulls gore the land. Where stacked cornshocks
stood last fall, an orange oil tank flaws
the spring; girders bloom with concrete blocks.
So far, your Concord has seen four more wars.
Vegetables are high. The streets are filled
with tourists. Cheap people in expensive cars
patrol the Sunday roads. An acre sold
in 1849 sells now two hundred times
the price. Lexington is houses sprawled
on desert-dusty streets with fertile names.
The arrogant inherit lust. Everywhere,
thick rows of sportsmen fish polluted streams,
or hunt the posted woods of their own fear.
Overhead, the tight-paired jets write
cryptic warnings in the thin blue air.

*

Too close to earth to show to those who scan
the sky for enemy, I walked last week
beyond the impulse caught on any radar screen.
In windworn March, halfway to dawn, I woke
to feel the growing day: the wind light North-
north-west, the morning luminous, a streak
of cloud between the sunward-turning earth
and yesterday's last stars. A rebel drummer
called me like the crows. The cross-lots path
I walked was wet with melting frost, a rumor
of frogs thawed the swamp, and toward town
I heard the hard first whack of a hammer.
A casual pilgrim to the phoebe's tune,
I whistled down the distant land where you
(this same month's end) tramped out to cut white pine
with Alcott's borrowed ax. Your Walden, now,
is still half yours: a summer swimmers' beach
corrupts the eastern bank, the sun-up view,
but you, who would be saint in a formal church,
are honored still on the further shores, preserved
in the commonwealth of hemlock, elm, and birch.
Your hut is marked by stone, the pond was saved
by taxes for a public park. Emerson's

strict laws of compensation have reserved
a parking space for Sunday lovers: beer cans
drift where you knelt soberly to drink,
and small boys smoke like truant puritans.
Such is August on the swimmers' bank,
but not my sharp March dawn. Between ice-out
and spring, I walk in time to hear the honk
of two stray geese, the song of a white-throat
soloing after his mate in your celibate woods.
It is the same, I tell you. Shadowy trout
rise like the swift perfection of your words,
the backyard journal of your human praise
is proved in the red oaks' blood-dark buds.
I like to think how animals would freeze
to see your stick, your crooked genius, poke
the leafy underbrush; until you froze
yourself, and all the thicket woodcock, duck,
and small scared beasts of Walden's shore
turned curious. Here, between the dark
and sudden milktrain day, halfway from fear,
halfway to spring, I say these natural names
to honor you as poet of the turning year.
Beside the ministry of waves, the times
of men are seasons, windfall seeds that spill
toward fruit: the perfect globe or wormy shames
of Adam. All poets climb back Eden's hill
within their own backyard. Woods and pond
were your recovery of the crop that's possible,
a harvest of good words grown from the land
that brings a whole world home. I cultivate
a different orchard, pruning under the sound
of probable war. The day's first silver jet
reflects first sunlight where I turn away
from Walden, turn, stop, look back, and start
again. Up the bank, I cross the highway
where a skunk got lost in headlights: traffic-
flat, his flowering intestines lie halfway
in sun. This new March day is sweetened thick
with death. But when was any season less?
You felt the cold fall snap of John Brown's neck,
owned a winter conscience, smelled slavery's grass-
fire torch the long dry land to civil war,

from Bull Run to Savannah to the Wilderness.
I tell you, Henry, distant as we are,
the good, the brave, are no more a majority
than when you walked this far spring shore.
Man, by his human nature, is not free,
but where his wildness is alive to swamp
and hill, he learns to live most naturally.
Still, a saunterer must make his camp
in strange unholy lands, begging alms
and passage for belief. I take no stump
except for liberty to listen to the elms,
to walk the cold wood, to sleep on bedrock
thought, and to say my winter psalms.
A century from where your wisdom struck
its temporary camp, I cross the middleground
toward truth. At home beneath both oak
and jet, praising what I halfway understand,
I walk this good March morning out
to say my strange love in a distant land.

Chronology of Important Dates

1817	Born, July 12, Concord, Massachusetts.
1833	Enters Harvard College.
1837	Graduates from Harvard College; teaches in the Concord school, but is dismissed for refusing to administer discipline; meets Emerson, and begins the *Journal*.
1838	Opens a private school with his brother John; lectures for the first time before the Concord Lyceum.
1839	August 31—September 13, excursions on the Concord and Merrimack rivers with John: the narrative basis of the *Week*.
1840	Publishes a critical essay in the newly-launched *Dial*.
1841	Takes up residence at Emerson's home.
1842	Brother John dies.
1843	Leaves Emerson for Staten Island.
1844	Returns home; makes pencils.
1845	Begins Walden experience in March; begins his residence there on July 4.
1846	First excursion to the Maine woods.
1847	Leaves Walden on September 6; takes up second residence with the Emersons.
1849	Returns to his father's house; publishes *A Week on the Concord and Merrimack Rivers* and "Civil Disobedience"; first visit to Cape Cod.
1850	Second visit to Cape Cod; goes to Canada.
1853	Second trip to the Maine woods.
1854	Delivers "Slavery in Massachusetts"; publishes *Walden*.
1855	Third visit to Cape Cod.
1856	Meets Walt Whitman in New York.
1857	Fourth visit to Cape Cod; third excursion to the Maine woods; meets John Brown.

1859   Delivers "A Plea for John Brown."

1860   Last camping excursion to Monadnock.

1861   Goes to Minnesota for his health.

1862   May 6, dies of tuberculosis at Concord.

Notes on the Editor and Contributors

SHERMAN PAUL, editor of the anthology, is the author of *Emerson's Angle of Vision* and *The Shores of America*. He is currently Professor of American Literature at the University of Illinois.

PHILIP BOOTH, Associate Professor of English at Syracuse University, is the author of *Letter From A Distant Land,* which was awarded the Lamont Prize of the Academy of American Poets.

WILLIAM DRAKE, after several years of professional conservation work, is now teaching English at the University of Arizona.

HEINZ EULAU, Professor of Political Science at Stanford University, is co-author of *Political Behavior, Legislative Behavior,* and *The Legislative System.*

EDWIN S. FUSSEL, Associate Professor of English and American Literature at Claremont Graduate School, has published essays and poems in various literary periodicals.

STANLEY EDGAR HYMAN of Bennington College is a staff writer for *The New Yorker* and the author of *The Armed Vision: A Study in the Method of Modern Literary Criticism.*

MAX LERNER, Professor of American Civilization at Brandeis University and columnist for the New York *Post,* is the author of many books, among them *America As A Civilization.*

R. W. B. LEWIS, Professor of English at Yale University, is the author of *The American Adam* and *The Picaresque Saints.*

F. O. MATTHIESSEN, who died in 1950, was Professor of English at Harvard University and the author of many distinguished studies, among them *American Renaissance* and *The Achievement of T. S. Eliot.*

LEWIS MUMFORD, philosopher of culture and civilization, is the author of twenty books, among them pioneer studies in American literature and architecture—*The Golden Day, Herman Melville, The Brown Decades.*

LAURENCE STAPLETON, Professor of English and of Political Theory at Bryn Mawr College, is the author of *Justice and World Society, The Design of Democracy,* and *H. D. Thoreau: A Writer's Journal.*

LEO STOLLER, a member of the English faculty of Wayne State University, is the author of *After Walden: Thoreau's Changing Views on Economic Man.*

HENRY W. WELLS, a member of the English faculty and Curator of the Brander Matthews Dramatic Museum of Columbia University, is the author of many literary studies, among them *The American Way of Poetry.*

The Editorial Board of *The Seven Arts* included JAMES OPPENHEIM, WALDO FRANK, VAN WYCK BROOKS, and RANDOLPH BOURNE.

Bibliography

WRITINGS OF THOREAU

Bode, Carl. *Collected Poems of Henry Thoreau.* New York: Packard & Co., 1943. Definitive edition.

Harding, Walter, and Carl Bode. *The Correspondence of Henry David Thoreau.* New York: New York University Press, 1958. Most complete edition of letters to and from Thoreau.

Miller, Perry. *Consciousness in Concord.* Boston: Houghton Mifflin Co., 1958. Includes the text of Thoreau's "lost" journal (1840-1941).

Thoreau, Henry David. *The Writings of Henry David Thoreau.* Boston: Houghton Mifflin Company, 1906. Vols. VII-XX contains the Journals. Standard edition.

BIOGRAPHICAL STUDIES

Canby, Henry S. *Thoreau.* Boston: Houghton Mifflin Co., 1939. The most complete study of Thoreau's life.

Channing, William E. *Thoreau, the Poet-Naturalist,* revised edition, edited by F. B. Sanborn. Boston: Goodspeed's Book Shop, 1902. By Thoreau's friend and walking companion.

Krutch, Joseph W. *Henry David Thoreau.* New York: William Sloane, 1948. Most recent biographical-critical appraisal.

Salt, Henry S. *The Life of Henry David Thoreau*. London: Richard Bentley, 1890; revised edition, Walter Scott Ltd., 1896. Still valuable English study.

Sanborn, F. B. *The Life of Henry David Thoreau*. Boston: Houghton Mifflin Co., 1917. By Thoreau's friend; valuable for Thoreau's college essays.

CRITICAL STUDIES

Cook, Reginald L. *Passage to Walden*. Boston: Houghton Mifflin Co., 1949. Thorough study of Thoreau's relation to nature.

Harding, Walter. *A Thoreau Handbook*. New York: New York University Press, 1959. A guide to Thoreau scholarship.

Harding, Walter. *Thoreau: A Century of Criticism*. Dallas: Southern Methodist University Press, 1954. Collected essays, including those by Emerson, Lowell, and Stevenson.

Leary, Lewis. "Thoreau," from *Eight American Authors*, edited by Floyd Stovall. New York: The Modern Language Association of America, 1956. An assessment of Thoreau scholarship.

Matthiessen, F. O. *American Renaissance: Art and Expression in the Age of Emerson and Whitman*. New York: Oxford University Press, 1941. Best study of Thoreau's aesthetics and style.

Paul, Sherman. *The Shores of America: Thoreau's Inward Exploration*. Urbana: University of Illinois Press, 1958. An inner biography based on a close reading of Thoreau's work.

Seybold, Ethel. *Thoreau: The Quest and the Classics*. New Haven: Yale University Press, 1951. A study of the relation of Thoreau's reading in the classics to his spiritual development.

Stanley, J. Lyndon. *The Making of Walden*. Chicago: University of Chicago Press, 1957. A study of the composition of Walden, containing the first version of the text.

Stoller, Leo. *After Walden: Thoreau's Changing Views on Economic Man*. Stanford: Stanford University Press, 1957. A major critical study treating the development of Thoreau's thought.